WHITAKER'S ALMANACK QUIZ BOOK

Second Edition

A&C BLACK PUBLISHERS
LONDON

A & C Black Publishers Ltd
36 Soho Square, London W1D 3QY

Whitaker's Almanack published annually since 1868

Reprinted 2009

ISBN 978–1–4081–0448–4

Typeset in Great Britain by RefineCatch Limited, Bungay, Suffolk
Printed in the UK by CPI Bookmarque, Croydon, CR0 4TD

A CIP catalogue record for this book is available from the British Library.

Editorial Staff
Editor-in-Chief: Inna Ward
Project Editor: Ruth Northey
Questions by: Rob Hardy, Mike Jakeman, Anna Krzyzanowska, Ruth Northey, Clare Slaven, Inna Ward

CONTENTS

ART AND DESIGN

ARCHITECTURE

15TH AND 16TH CENTURY

17TH AND 18TH CENTURY

19TH AND 20TH CENTURY

IMPRESSIONISTS

FASHION

CONTEMPORARY ART

HOAXES, HEISTS AND FORGERIES

DESIGN OBJECTS

DESIGNERS

FASHION FADS

BRITISH ART

MUSEUMS AND GALLERIES

BUILDINGS AND MONUMENTS

ANCIENT ART

MOVERS AND SHAKERS

Q ARCHITECTURE

1 Which architects designed the Houses of Parliament in Westminster, completed in 1860?

a) Sir Charles Barry and Augustus Pugin

b) Augustus Pugin and Sir George Gilbert Scott

c) Sir Charles Barry and Sir George Gilbert Scott

2 Which of the following landmark 20th-century buildings was designed by the Danish architect Jorn Utzon?

a) The Pompidou Centre

b) Lloyds of London Building

c) Sydney Opera House

3 Which architect created the concept of a house as a 'machine for living'?

a) Frank Lloyd Wright

b) Norman Foster

c) Le Corbusier (Charles Edouard Jeanneret)

4 In which Spanish city can almost all the buildings designed by Antoni Gaudi be seen?

a) Barcelona

b) Madrid

c) Seville

5 Who designed the Millennium Dome, the Lloyd's building and Terminal 5 at Heathrow?

a) Norman Foster

b) Richard Rogers

c) James Stirling

6 Which of the following styles of architecture was the earliest?

a) Doric

b) Corinthian

c) Ionic

---

7 Which Roman author wrote *Ten Books on Architecture*, a work which has continued to influence Western architecture through the centuries?

a) Cicero

b) Vitruvius

c) Columella

---

8 Who founded the Bauhaus School of Art, Design and Architecture in 1919?

a) Mies van der Rohe

b) Walter Benjamin

c) Walter Gropius

---

9 Which bridge was designed by Benjamin Baker and Sir John Fowler and opened in 1890 by the Prince of Wales?

a) The Golden Gate Bridge, San Francisco

b) The Sydney Harbour Bridge

c) The Forth Rail Bridge, Scotland

---

10 Which architect designed the pyramids outside the Louvre in Paris?

a) Frank Gehry

b) I. M. Pei

c) Renzo Piano

A

1	a
2	c
3	c
4	a
5	b
6	a
7	b
8	c
9	c
10	b

Q 15TH AND 16TH CENTURY

1 **Which Italian painter is best known for his portraits of heads made up of fruit and vegetables?**

a) Sandro Botticelli

b) Giuseppe Arcimboldo

c) Giovanni Bellini

2 **Which artist is buried in the Pantheon in Rome?**

a) Raphael

b) Michelangelo

c) Leonardo da Vinci

3 **Which Renaissance artist and former pupil of Giovanni Bellini painted the *Venus of Urbino* in 1538?**

a) Botticelli

b) Titian

b) Velázquez

4 **Which of the following artists did not add a moustache to their re-working of Leonardo da Vinci's *Mona Lisa*?**

a) Marcel Duchamp

b) Salvador Dalí

c) Andy Warhol

5 **Donatello, Michelangelo, Fra Angelico and Lippi were all members of which school of artists?**

a) Bolognese School

b) School of Ferrara

c) Florentine School

6 **Michelangelo's *The Last Judgment* can be found above the altar of which church?**

a) Sistine Chapel, Rome

b) Cathedral of Santa Maria Assunta, Venice

c) Basilica of San Lorenzo, Florence

---

7 **What is the modern name of the country in which Hieronymus Bosch was born in 1450?**

a) Belgium

b) The Netherlands

c) Germany

---

8 **German painter and engraver Albrecht Dürer is also known for his work in which other academic field?**

a) Mathematics

b) Astronomy

c) Philosophy

---

9 **Which of the following is not a work by Dutch artist Pieter Bruegel the Elder?**

a) *The Tower of Babel*

b) *The Garden of Earthly Delights*

c) *The Triumph of Death*

---

10 **Which German artist painted the portrait of Anne of Cleves presented to Henry VIII?**

a) Hans Holbein the Elder

b) Ambrosius Holbein

c) Hans Holbein the Younger

A

1 b
2 a
3 b
4 c
5 c
6 a
7 b
8 a
9 b
10 c

Q 17TH AND 18TH CENTURY

1 Who painted *The Night Watch*?

a) Rubens

b) Rembrandt

c) Renoir

2 *Las Meninas (The Maids of Honour)* painted in 1656 by Velázquez was reinterpreted in 1957 by which equally famous Spanish artist?

a) Pablo Picasso

b) Joan Miró

c) Salvador Dalí

3 Which Flemish artist became the principal court painter to Charles I?

a) Frans Snyders

b) Peter Paul Rubens

c) Anthony van Dyck

4 Which Italian artist is believed to have fled Rome in 1606 after killing a man in an argument over a game of tennis?

a) Correggio

b) Caravaggio

c) Canaletto

5 In which town did the Dutch artist Jan Vermeer live and work all his life?

a) Amsterdam

b) Delft

c) Leiden

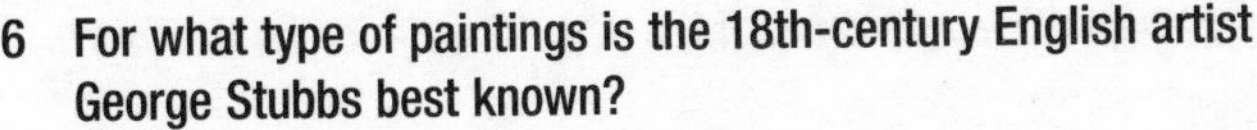

6 **For what type of paintings is the 18th-century English artist George Stubbs best known?**

a) Still life

b) Animal painting

c) Portraiture

7 **What is the name of the ornate and decorative style consisting of undulating lines, s-curves and carved stucco which originated in France in the early 18th century?**

a) Gothic

b) Neoclassical

c) Rococo

8 **Which of the following literary works was not illustrated by William Blake?**

a) *Original Stories from Real Life* by Mary Wollstonecraft

b) *Paradise Lost* by John Milton

c) *The Works of Virgil* by John Dryden

9 **Prints of which artist's work were distributed as propaganda in support of the 1751 Gin Act?**

a) William Hogarth

b) Francis Hayman

c) Richard Wilson

10 **Which of the following portrait-painters and foundation members of the Royal Academy of Arts was not born in England?**

a) Nathaniel Hone

b) Thomas Gainsborough

c) Joshua Reynolds

A

1 b
2 a
3 c
4 b
5 b
6 b
7 c
8 c
9 a
10 a

Q 19TH AND 20TH CENTURY

1 Which 20th-century artist painted *The Persistence of Memory*?

a) Salvador Dalí

b) Pablo Picasso

c) Henri Matisse

2 Which artist did the 19th-century critic John Ruskin accuse of 'flinging a pot of paint in the public's face'?

a) James Whistler

b) J. M. W. Turner

c) Claude Monet

3 Which 20th-century American artist was born Emmanuel Radnitzky?

a) Mark Rothko

b) Jasper Johns

c) Man Ray

4 With which 20th-century art movement is the painter Roy Lichtenstein chiefly associated?

a) Surrealism

b) Abstract Expressionism

c) Pop Art

5 Who played the abstract expressionist painter Jackson Pollock in the 2000 film *Pollock*?

a) Ed Harris

b) Brad Pitt

c) Val Kilmer

6 How is the 19th-century painting entitled *Arrangement in Black and Grey* better known?

a) *Whistler's* Mother

b) *The Fighting Temeraire*

c) *The Stag at Bay*

7 What was unusual about the abstract expressionist painter Nat Tate?

a) He suffered from a retinal detachment after being hit by a car as a child

b) He was fictional, created by the author William Boyd and musician David Bowie as a prank

c) He spent his entire adult life renting a room in a Romanian orphanage

8 Who created a work called *The Bride Stripped Bare by Her Bachelors, Even*?

a) Max Ernst

b) Damien Hirst

c) Marcel Duchamp

9 Which of the following is not the name of a 20th-century art movement?

a) Vorticism

b) Resistentialism

c) Rayonism

10 Which 20th-century American artist painted a work entitled *Nighthawks*?

a) Edward Hopper

b) Georgia O'Keeffe

c) Grant Wood

A

1 a
2 a
3 c
4 c
5 a
6 a
7 b
8 c
9 b
10 a

IMPRESSIONISTS

1 From what did the Impressionist movement derive its name?

a) The process of making multiple versions or impressions of a single work

b) The work *Impression, Sunrise* by Claude Monet

c) Edgar Degas' description of his finished works as 'impressions' of what he saw

2 What was considered unusual about the way the Impressionists chose to paint?

a) They often painted 'en plein air', or in the open air

b) Groups of artists would gather to paint in the same room

c) They favoured painting under very bright lights

3 Which of these painters was not considered to be an Impressionist?

a) Camille Pissaro

b) Vincent van Gogh

c) Alfred Sisley

4 When did the Impressionist movement develop?

a) 18th century

b) 19th century

c) 20th century

5 Who painted *Le Bal au Moulin de la Galette*?

a) Pierre-Auguste Renoir

b) Édouard Manet

c) Frédéric Bazille

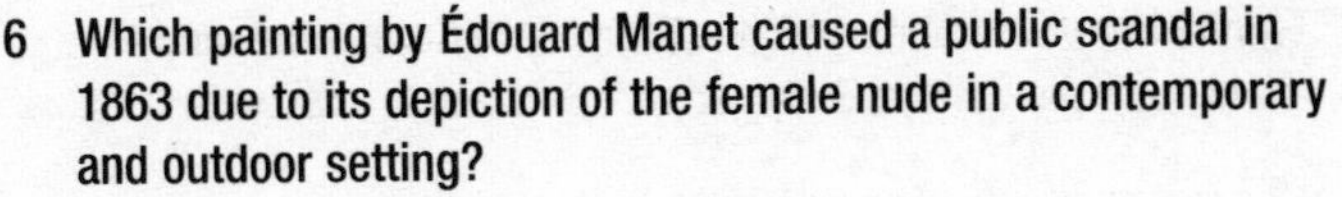

6 **Which painting by Édouard Manet caused a public scandal in 1863 due to its depiction of the female nude in a contemporary and outdoor setting?**

a) *Le Déjeuner sur l'herbe*

b) *Le Bar aux Folies-Bergère*

c) *Olympia*

7 **Which Impressionist was particularly known for their portraits of dancers?**

a) Pierre-Auguste Renoir

b) Edgar Degas

c) Mary Cassatt

8 **How was painter Berthe Morisot related to fellow Impressionist Édouard Manet?**

a) She was his half-sister

b) She was his stepmother

c) She was his sister-in-law

9 **Which Post-Impressionist, whose work was particularly influenced by Manet and Degas, was only 1.5m (4ft 11in) because his legs stopped growing during childhood?**

a) Henri de Toulouse-Lautrec

b) Paul Gauguin

c) Paul Cézanne

10 **Claude Monet painted which series of paintings at his garden in Giverny?**

a) *Poplars*

b) *Haystacks*

c) *Waterlilies*

A

1 b

2 a

3 b

4 b

5 a

6 a

7 b

8 c

9 a

10 c

FASHION

1 **The 1947 collection of which couture house was christened the 'New Look' by Carmel Snow, editor of American *Harper's Bazaar*?**

a) Fath

b) Balenciaga

c) Christian Dior

2 **Which world-famous designer originally had the surname Lifshitz?**

a) Calvin Klein

b) Ralph Lauren

c) Charles Frederick Worth

3 **For what fashion 'crime' was Australian swimmer and actress Annette Kellerman arrested for in 1907?**

a) For not wearing gloves during an evening visit to the theatre in New York

b) For wearing one of her fitted one-piece swimming costumes on Boston beach

c) For not wearing anything at all in the film *A Daughter of the Gods*

4 **Which fashion designer founded the Fashion and Textile Museum in London which opened in 2003?**

a) Zandra Rhodes

b) Celia Birtwell

c) Vivienne Westwood

5 **The Irishman Philip Treacy is renowned for his designs of what?**

a) Hats

b) Shoes

c) Handbags

6 Which French fashion designer said: 'There is time for work. And time for love. That leaves no other time.'

a) Jean-Paul Gaultier

b) Coco Chanel

c) Pierre Cardin

7 What was the 'utility clothing scheme'?

a) A second world war competition to design practical female workwear

b) A 1950s mail order service for dress patterns

c) A British wartime initiative offering government-approved clothing at fixed prices

8 Which 1960s fashion designer is epitomised by the miniskirt, hot-pants and multi-coloured patterned tights?

a) Mary Quant

b) Ossie Clark

c) Barbara Hulanicki

9 Which shoe designer opened a shop called *Cobblers to the World* on King's Road in 1972?

a) Patrick Cox

b) Manolo Blahnik

c) Terry de Havilland

10 Which fashion designer is known as the 'enfant terrible'?

a) John Paul Gaultier

b) John Galliano

c) Karl Lagerfeld

A

1	c
2	b
3	b
4	a
5	a
6	b
7	c
8	a
9	c
10	a

Q CONTEMPORARY ART

1 Which artist has formed works of art from materials including lamb's tongue, fur, flowers, urine, meat, household cleaning fluids and chocolate?

a) Damien Hirst

b) Helen Chadwick

c) Tracey Emin

2 Anthony Gormley's *Another Place*, consisting of 100 cast iron figures facing out to sea, can be found on which UK beach?

a) Holkham Bay, Norfolk

b) Sandhaven Beach, South Shields

c) Crosby Beach, Liverpool

3 With which art movement is Bridget Riley most associated?

a) Op Art

b) Dadaism

c) Cubism

4 Martin Creed won the 2001 Turner prize for an installation which manipulated the gallery's existing light fittings, what was the name of the piece?

a) *The lights are too bright*

b) *The light bulbs need changing*

c) *The lights going on and off*

5 *Little Sparta* located in the Pentland Hills near Edinburgh is the famous garden of which contemporary artist?

a) Ian Hamilton Finlay

b) Derek Jarman

c) Richard Long

6 **What is the name of the art movement formed in 1999 by Billy Childish and Charles Thomson to promote figurative painting in opposition to conceptual art?**

a) Brit Art

b) Stuckism

c) Superflat

7 **What was the title of the piece of work exhibited by Tracey Emin for the 1999 Turner prize which caused a media furore?**

a) *My Bed*

b) *Unmade Bed*

c) *Dirty Bed Linen*

8 **Which of the following has not been pickled by Damien Hirst?**

a) A sheep

b) A pig

c) A goat

9 **What is the name of ceramicist Grayson Perry's transvestite alter ego?**

a) Mary

b) Claire

c) Joan

10 **Which of the following pair of artistic collaborators are also twins?**

a) Gilbert and George

b) Jake and Dinos Chapman

c) Jane and Louise Wilson

A

1 b

2 c

3 a

4 c

5 a

6 b

7 a

8 c

9 b

10 c

Q HOAXES, HEISTS AND FORGERIES

1 **Which of these has not been stolen?**

a) A sheep preserved in formaldehyde by Damien Hirst

b) A Henry Moore bronze sculpture weighing two tonnes

c) A piece of wall featuring a work by Banksy

2 **Stephen Jory (1949–2006) is thought to have been Britain's most prolific counterfeiter, what was the name of his gang?**

a) Stamford Hill posse

b) Lavender Hill mob

c) Primrose Hill gang

3 **Norwegian artist Edvard Munch painted several versions of his iconic image *The Scream*, how many versions have been stolen?**

a) One

b) Two

c) Three

4 **Who wrote *The Art Forger's Handbook*?**

a) Eric Hebborn

b) Elmyr de Hory

c) John Drewe

5 **How did Vincenzo Perugia steal the *Mona Lisa* from the Louvre in 1911?**

a) He replaced it with a forgery overnight

b) He overpowered a tour guide

c) He walked out with it under his smock

6 Where was *Russian Schoolroom*, a stolen Norman Rockwell painting, found?

a) In a car park in Switzerland

b) In a pensioner's loft

c) In Stephen Spielberg's private collection

7 In 2003 thieves stole diamonds worth £67m in one of the largest robberies in history – which city did this take place in?

a) Antwerp

b) Rome

c) Berlin

8 How was a forgery of Gauguin's *Vase de Fleurs* discovered?

a) There was a spelling mistake in the signature

b) The same painting was auctioned at two rival auction houses in the same month

c) An x-ray revealed a landscape painting underneath

9 Who was convicted of forgery, then went on to have his own exhibition, *Genuine Fakes*?

a) Han van Meegeren

b) John Myatt

c) Stephen Greenhalgh

10 How were £150m of paintings stolen from the Isabella Stewart Gardner Museum?

a) They were taken while the directors were in a meeting about art theft

b) They were replaced with copies that went unnoticed for two days

c) The thieves disguised themselves as police officers to break in

1 a
2 b
3 b
4 a
5 c
6 c
7 a
8 b
9 b
10 c

DESIGN OBJECTS

ART AND DESIGN

1 Which of the following familiar sights was designed by the British architect Giles Gilbert Scott?

a) The red telephone kiosk

b) The London Transport Routemaster bus

c) The Royal Mail red pillar box

2 The *Constellation* vacuum cleaner, featuring a hovercraft mechanism for manoeuvrability, was manufactured by which company?

a) Dyson

b) Hoover

c) Electrolux

3 What are the colours of the five interlocking rings of the Olympic Games emblem designed by Pierre de Coubertin in 1913?

a) Blue, black, red, yellow and green

b) Blue, black, red, yellow and purple

c) Blue, black, red, purple and green

4 Which of the following Ford Motor Company automobiles was produced first?

a) Ford Model F

b) Ford Model A

c) Ford Model T

5 Whose three-legged lemon squeezer became a design classic?

a) Terence Conran

b) Philippe Starck

c) Wayne Hemingway

6 **In which year did the British Motor Corporation produce its first Mini?**

a) 1949

b) 1959

c) 1969

7 **Who designed the moulded plastic *S-chair* manufactured by Vitra in 1968?**

a) Verner Panton

b) Charles Eames

c) Harry Bertoia

8 **What did Harry Beck design in 1933?**

a) The London Underground sign and logo

b) Stockwell London Underground station

c) The first diagrammatic map of the London Underground

9 **The Sony Walkman personal stereo was originally marketed in the UK in 1979 under what name?**

a) The Stowaway

b) The Hideaway

c) The Soundabout

10 **How did the Vespa ('wasp') motor scooter manufactured by Piaggio get its name?**

a) Vespa was the first name of the designer Corradino d'Ascanio's mother

b) Like the wasp, it was good at travelling short distances

c) The high-pitched noise of the engine sounded like a wasp

A

1	a
2	b
3	a
4	a
5	b
6	b
7	a
8	c
9	a
10	c

DESIGNERS

1 What was the relationship between American furniture designers Charles and Ray Eames?

a) Father and son

b) Brother and sister

c) Husband and wife

2 Which graphic designer and typographer, closely associated with the Bauhaus movement, designed the Universal typeface in 1925?

a) Adrian Frutiger

b) Herbert Bayer

c) Eric Gill

3 Where was art nouveau silver and pewter ware designer Archibald Knox born?

a) Isle of Wight

b) Isle of Skye

c) Isle of Man

4 *Designing for People* (1955) was the seminal work by which pioneer of ergonomic principles in industrial design?

a) Alvin Tilley

b) Niels Diffrient

c) Henry Dreyfuss

5 Who designed the Glasgow School of Art?

a) Charles Rennie Macintosh

b) Arthur Heygate Macmurdo

c) Philip Webb

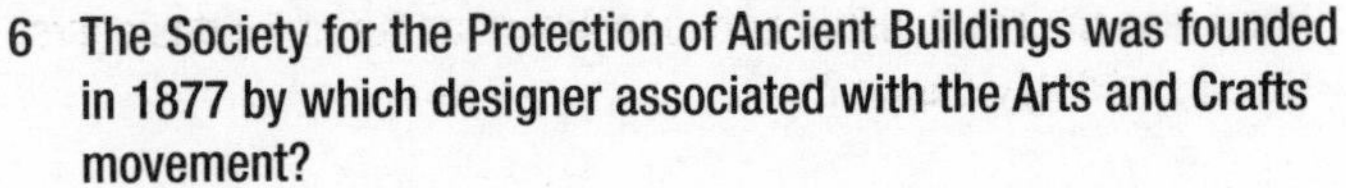

6 The Society for the Protection of Ancient Buildings was founded in 1877 by which designer associated with the Arts and Crafts movement?

a) Charles Voysey

b) William Morris

c) Herbert Tudor Buckland

7 What is engineer and architect R. Buckminster Fuller most famous for designing?

a) The skyscraper

b) The geodesic dome

c) The prefabricated house

8 In which Indian city can the Viceroy's House designed by British architect Sir Edwin Lutyens be found?

a) Delhi

b) Calcutta

c) Bombay

9 Who was commissioned to design the furniture for the Royal Festival Hall built in 1951 as part of the Festival of Britain?

a) Robin Day

b) Lucienne Day

c) Terence Conran

10 French Art Nouveau designer René Lalique is particularly renowned for his work in which medium?

a) Wood

b) Textiles

c) Glass

A

1 c

2 b

3 c

4 c

5 a

6 b

7 b

8 a

9 a

10 c

Q FASHION FADS

1 What is a chopine?

a) A high platform shoe popular in Venice in the 16th century

b) A high collar held up with wire or whalebone popular in the early 20th century

c) A high 'roll' hairstyle popular at the 18th-century French court

2 In the 1920s young women who danced the Charleston, wore rolled-down stockings, T-bar shoes and short skirts were commonly known as what?

a) Flippers

b) Flappers

c) Floppers

3 What are loon pants?

a) A trouser that flared from the knee, popular in the 1970s

b) A trouser with skirt attached, popular in the 1990s

c) A pyjama-style trouser, popular in the 1920s

4 A small woman's hat with a flat crown and straight upright sides is known as what?

a) A beret

b) A pillbox hat

c) A cloche hat

5 What design was commonly appliquéd on to wide swing skirts worn by American teenage girls in the 1950s?

a) A greyhound

b) A terrier

c) A poodle

6 Men who wore drape jackets, drainpipe trousers and crepe-soled shoes where know by what name?

a) Mods

b) Teddy boys

c) Dandies

7 Who designed the aptly named 'hobble skirt' popular for a brief period in the early 20th century?

a) Paul Poiret

b) Madame Paquin

c) Jacques Doucet

8 What is the name of the 18th-century undergarment worn at each side of the hips to widen a skirt?

a) Pannier

b) Bustle

c) Stay

9 What is a pompadour?

a) An undergarment

b) A dress

c) A hairstyle

10 What were the main ingredients of ceruse, makeup used by wealthy Tudor women to achieve a pale complexion?

a) Chalk and water

b) Flour and vinegar

c) White lead and vinegar

A

1 a
2 b
3 a
4 b
5 c
6 b
7 a
8 a
9 c
10 c

BRITISH ART

1 Which artist became known as 'the painter of light'?

a) Joseph Turner

b) John Ruskin

c) John Constable

2 Who painted *The Blue Boy* (*c.* 1770)?

a) Francis Hayman

b) Joshua Reynolds

c) Thomas Gainsborough

3 What is the title of the series of paintings by William Hogarth that depict the life of excess led by Tom Rakewell?

a) *Birth to Bedlam*

b) *Marriage á-la-Mode*

c) *A Rake's Progress*

4 Which institution is dedicated to British artists?

a) The Royal Academy

c) The British Academy

c) The Royal Society

5 Which British poet illustrated his own books, and was as well known for his art as for his writing?

a) Geoffrey Chaucer

b) John Milton

c) William Blake

6 *The Hay Wain* was painted in 1821 by which famous British landscape painter?

a) Joseph Turner

b) John Constable

c) Thomas Girtin

7 The Pre-Raphaelites signed their work 'PRB', what does the 'B' stand for?

a) Band

b) Brethren

c) Brotherhood

8 Dante Gabriel Rossetti's painting *Beata Beatrix* is also a portrayal of which of the women in his life?

a) His wife, Elizabeth Siddal

b) His mistress, Fanny Cornforth

c) William Morris' wife, Jane Burden

9 Which Yorkshire-born modernist sculptor spent the last 26 years of his or her life in St Ives, Cornwall?

a) Henry Moore

b) Barbara Hepworth

c) Jacob Epstein

10 Which British artist has produced a series of paintings based on the theme of the swimming pool?

a) David Hockney

b) Patrick Caulfield

c) Gary Hume

A

1 a
2 c
3 c
4 a
5 c
6 b
7 c
8 a
9 b
10 a

Q MUSEUMS AND GALLERIES

1 Which of the following was named European Capital of Culture in 2008?

a) Liverpool

b) Leeds

c) London

2 In which museum can the Rosetta Stone be seen?

a) The Louvre

b) The British Museum

c) The Cairo Museum of Antiquities

3 Which gallery can be found in Kensington Gardens?

a) Photographers'

b) Saatchi

c) Serpentine

4 Which museum contains *Launchpad*, an interactive gallery?

a) Royal Air Force Museum

b) Science Museum

c) Greenwich Royal Observatory

5 Which writer has a museum dedicated to his life and works in Chatham?

a) Charles Dickens

b) William Shakespeare

c) William Blake

6 The Peggy Guggenheim collection is located in which city?

a) New York

b) Venice

c) Paris

7 Which London museum complex was forced to close its permanent gallery of artworks from St Petersburg's State Hermitage Musuem in 2007?

a) The Tate

b) The National Gallery

c) Somerset House

8 The Prado is the national museum of Spain. What does Prado mean in Spanish?

a) Palace

b) Meadow

c) Bridge

9 Who was the subject for the first waxwork modelled by Marie Tussaud?

a) Voltaire

b) Louis XIV

c) Her husband

10 Which of the following London landmarks contains a museum?

a) 30 St Mary Axe

b) Tower Bridge

c) St Paul's Cathedral

A

1 a
2 b
3 c
4 b
5 a
6 b
7 c
8 b
9 a
10 b

Q BUILDINGS AND MONUMENTS

1 Which is the largest inhabited castle in the world?

a) Windsor

b) Balmoral

c) Floors

2 Which English cathedral suffered a major fire in July 1984?

a) St Paul's, London

b) Chichester

c) York Minster

3 The Collegiate Church of St Peter is the formal name for which place of worship?

a) Westminster Abbey

b) Canterbury Cathedral

c) York Minster

4 Marble Arch was built originally as the entrance to which building?

a) St James's Palace

b) The Tower of London

c) Buckingham Palace

5 Which of the following has the Hagia Sophia in Istanbul not been used as?

a) Mosque

b) Cathedral

c) Synagogue

6 **Which of the following great houses can be found on the Isle of Wight?**

a) Chatsworth House

b) Blenheim Palace

c) Osborne House

---

7 **Which of the following cities does not contain an Egyptian obelisk named Cleopatra's Needle?**

a) London

b) Moscow

c) Paris

---

8 **Where is the temple of Angkor Wat?**

a) Cambodia

b) Thailand

c) Afghanistan

---

9 **What was Machu Picchu in Peru?**

a) A temple

b) A city

c) A statue

---

10 **Which New York skyscraper, designed by William van Alen, stands at 405 Lexington Avenue, between 42nd and 43rd Street?**

a) The Empire State Building

b) The Rockefeller Centre

c) The Chrysler Building

A

1 a

2 c

3 a

4 c

5 c

6 c

7 b

8 a

9 b

10 c

ANCIENT ART

1 Where are the *Black Frieze* prehistoric cave paintings?

a) Altamira, Northern Spain

b) Pech Merle, Quercy, France

c) Creswell Crags, Northern England

2 Which ancient artists developed a complex series of rules for depicting figures and objects over a flat picture plane?

a) The Egyptians

b) The Greeks

c) The Romans

3 In which country was the figurine of the *Venus of Tan-Tan*, thought to date between 300,000 and 500,000 BC, found?

a) Morocco

b) Iran

c) Turkey

4 What is the main ingredient in Egyptian Faience ware?

a) Clay

b) Quartz

c) Papyrus

5 The *Terracotta Army* was found buried in the tomb of Emperor Qin Shi Huang – which Chinese dynasty did he belong to?

a) The Qin Dynasty

b) The Shang Dynasty

c) The Zhou Dynasty

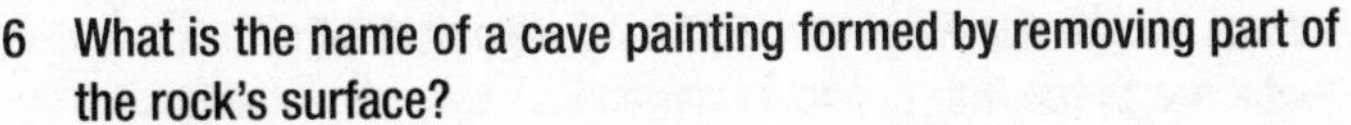

6 **What is the name of a cave painting formed by removing part of the rock's surface?**

a) Petroform

b) Pictograph

c) Petroglyph

7 **What is the *Standard of Ur*, a Sumerian artefact excavated in the 1920s from the ancient city of Ur in Iraq?**

a) A necklace made of mother of pearl and lapis lazuli

b) An intricately carved spear made of bone

c) A hollow wooden box inlaid with a mosaic of shell, red limestone and lapis lazuli

8 **Which artefact was discovered by a Napoleonic army captain in Egypt in 1798?**

a) A bust of Queen Nefertiti

b) The Dendera Zodiac relief

c) The Rosetta Stone

9 **What is the name of the Celtic figure carved into the chalk of Windover Hill in Sussex?**

a) The Long Man of Wilmington

b) The Cerne Abbas Giant

c) The Great Red Horse

10 **Where are the Roman mosaics of the House of Dionysus, the House of Theseus and the House of Aion?**

a) Athens, Greece

b) Paphos, Cyprus

c) Heraklion, Crete

A

1 b
2 a
3 a
4 b
5 a
6 c
7 c
8 c
9 a
10 b

ART AND DESIGN

MOVERS AND SHAKERS

1 **What was the name of the 1997 exhibition at the Royal Academy which was the first to show Charles Saatchi's art collection of Young British Artists en masse?**

a) *Sensation*

b) *Revelation*

c) *Perversion*

2 **Jay Joplin, art dealer and owner of London's *White Cube* galleries is married to which Turner prize-shortlisted artist?**

a) Sarah Morris

b) Catherine Yass

c) Sam Taylor-Wood

3 **What was the name of Andy Warhol's studio in New York where he produced a vast body of work in the 1960s?**

a) The Studio

b) The Factory

c) The Assembly Line

4 **The National Gallery of British Art, which opened in 1897, was founded by which art philanthropist?**

a) John D. Rockefeller

b) Andrew Carnegie

c) Henry Tate

5 **In 2006 which work became the most expensive painting ever to be sold?**

a) *Adele Bloch-Bauer I* by Gustav Klimt

b) *No 5, 1948* by Jackson Pollock

c) *Garçon à la Pipe* by Pablo Picasso

A

1 a

2 c

3 b

4 c

5 a

BUSINESS

ADVERTISING SLOGANS

BRITISH ENTERPRISE

BIG BUSINESS

IMPORTS AND EXPORTS

ECONOMICS AND ECONOMISTS

PEOPLE IN BUSINESS

ADVERTISING CAMPAIGNS

ENTREPRENEURS

MONEY MATTERS

BOOM AND BUST

BUSINESS TERMS

CURRENCIES

ADVERTISING SLOGANS

1 The slogan 'I'd rather die of thirst than drink from the cup of mediocrity' was used to advertise which premium lager?

a) Kronenberg

b) Stella Artois

c) Heineken

2 Which country wanted to know 'Where the bloody hell are you?'

a) USA

b) Canada

c) Australia

3 What was the slogan promoted by Nancy Reagan as part of the US government's war on drugs?

a) 'Just say no'

b) 'Above the influence'

c) 'Stay clean'

4 Which celebrity was used by John Smith's bitter in their 'No nonsense' advertising campaign in the 1990s?

a) Gary Lineker

b) Alan Davies

c) Jack Dee

5 Why did Heinz drop the 'Beanz meanz Heinz' slogan after using it for thirty years?

a) It had received too many complaints about the misspellings

b) It wanted to ensure its brand was associated with more than just baked beans

c) The Trading Standards Authority felt that the slogan was misleading

6 Which organisation's slogan is 'don't be evil'?

a) The CIA

b) Google

c) Gap

7 What is the title of the book by Naomi Klein which looked at the branding and advertising techniques of multinational corporations?

a) *No Space*

b) *No Choice*

c) *No Logo*

8 Which company asked 'Where do you want to go today?'

a) Thomas Cook

b) Microsoft

c) Volkswagen

9 The original logo of which company featured Isaac Newton?

a) Intel

b) Microsoft

c) Apple

10 'Clunk click every trip', the public information film slogan for seatbelts in the 1970s, was spoken by which celebrity?

a) Bob Monkhouse

b) Bruce Forsyth

c) Jimmy Saville

1 b
2 c
3 a
4 c
5 b
6 b
7 c
8 b
9 c
10 c

Q BRITISH ENTERPRISE

1 **Which is the oldest: Harrods, Selfridges or Liberty?**

a) Harrods

b) Selfridges

c) Liberty

2 **Which global car manufacturer bought Bentley in 1998?**

a) BMV

b) Volkswagen

c) General Motors

3 **Why are Strelley and Wollaton significant in the history of British industry?**

a) John Strelley and Peter Wollaton invented the piston engine

b) They are two towns in Nottinghamshire linked by Britain's first railway

c) They were the first two companies listed on the original FTSE index

4 **Which British electronics manufacturer produced the CPC range of computers?**

a) Amstrad

b) Alba

c) Linn

5 **In which year did Railtrack go into liquidation?**

a) 1997

b) 1999

c) 2001

6 **The fictitious Coketown – modelled on Preston – was the setting for which novel about Britain in the industrial revolution?**

a) Elizabeth Gaskell's *Mary Barton*

b) Charles Dickens' *Hard Times*

c) Benjamin Disraeli's *Sybil*

7 **When did the last deep coal mine in Wales – Tower Colliery in Hirwaun, Rhondda Cynon Taf – close down?**

a) 2002

b) 2005

c) 2008

8 **Which city links Boots the Chemist, the Raleigh Cycle Company and John Player & Sons?**

a) Leeds

b) Nottingham

c) Bath

9 **Whittard – the luxury tea and coffee retailer – is 'of' which London neighbourhood?**

a) Kensington

b) Chelsea

c) Hampstead

10 **Which aircraft manufacturer founded in 1934 was nationalised and merged with the British Aircraft Corporation and Scottish Aviation to form British Aerospace in 1977?**

a) A. V. Roe and Company

b) Armstrong Whitworth

c) Hawker Siddeley

A

1 a
2 b
3 b
4 a
5 c
6 b
7 c
8 b
9 b
10 c

Q BIG BUSINESS

1 How did Ray Kroc wisely spend $2.7m in 1961?

a) He founded Abbey Road studios, prior to the success of the Beatles

b) He bought out the McDonald brothers

c) He loaned it to Ralph Lauren, then a young fashion designer

2 In Armando Iannucci's satirical comedy show *Time Trumpet*, what does Tesco invade to create the world's first 'retail country'?

a) Isle of Wight

b) Denmark

c) Australia

3 Why did Henry Ford insist his Model T car was available in 'any colour . . . so long as it is black'?

a) Black enabled a lucrative deal for Ford to supply the cars for use as hearses

b) It was his wife's favourite colour

c) Black paint had a quick drying time

4 Which sportswear company, founded by Bill Bowerman and Philip Knight in 1964, was originally called Blue Ribbon Sports?

a) Adidas

b) Nike

c) Puma

5 Which corporation owns the Pot Noodle, Peperami and Marmite brands?

a) Unilever

b) Procter and Gamble

c) Nestlé

6 **Which of the following chocolate and confectionary makers did not have a factory in York?**

a) John Cadbury

b) Henry Rowntree

c) Joseph Terry

7 **To which cosmetics giant did Anita Roddick sell The Body Shop for £652m in 2006?**

a) Max Factor

b) L'Oréal

c) Estée Lauder

8 **According to UK law, what percentage of a market controlled by a single business constitutes a monopoly?**

a) 25 per cent

b) 50 per cent

c) 75 per cent

9 **What did the Nintendo company make when it first started business in the 19th century?**

a) Confectionery

b) Playing cards

c) Dolls

10 **Which company is nicknamed 'Big Blue'?**

a) BMV

b) IBM

c) TDK

A

1 b
2 b
3 c
4 b
5 a
6 a
7 b
8 a
9 b
10 b

Q IMPORTS AND EXPORTS

1 What British product was subject to a worldwide export ban in 1996?

a) Chicken

b) Cheddar

c) Beef

2 Which country is the world's largest exporter of coal?

a) Australia

b) China

c) Russia

3 Until the 19th century, where did the vast majority of tea drunk in Britain come from?

a) India

b) China

c) West Indies

4 Which national flag is the same as that of the original flag of the former British East India Company?

a) USA

b) India

c) Hawaii

5 On which continent is the MERCOSUR free trade initiative active?

a) Africa

b) Asia

c) South America

6 **In which African country did coffee originate?**

a) Kenya

b) Ethiopia

c) Egypt

7 **Which country was the original 'banana republic' as defined by American satirist O. Henry?**

a) Honduras

b) Brazil

c) The Bahamas

8 **According to the UN, which country is the world's largest producer of cocoa?**

a) USA

b) Cote d'Ivoire

c) Indonesia

9 **With which country did Britain go to war in the 19th century after its government banned the importing of opium?**

a) India

b) China

c) Japan

10 **Who was US president when the North American Free Trade Agreement began?**

a) Ronald Reagan

b) George Bush

c) Bill Clinton

A

1 c
2 a
3 b
4 c
5 c
6 b
7 a
8 b
9 b
10 c

Q ECONOMICS AND ECONOMISTS

1 Which economist is best known for his views on population growth, in which he predicted the human race would reproduce beyond all control and cause a worldwide catastrophe?

a) Thomas Doubleday

b) Thomas Hood

c) Thomas Malthus

2 In which English city did Friedrich Engels work for a textile firm, an experience which inspired his first book *The Condition of the Working Class in England*?

a) Sheffield

b) Leeds

c) Manchester

3 What did Thomas Carlyle call economics (or political economy, as it was known in his day)?

a) The doubtful science

b) The dreadful science

c) The dismal science

4 Which of the following people attended the London School of Economics?

a) Pete Townsend

b) Mick Jagger

c) Elton John

5 Who wrote *The Affluent Society*, first published in the 1950s?

a) J. K. Galbraith

b) Friedrich Hayek

c) Milton Friedman

6 **Which economist caused controversy by linking the fall in crime in US cities during the 1990s with the legalisation of abortion in 1973?**

a) Steven Levitt

b) Tim Harford

c) Ariel Rubenstein

7 **Which of the following words was coined in 1968 by Karl Brunner to describe the economic theories of Milton Friedman?**

a) Macroeconomics

b) Monetarism

c) Short-termism

8 **At which University of London college is the body of Jeremy Bentham on display?**

a) University College London

b) The School of Oriental and African Studies

c) London School of Economics and Political Science

9 **Who succeeded Alan Greenspan as chair of the US Federal Reserve?**

a) Ben Bernanke

b) Donald Rumsfeld

c) Paul Wolfowitz

10 **Which politician served as Chancellor of the Exchequer four times in his career?**

a) William Pitt the Younger

b) William Gladstone

c) William Harcourt

A

1 c
2 c
3 c
4 b
5 a
6 a
7 b
8 a
9 a
10 b

Q PEOPLE IN BUSINESS

1 What is the name of the autobiography of Jacqueline Gold, chief executive of Ann Summers?

a) *Good Vibrations*

b) *In the Heat of the Night*

c) *Knickerbockerglory*

2 Which American politician was once CEO of Halliburton, a company much involved in the rebuilding of Iraq after the second Gulf War?

a) Colin Powell

b) Donald Rumsfeld

c) Dick Cheney

3 Who started his business career with a successful 'five and dime' store in Lancaster, Pennsylvania?

a) Frank Woolworth

b) Richard W. Sears

c) Joseph Bloomingdale

4 Which businessman and philanthropist made a particularly large donation to the Bill and Melinda Gates Foundation in 2006?

a) Steve Jobs

b) Warren Buffett

c) Carlos Slim

5 Which software company was founded by a Harvard drop-out in 1975?

a) IBM

b) Apple Computers

c) Microsoft

6 **Which one of the following high street chains is not owned by Philip Green?**

a) Topshop

b) Dorothy Perkins

c) Marks and Spencer

7 **Which football club did Mohammed Al Fayed buy in 1997?**

a) Chelsea

b) Fulham

c) Tottenham Hotspur

8 **In which year was Sainsbury's founded by John James and Mary Ann Sainsbury?**

a) 1869

b) 1900

c) 1952

9 **Jeff Bezos created which online retailer?**

a) Amazon

b) Lastminute

c) Play

10 **The Miss Universe Organisation is owned by which businessman?**

a) Sean 'P Diddy' Combs

b) Donald Trump

c) Harvey Weinstein

A

1 a
2 c
3 a
4 b
5 c
6 c
7 b
8 a
9 a
10 b

BUSINESS

Q ADVERTISING CAMPAIGNS

1 **In which year did the Tipps family of chimpanzees begin to advertise PG Tips tea?**

a) 1956

b) 1966

c) 1976

2 **Michael Winner – and his 'Calm down dear' catchphrase – appeared in adverts for which insurance company?**

a) Direct Line

b) esure

c) Churchill

3 **Who directed the original Scottish widow television advert?**

a) Anthony Minghella

b) David Bailey

c) Lucian Freud

4 **Which of the following has not been a Cadbury's Flake girl?**

a) Joss Stone

b) Alyssa Sutherland

c) Amanda Lamb

5 **Which of these photographers has not shot a Pirelli calendar?**

a) Annie Leibovitz

b) Mario Testino

c) David LaChapelle

6 The characters of Papa and Nicole were created for which car manufacturer?

a) Renault

b) Citroën

c) Fiat

7 Which England footballer made a series of cameo appearances alongside the honey monster in adverts for Sugar Puffs?

a) Ian Wright

b) Alan Shearer

c) Paul Gascoigne

8 Which model fronted the 'hello boys' UK Wonderbra campaign?

a) Eva Herzigova

b) Elle Macpherson

c) Elizabeth Hurley

9 Which of the following was the first advert to feature a song by the Beatles?

a) Garmin GPS, 'The Long and Winding Road'

b) South-West Trains, 'It Won't Be Long'

c) Luvs nappies, 'All you need is Luvs'

10 Who, alongside Sharon Maugham, formed the Nescafé Gold Blend couple?

a) Ray Winstone

b) Anthony Head

c) Nigel Havers

A

1 a
2 b
3 b
4 c
5 c
6 a
7 b
8 a
9 c
10 b

Q ENTREPRENEURS

1 How did Phineas Barnum make his fortune in the 19th century?

a) He discovered gold while working at a lumber mill in California

b) He invented a prototype of the electric chair and marketed it as a tool for parents to use to discipline their children

c) He was a showman who organised freak shows, set-up a museum of curiosities and founded a circus

2 Who co-founded Google with Sergey Brin?

a) Mark Zuckerberg

b) Larry Page

c) Steve Jobs

3 In which television programme do contestants pitch their business idea to try and get a successful entrepreneur to invest in their business?

a) *Dragons' Den*

b) *The Apprentice*

c) *Risking It All*

4 Which entrepreneur started out by selling electrical goods out of a van?

a) Richard Branson

b) Alan Sugar

c) Bill Gates

5 What is the name of Oprah Winfrey's company?

a) OPFREY Multimedia

b) OWIN Television

c) HARPO Productions

6 **According to the 2008 *Forbes* list, who was the world's richest woman?**

a) Liliane Bettencourt

b) J. K. Rowling

c) Margaret Whitman

7 **Which entrepreneur used to chair Millwall FC?**

a) Peter Jones

b) Theo Paphitis

c) Duncan Bannatyne

8 **Which film studio is owned by Rupert Murdoch?**

a) Paramount

b) United Artists

c) 20th Century Fox

9 **How much was the deal worth which secured Chelsea FC for Russian billionaire Roman Abramovich in 2003?**

a) £4m

b) £140m

c) £400m

10 **Which entrepreneur lost a son in the *Titanic* disaster?**

a) John D. Rockefeller

b) Meyer Guggenheim

c) Andrew Carnegie

A

1 c
2 b
3 a
4 b
5 c
6 a
7 b
8 c
9 b
10 b

Q MONEY MATTERS

1 In which year was the UK £1 note abolished?

a) 1978

b) 1988

c) 1998

2 Where was the world's first stock exchange established?

a) London

b) Antwerp

c) Florence

3 In the 17th century, which European country was the first to use paper money?

a) Sweden

b) Spain

c) Switzerland

4 On which stock market is the share index known as the Hang Seng?

a) Shanghai

b) Tokyo

c) Hong Kong

5 Who won an Oscar for his portrayal of stockbroker Gordon Gekko in the film *Wall Street*?

a) Tommy Lee Jones

b) Michael Douglas

c) Harrison Ford

BUSINESS

6 Which bank employed Jérôme Kerviel, who lost £3.7bn on unauthorised trading of derivatives in 2008?

a) BNP Paribas

b) Bear Stearns

c) Société Générale

7 What term is used to describe the process of sending spam emails purporting to be from a bank with the aim of defrauding the recipient?

a) Phishing

b) Phrogging

c) Phoxing

8 What is the name of the Nobel laureate who pioneered 'microcredit' loans for small businesses in developing companies?

a) Rehman Sobhan

b) Muhammad Yunus

c) Fakhruddin Ahmed

9 What was the Paris Bourse renamed as in 2000?

a) EuroStock Paris

b) Euronext Paris

c) Paris Gateway

10 On which London street does the Bank of England stand?

a) Chancery Lane

b) Cheapside

c) Threadneedle Street

A

1 b
2 b
3 a
4 c
5 b
6 c
7 a
8 b
9 b
10 c

Q BOOM AND BUST

1 In which month of the year was the Wall Street Crash of 1929?

a) February

b) June

c) October

2 At the height of the German hyperinflationary crisis of 1923, how long did it take for prices to double?

a) 2 days

b) 1 week

c) 2 weeks

3 How much did AOL pay for Time Warner in 2001 at the height of the dotcom bubble?

a) $1.64bn

b) $16.4bn

c) $164bn

4 Who played Nick Leeson in the 1999 biopic *Rogue Trader*?

a) Ewan McGregor

b) Christopher Ecclestone

c) Robert Carlyle

5 Who were 'the 49ers'?

a) Baby boomers born in 1949 that are predicted to put an unprecedented strain on the US social security system

b) Speculators who rushed to California in 1849 prompted by the gold rush

c) Brokers on the 49th floor of the New York Stock Exchange who leapt to their deaths during the Wall Street Crash

6 **Which of the following John Steinbeck novels is not set against the backdrop of America's Great Depression?**

a) *Of Mice and Men*

b) *The Pearl*

c) *The Grapes of Wrath*

7 **The term BRIC refers to four developing economies predicted to boom during this century. What does the C stand for?**

a) Canada

b) Czech Republic

c) China

8 **Which American company collapsed in December 2001 in the largest bankruptcy in US history?**

a) Exxon

b) Enron

c) General Motors

9 **On which 'black' day of the week did the British government withdraw the pound from the European Exchange Rate Mechanism in 1992?**

a) Monday

b) Wednesday

c) Friday

10 **Which of the following people has never filed for bankruptcy?**

a) Walt Disney

b) Donald Trump

c) Steve Wozniak

A

1	c
2	a
3	c
4	a
5	b
6	b
7	c
8	b
9	b
10	c

Q BUSINESS TERMS

What do the following acronyms stand for?

1 BACS

a) Bankers Associated Clearing System

b) Bankers Automatic Clearing System

c) Bankers Automated Clearing System

2 ERM

a) External Retail Market

b) Exchange Rate Mechanism

c) European Regional Market

3 LSE

a) London Services Exchange

b) London Shares Exchange

c) London Stock Exchange

4 NYMEX

a) New York Money Exchange

b) New York Mercantile Exchange

c) New York Metal Exchange

5 LIBOR

a) London Interbank Offered Rate

b) London International Banking Open Rate

c) London Interest Borrowing Offered Rate

BUSINESS

6 NASDAQ

a) National Association of Securities Dealers Automated Quotation

b) North American Securities Dealers Automated Quotation

c) North Atlantic Securities Dealers Automated Quotation

7 HSBC

a) Hong Kong and Shanghai Banking Corporation

b) Hang Seng Banking Corporation

c) High Street Banking Corporation

8 APR

a) Appropriate Payment Rate

b) Annual Percentage Rate

c) Annual Payment Rate

9 AER

a) Annual Estimated Rate

b) Annual Extended Rate

c) Annual Equivalent Rate

10 FSA

a) Financial Services Authority

b) Financial Savings Authority

c) Financial Selling Authority

A

1 c
2 b
3 c
4 b
5 a
6 a
7 a
8 b
9 c
10 a

Q CURRENCIES

In which country would you spend the following?

1 Shekel

a) Venezuela
b) Israel
c) Nigeria

2 Dong

a) Vietnam
b) Laos
c) The Philippines

3 Zloty

a) Georgia
b) Azerbaijan
c) Poland

4 Ringgit

a) India
b) Pakistan
c) Malaysia

5 Balboa

a) Colombia
b) Panama
c) Guatemala

6 Pa'anga

a) Tonga
b) Fiji
c) Tuvalu

7 Riyal

a) Iran
b) Iraq
c) Saudi Arabia

8 Forint

a) Hungary
b) Czech Republic
c) Slovenia

9 Won

a) South Korea
b) Japan
c) Indonesia

10 Rand

a) Zimbabwe
b) Ghana
c) South Africa

A

1 b
2 a
3 c
4 c
5 b
6 a
7 c
8 a
9 a
10 c

ENTERTAINMENT

RADIO

THEATRE

DANCE

ADAPTATIONS

ANIMATION

FILM SEQUELS AND REMAKES

EPICS

ACTORS AND ACTRESSES

BRITISH FILM

AWARD WINNERS

TELEVISION COMEDY

SOAPS

CHILDREN'S TELEVISION

GUESS THE FILM

MURDER MYSTERY

DOCUMENTARIES

MUSICALS

ENTERTAINERS

HORROR

TAG LINES

RADIO

1 Who was the first female presenter on BBC Radio 1?

a) Jo Whiley

b) Mary Anne Hobbs

c) Annie Nightingale

2 Humphrey Lyttelton was the chair of which BBC Radio quiz?

a) *Just a Minute*

b) *I'm Sorry I Haven't a Clue*

c) *The News Quiz*

3 Which journalist and broadcaster presented the long-running BBC Radio series *Letter from America*?

a) Alistair Cooke

b) Roy Plomley

c) John Humphrys

4 What was the original name of *The Goon Show*?

a) *It's A Mad World*

b) *Crazy People*

c) *Loons at Large*

5 Which of the following records has not been subjected to a ban on BBC Radio?

a) George Formby's 'When I'm Cleaning Windows'

b) The Beatles' 'Come Together'

c) The Prodigy's 'Firestarter'

6 In 1938 who broadcast a radio adaptation of H. G. Wells' *The War of the Worlds* which persuaded millions of Americans that Martians had landed on Earth?

a) Orson Welles

b) Alfred Hitchcock

c) Cecil B. DeMille

7 Which radio programme is introduced by the music *Sailing By* by Ronald Binge?

a) *Desert Island Discs*

b) The late night *Shipping Forecast*

c) *Woman's Hour*

8 Which classic radio comedy show included the characters Rambling Syd Rumpo, Binkie Huckaback and Dame Celia Molestrangler?

a) *I'm Sorry, I'll Read That Again*

b) *ITMA*

c) *Round the Horne*

9 Which legendary DJ produced an annual 'Festive 50'?

a) Alan Freed

b) John Peel

c) Dave Lee Travis

10 In 1965 which well-known playwright wrote five episodes for *Mrs. Dale's Diary*, the first post-war soap on British radio?

a) Tom Stoppard

b) Harold Pinter

c) John Osborne

A

1 c

2 b

3 a

4 b

5 c

6 a

7 b

8 c

9 b

10 a

Q THEATRE

1 Whose play *The Mousetrap* holds the record for the longest-running stage production?

a) Terence Rattigan

b) Noel Coward

c) Agatha Christie

2 Who wrote the plays *The Homecoming* and *The Birthday Party*?

a) Alan Bennett

b) Tom Stoppard

c) Harold Pinter

3 Which world leader wrote a play called *The Jeweller's Shop* which was adapted into a film starring Burt Lancaster?

a) Bill Clinton

b) Vaclav Havel

c) Pope John Paul II

4 An actress using which word shocked some of the audience at the first performance of George Bernard Shaw's play *Pygmalion* in 1914?

a) Bloody

b) Bugger

c) Bastard

5 In the theatre what is a 'scrim'?

a) A 'see-through' curtain

b) A makeup artist

c) An area of the stage

ENTERTAINMENT

6 In which century did women first appear on a public stage in England?

a) 16th

b) 17th

c) 18th

7 Which West End theatre has the biggest capacity?

a) The Apollo Victoria

b) The London Coliseum

c) The London Palladium

8 Which former London theatre got past the censor by presenting its nude girls in motionless poses in the 1930s and 40s?

a) The Windmill

b) The Opera Comique

c) The Scala Theatre

9 Who was the first actor to be knighted?

a) Laurence Olivier

b) Henry Irving

c) Herbert Beerbohm Tree

10 Which actress lost a leg to gangrene?

a) Sarah Bernhardt

b) Mrs Patrick Campbell

c) Anne Bracegirdle

1 c
2 c
3 c
4 a
5 a
6 b
7 b
8 a
9 b
10 a

DANCE

1 **Which dancer starred in *The Prince of the Pagodas* in 1989, becoming the youngest ballerina to take a principal role at the Royal Ballet?**

a) Viviana Durante

b) Darcy Bussell

c) Sarah Wildor

2 **What year did Marie Rambert form her school of dance?**

a) 1890

b) 1910

c) 1920

3 **Which of the following was originally devised by a dancer?**

a) Laban Movement Analysis

b) The Pilates Method

c) The Alexander Technique

4 **Who choreographed the first performances of Tchaikovsky's ballets *Swan Lake* and *The Sleeping Beauty*?**

a) Jules Perrot

b) Marius Petipa

c) Arthur Saint-Léon

5 **In which ballet do the characters Count Albrecht and Hilarion appear?**

a) *Giselle*

b) *Swan Lake*

c) *Coppélia*

ENTERTAINMENT

6 Which pioneer of modern dance died when her long headscarf was caught on the wheel of her car?

a) Isadora Duncan

b) Twyla Tharp

c) Martha Graham

7 Which well-known 20th century dancer was born Frederick Austerlitz?

a) Frederick Ashton

b) Anton Dolin

c) Fred Astaire

8 Who took the role of the dancer Victoria Page in the 1948 Powell and Pressburger film *The Red Shoes*?

a) Moira Shearer

b) Margot Fonteyn

c) Margaret Lockwood

9 In which year did Rudolf Nureyev defect from Russia to the West?

a) 1961

b) 1964

c) 1969

10 How does the waltz get its name?

a) From the small Austrian town of Waltz where it originated

b) From Friedrich von Waltz who was the first composer to write waltzes

c) From the German word *waltzen*, meaning to revolve

1 b

2 c

3 a

4 b

5 a

6 a

7 c

8 a

9 a

10 c

ADAPTATIONS

1 Which of Thomas Harris' Hannibal Lecter novels has been filmed twice?

a) *The Silence of the Lambs*

b) *Red Dragon*

c) *Hannibal Rising*

2 Whose album *No Promises* features poems by W. B. Yeats, Emily Dickinson and Christina Rossetti set to music?

a) Vanessa Paradis

b) Charlotte Gainsbourg

c) Carla Bruni

3 The 1995 film, *Clueless*, starring Alicia Silverstone, is (loosely) based on which classic English novel?

a) Jane Austen's *Emma*

b) Charlotte Bronte's *Jane Eyre*

c) Thomas Hardy's *Tess of the D'Urbervilles*

4 In the Oscar-winning film *Adaptation*, which novel is protagonist Charlie Kaufman attempting to rewrite for the screen?

a) David Guterson's *Snow Falling on Cedars*

b) J. D. Salinger's *The Catcher in the Rye*

c) Susan Orlean's *The Orchid Thief*

5 What was the *Pirates of the Caribbean* trilogy adapted from?

a) A video game

b) A theme park ride

c) A comic book

6 **Gus Van Sant's film *My Own Private Idaho* is loosely based on which Shakespeare play?**

a) *Othello*

b) *King Lear*

c) *Henry IV, Part 1*

7 **Which role in *The Importance of Being Earnest* has been played on screen by both Michael Redgrave and Colin Firth?**

a) Jack Worthing

b) Algernon Moncrieff

c) Dr Chasuble

8 **Who directed *Tommy*, the film adaptation of The Who's rock opera?**

a) Alex Cox

b) Ken Russell

c) Mike Leigh

9 **Which Italian director adapted Boccaccio's *Decameron* and Chaucer's *Canterbury Tales*?**

a) Federico Fellini

b) Michelangelo Antonioni

c) Pier Paolo Pasolini

10 **Which poem by Lewis Carroll was used as the basis for a film by Terry Gilliam?**

a) 'The Walrus and the Carpenter'

b) 'Jabberwocky'

c) 'The Hunting of the Snark'

A

1 b
2 c
3 a
4 c
5 b
6 c
7 a
8 b
9 c
10 b

Q ANIMATION

1 **What was the first feature-length animated film made by Walt Disney?**

a) *Fantasia*

b) *Snow White and the Seven Dwarfs*

c) *Dumbo*

2 **Which of the following is not a genuine episode of the controversial *South Park*?**

a) 'Osama Bin Laden Has Farty Pants'

b) 'The Passion of the Jew'

c) 'Cartman Trapped in the Closet'

3 **Which animator was responsible for the creation of Daffy Duck, Droopy and Bugs Bunny?**

a) Fred Quimby

b) Bob Clampett

c) Tex Avery

4 **Peter, Lois, Chris, Meg, Brian and Stewie are characters in which animated show?**

a) *American Dad*

b) *Family Guy*

c) *Futurama*

5 **In *SpongeBob SquarePants*, what kind of creature is Patrick, SpongeBob's best friend and neighbour?**

a) Starfish

b) Squid

c) Prawn

ENTERTAINMENT

6 **Which of the following cartoon characters was first created by E. C. Segar in the 1920s and went on to become the star of animated films produced by Max Fleischer?**

a) Huckleberry Hound

b) Felix the Cat

c) Popeye

7 **Which cartoon characters made their first appearance in a 1940 short called *Puss Gets the Boot*?**

a) Sylvester and Tweety Pie

b) Tom and Jerry

c) Goofy and Pluto

8 **In *Wacky Races*, what is Dick Dastardly and Mutley's car called?**

a) The Mean Machine

b) The Creepy Coupe

c) The Bulletproof Bomb

9 **With whom did the Teenage Mutant Ninja Turtles share their names?**

a) Italian artists

b) Planets

c) American states

10 **Whose dog is called Santa's Little Helper?**

a) The Flintstones'

b) The Simpsons'

c) The Munsters'

A

1 b
2 c
3 c
4 b
5 a
6 c
7 b
8 a
9 a
10 b

Q FILM SEQUELS AND REMAKES

1 Who took the role of Catwoman in the 1992 film *Batman Returns*?

a) Uma Thurman

b) Michelle Pfeiffer

c) Kim Basinger

2 Who played the role of Charlie Croker, originally made famous by Michael Caine, in the 2003 remake of *The Italian Job*?

a) Mark Wahlberg

b) Sylvester Stallone

c) Kiefer Sutherland

3 In *Home Alone 2*, in which city was Macaulay Culkin lost?

a) Los Angeles

b) Chicago

c) New York

4 Which former England footballer is killed by Sharon Stone's Catherine Tramell in the opening scene of *Basic Instinct 2*?

a) Paul Gascoigne

b) Stan Collymore

c) Tony Adams

5 Which film was made in 1922, starring Max Schreck, and in 1980, starring Klaus Kinski?

a) *The Island of Dr Moreau*

b) *Nosferatu*

c) *Frankenstein*

ENTERTAINMENT

6 **Which original film directed by Howard Hawks was remade by Brian de Palma?**

a) *The Big Sleep*

b) *Body Double*

c) *Scarface*

7 **Which film did Alfred Hitchcock direct twice?**

a) *The Man Who Knew Too Much*

b) *Sabotage*

c) *To Catch a Thief*

8 **Who is missing from this sequence: Ridley Scott, James Cameron, David Fincher, _______________?**

a) Steven Soderbergh

b) Jean-Pierre Jeunet

c) Michael Mann

9 ***Never Say Never Again* was the second film adaptation of which of Ian Fleming's James Bond novels?**

a) *Thunderball*

b) *Goldfinger*

c) *Moonraker*

10 **Akira Kurosawa's *Shichinin no samurai* was remade into which classic Hollywood western?**

a) *High Noon*

b) *The Magnificent Seven*

c) *The Good, The Bad and The Ugly*

A

1 b
2 a
3 c
4 b
5 b
6 c
7 a
8 b
9 a
10 b

EPICS

1 **In which film did Oliver Reed make his final screen appearance?**

a) *Gladiator*

b) *The Thin Red Line*

c) *Titanic*

2 **Who created the special effects for the films *Jason and the Argonauts* and *The Golden Voyage of Sinbad*?**

a) Max Fleischer

b) Willis O'Brien

c) Ray Harryhausen

3 **Which actor plays Jesus in Mel Gibson's *The Passion of the Christ*?**

a) James Caan

b) Jim Caviezel

c) John Cusack

4 **Which film had the tag line 'Makes Ben-Hur look like an epic'?**

a) *Monty Python and the Holy Grail*

b) *The Mummy*

c) *Indiana Jones and the Temple of Doom*

5 **Which epic film's failure at the box office led to the collapse of its studio?**

a) *The Postman*

b) *Waterworld*

c) *Heaven's Gate*

6 What is Vito Corleone's real surname, as revealed in *The Godfather Part II*?

a) Andolini

b) Giovanni

c) Panucci

7 Which Native American language is featured in *Dances With Wolves*?

a) Navajo

b) Lakota

c) Chickasaw

8 Which film did veteran film critic Roger Ebert describe as 'sickening, utterly worthless, shameful trash'?

a) *Alexander*

b) *Troy*

c) *Caligula*

9 Who directed *Spartacus*?

a) Stanley Kubrick

b) Sidney Lumet

c) Richard Attenborough

10 For which of these films did David Lean not win a Best Director Oscar?

a) *Lawrence of Arabia*

b) *The Bridge on the River Kwai*

c) *Doctor Zhivago*

A

1 a
2 c
3 b
4 a
5 c
6 a
7 b
8 c
9 a
10 c

ENTERTAINMENT

Q ACTORS AND ACTRESSES

1 What curious role did Val Kilmer take in the 1993 film *True Romance*?

a) An alien

b) The ghost of Elvis Presley

c) A corpse

2 Who played Fleance in Roman Polanski's 1971 film of *Macbeth*?

a) Keith Chegwin

b) Jonathan Ross

c) Shane Richie

3 What is Sigourney Weaver's real first name?

a) Susan

b) Simone

c) Sharon

4 Which movie tough guy once remarked that, 'I look like a rock quarry that someone has dynamited'?

a) Humphrey Bogart

b) Ernest Borgnine

c) Charles Bronson

5 Which film actress married Humphrey Bogart in 1945?

a) Lauren Bacall

b) Kim Novak

c) Katherine Hepburn

6 **Who provided the baby's voice in the 1989 film *Look Who's Talking*?**

a) Sylvester Stallone

b) Bruce Willis

c) Mel Gibson

7 **Which star of gangster movies started his career as a female impersonator?**

a) Humphrey Bogart

b) George Raft

c) James Cagney

8 **Which British TV and film actress is married to the Hollywood director Taylor Hackford?**

a) Helen Mirren

b) Joanna Lumley

c) Amanda Burton

9 **Where was Russell Crowe born?**

a) New Zealand

b) New Guinea

c) Australia

10 **In which 1973 film did Steve McQueen play a prisoner trying to escape from a French penal colony?**

a) *Escape from Devil's Island*

b) *The Great Escape*

c) *Papillon*

A

1 b
2 a
3 a
4 c
5 a
6 b
7 c
8 a
9 a
10 c

Q BRITISH FILM

1 *The Madness of King George* is based on which British king?

a) George II

b) George III

c) George IV

2) In which city do the events of the 1996 film *Trainspotting* take place?

a) London

b) Edinburgh

c) Manchester

3 What was the first British film to win a Best Picture Oscar?

a) Laurence Olivier's *Hamlet*

b) Carol Reed's *The Third Man*

c) David Lean's *Great Expectations*

4 Which of the following Shakespeare plays has not been adapted for screen by Kenneth Branagh?

a) *Love's Labour's Lost*

b) *As You Like It*

c) *A Midsummer Night's Dream*

5 In which Ealing comedy does Alec Guinness play eight siblings?

a) *Kind Hearts and Coronets*

b) *Whisky Galore!*

c) *The Ladykillers*

6 **Michael Winterbottom's 2006 film, *A Cock And Bull Story*, is based on which 18th-century novel?**

a) *Tom Jones*

b) *Tristram Shandy*

c) *Clarissa*

7 ***The Night of the Hunter*, released in 1955 and starring Robert Mitchum, is the only film directed by which famous British actor?**

a) Lawrence Olivier

b) Charles Laughton

c) Richard Burton

8 **The classic documentary *Night Mail* features rhyming verse by which poet?**

a) T. S. Eliot

b) W. H. Auden

c) Y. B. Yeats

9 ***The Full Monty* is set in which English city?**

a) Sheffield

b) Leeds

c) Manchester

10 **The music of which composer features in *Brief Encounter*?**

a) Frederic Chopin

b) Sergei Rachmaninov

c) Pyotr Tchaikovsky

A

1 b

2 b

3 a

4 c

5 a

6 b

7 b

8 b

9 a

10 b

Q AWARD WINNERS

1 What was the first winner of the Best Animated Feature award at the Oscars?

a) *Shrek*

b) *Ice Age*

c) *Monsters, Inc.*

2 Which Hollywood figure founded the Sundance Film Festival?

a) Steven Spielberg

b) Samuel Goldwyn

c) Robert Redford

3 Who is the oldest person to win the Oscar for Best Actress?

a) Jessica Tandy for *Driving Miss Daisy*

b) Katherine Hepburn for *On Golden Pond*

c) Marie Dressler for *Min and Bill*

4 In 1941 which now-forgotten movie beat *Citizen Kane* and *The Maltese Falcon* to take the Oscar for Best Picture?

a) *How Green Was My Valley*

b) *The Little Foxes*

c) *Sergeant York*

5 For which movie did John Wayne win his first and only Oscar for Best Actor?

a) *Stagecoach*

b) *The Searchers*

c) *True Grit*

6 At which film festival does the best picture receive the Golden Bear award?

a) Cannes

b) Berlin

c) Venice

7 Which film awards are traditionally held inside a tent on a beach in Santa Monica, California, the night before the Oscars?

a) Golden Globes

b) Independent Spirit Awards

c) Golden Raspberry Awards

8 Which film won Best Picture at the first ever Oscars ceremony in 1927?

a) *The Jazz Singer*

b) *All Quiet on the Western Front*

c) *Wings*

9 Which of the following singers has been nominated for a Best Actress Oscar?

a) Diana Ross

b) Whitney Houston

c) Madonna

10 Which actor was nominated for the Best Actor Oscar for four consecutive years between 1951 and 1954?

a) Humphrey Bogart

b) Marlon Brando

c) Gregory Peck

1 a
2 c
3 a
4 a
5 c
6 b
7 b
8 c
9 a
10 b

Q TELEVISION COMEDY

1 In *Hancock's Half-Hour*, where did Tony Hancock live?

a) The Laurels, Brickfield Terrace, Holloway

b) 42 Viaduct Way, Ruislip

c) 23 Railway Cuttings, East Cheam

2 In an episode of which TV series does a much-loved Siberian hamster turn out to be a common-or-garden rat?

a) *Fawlty Towers*

b) *'Allo 'Allo*

c) *Only Fools and Horses*

3 Who played Richard III in an episode of *Blackadder*?

a) Rik Mayall

b) Peter Cook

c) Spike Milligan

4 What was the name of the character played by David Jason in *Porridge*?

a) Blanco

b) Bunco

c) Danko

5 Which TV comedian used the catchphrase, 'Ooh, you are awful. But I like you'?

a) Tommy Cooper

b) Dick Emery

c) Eric Morecambe

6 **Which scriptwriter created the sitcoms *The Liver Birds* and *Bread*?**

a) John Sullivan

b) Phil Redmond

c) Carla Lane

7 **Which TV comedy series was largely set in a small town called Royston Vasey?**

a) *The Office*

b) *Fawlty Towers*

c) *The League of Gentlemen*

8 **Which member of the *Red Dwarf* crew has an insufferable brother called Ace?**

a) Arnold Rimmer

b) Kristine Kochanski

c) David Lister

9 **In which classic American sitcom did characters called Lurch, Pugsley and Fester appear?**

a) *The Munsters*

b) *The Beverley Hillbillies*

c) *The Addams Family*

10 **In *Dad's Army* what was Private Fraser's occupation?**

a) Butcher

b) Undertaker

c) Chemist

1 c
2 a
3 b
4 a
5 b
6 c
7 c
8 a
9 c
10 b

SOAPS

1 In which soap did the body of wife-beater and child-abuser Trevor Jordache remain undisturbed under the patio for a year?

a) *EastEnders*

b) *Emmerdale*

c) *Brookside*

2 How did Pauline Fowler die in *EastEnders* – and who was responsible?

a) Daughter-in-law Sonia poisoned her tea

b) Husband Joe hit her over the head with a frying pan

c) Son Martin, distracted by sending a text message, ran over her in his car

3 Which future Oscar winner played Irma Ogden's boyfriend in *Coronation Street*?

a) Daniel Day-Lewis

b) Ben Kingsley

c) Ranulph Fiennes

4 How was Harold Bishop's five-year absence from *Neighbours* explained?

a) After surviving a fall from a cliff, he suffered from amnesia and forgot about his former life

b) He was kidnapped on holiday and held hostage by a terrorist group

c) He left Erinsborough in shame after his wife discovered his affair with her sister

5 Where is the soap *Hollyoaks* set?

a) Liverpool

b) Chester

c) Warrington

6 **Which soap featured a Lockerbie-inspired plane crash?**

a) *EastEnders*

b) *Emmerdale*

c) *Family Affairs*

7 **What is the name of the tube station featured in *EastEnders*?**

a) Albert Square

b) George Street

c) Walford East

8 **Which Australian soap was built around foster parents Tom and Pippa Fletcher?**

a) *Home and Away*

b) *Sons and Daughters*

c) *Pacific Drive*

9 **Who was 'The Weatherfield One'?**

a) Alma Barlow

b) Gail Platt

c) Deirdre Rachid

10 **In which soap was Bouncer the dog granted a whole episode shot from his canine perspective, ending in a marriage to his pedigree chum, Rosie?**

a) *Neighbours*

b) *Eldorado*

c) *Sunset Beach*

A

1 c

2 b

3 b

4 a

5 b

6 b

7 c

8 a

9 c

10 a

Q CHILDREN'S TELEVISION

1 **What animal was George in *Rainbow*?**

a) A pig

b) A hippo

c) A bear

2 **What did Mr Benn usually wear?**

a) Pyjamas

b) A suit with bowler hat

c) A spacesuit

3 **Who provided the voice for Bob the Builder?**

a) Neil Morrissey

b) Martin Clunes

c) Rik Mayall

4 **In which TV series does the banjo-playing toad, Gabriel the Croaker appear?**

a) *Fingermouse*

b) *Bagpuss*

c) *The Clangers*

5 **In *Trumpton*, who were Pugh, Pugh, Barney McGrew, Cuthbert, Dibble and Grubb?**

a) The village police force

b) The village band

c) The village fire brigade

ENTERTAINMENT

6 **Whose sidekick was called Penfold?**

a) The Flowerpot Men

b) DangerMouse

c) Supergran

7 **Which of the following series was narrated by Bernard Cribbins?**

a) *The Wombles*

b) *Thomas the Tank Engine*

c) *Tales of the Riverbank*

8 **Who was the first Doctor Who?**

a) Patrick Troughton

b) William Hartnell

c) Peter Cushing

9 **Whose arch enemy was Texas Pete?**

a) Bagpuss

b) Deputy Dawg

c) SuperTed

10 **Who created *Grange Hill*?**

a) Tony Warren

b) Carla Lane

c) Phil Redmond

A

1 b
2 b
3 a
4 b
5 c
6 b
7 a
8 b
9 c
10 c

Q GUESS THE FILM

Identify the film through the list of principal characters or actors:

1 Anton Chigurh, Llewelyn Moss, Ed Tom Bell

a) *No Country For Old Men*

b) *LA Confidential*

c) *Heat*

2 Andy Dufresne, Ellis Boyd Redding

a) *The Green Mile*

b) *The Shawshank Redemption*

c) *Midnight Express*

3 Jack Nicholson, Shelley Duvall, Danny Lloyd

a) *The Postman Always Rings Twice*

b) *The Shining*

c) *One Flew Over the Cuckoo's Nest*

4 Marilyn Monroe, Tony Curtis, Jack Lemmon

a) *Some Like it Hot*

b) *All About Eve*

c) *The Seven Year Itch*

5 Martin Brody, Quint, Matt Hooper

a) *Apocalypse Now*

b) *Jaws*

c) *Easy Rider*

ENTERTAINMENT

6 Tony Montana, Elvira Hancock, Manny Ribera

a) *Goodfellas*

b) *Once Upon a Time in America*

c) *Scarface*

7 Cary Grant, Eva Marie Saint, James Mason

a) *To Catch a Thief*

b) *Strangers on a Train*

c) *North By Northwest*

8 Dean Keaton, Fred Fenster, Roger 'Verbal' Kint

a) *The Usual Suspects*

b) *The Dirty Dozen*

c) *The Good, The Bad and The Ugly*

9 Dickie Greenleaf, Marge Sherwood, Meredith Logue

a) *The English Patient*

b) *The Talented Mr Ripley*

c) *The Cook, The Thief, His Wife & Her Lover*

10 Vincent Vega, Jules Winnfield, Mia Wallace

a) *Grease*

b) *Saturday Night Fever*

c) *Pulp Fiction*

1 a

2 b

3 b

4 a

5 b

6 c

7 c

8 a

9 b

10 c

Q MURDER MYSTERY

1 What is the first name of Inspector Morse?

a) Isambard

b) Invincible

c) Endeavour

2 Who originally adapted *Midsomer Murders* for television?

a) Roald Dahl

b) Gillian Cross

c) Anthony Horowitz

3 Which of the following has not played one of Jonathan Creek's sidekicks?

a) Caroline Quentin

b) Amanda Holden

c) Julia Sawalha

4 Superintendent Norman Mullett is the beleaguered boss of which police station?

a) Sun Hill

b) Denton

c) Aidensfield

5 In which American city is *Columbo* set?

a) New York

b) San Francisco

c) Los Angeles

6 Who plays Gil Grissom in the American crime series *CSI*?

a) David Caruso

b) Michael Douglas

c) William Petersen

7 What is the name of the forensic psychologist in *Waking the Dead*?

a) Dr Eddie Fitzgerald

b) Dr Grace Foley

c) Dr Tony Hill

8 What is the name of the central character in *Prime Suspect*?

a) Samantha Ryan

b) Jane Tennison

c) Lynda La Plante

9 What is the surname of Buffy the Vampire Slayer?

a) Summers

b) Spring

c) Winters

10 In which series does Jack Malone lead a missing persons unit?

a) *Without a Trace*

b) *Vanished*

c) *NCS: Manhunt*

A

1 c
2 c
3 b
4 b
5 c
6 c
7 b
8 b
9 a
10 a

Q DOCUMENTARIES

1 Which was the first major series presented by David Attenborough?

a) *Life on Earth*

b) *The Living Planet*

c) *Trials of Life*

2 In Morgan Spurlock's film, *Super Size Me*, how does McDonalds label its most frequent customers?

a) Gold customers

b) Super heavy users

c) Ronald McDonalds

3 In *Fahrenheit 9/11*, what did Michael Moore claim George W. Bush's actions were in the aftermath of the attacks on the World Trade Center?

a) He had a secret meeting with leaders in Afghanistan

b) He flew members of the Bin Laden family to safety

c) He claimed they were not terrorist attacks

4 Which of these films won an Oscar for Best Documentary Feature?

a) *Buena Vista Social Club*

b) *The Story of the Weeping Camel*

c) *One Day in September*

5 Who narrated the classic TV documentary *The World at War*?

a) Laurence Olivier

b) John Gielgud

c) Brian Blessed

ENTERTAINMENT

6 When was *Seven Up*, a documentary series that would follow its participants at seven-year intervals through their lives, first broadcast?

a) 1950

b) 1957

c) 1964

7 What was the subject of the 2002 documentary film *Spellbound*?

a) A spelling competition

b) Modern day white witches

c) An amnesia patient

8 What is unusual about the 2006 documentary *Into Great Silence* which follows monastic life in the Carthusian Order?

a) The whole film is in Latin

b) The whole film is silent apart from the monks' chanting

c) It is filmed in real time

9 Who narrated the English-language version of *March of the Penguins*?

a) Morgan Freeman

b) Samuel L. Jackson

c) Edward Norton

10 Which of the following is not a documentary presented by Stephen Fry?

a) *HIV and Me*

b) *The Secret Life of the Manic Depressive*

c) *Who do you think you are?*

1	a
2	b
3	b
4	c
5	a
6	c
7	a
8	b
9	a
10	c

Q MUSICALS

1 Who wrote the song 'I Get a Kick out of You', from the musical *Anything Goes*?

a) Cole Porter

b) Irving Berlin

c) George Gershwin

2 In which city is *The Sound of Music* set?

a) Strasbourg

b) Salzburg

c) Vienna

3 Which is the longest running musical in the West End?

a) *The Phantom of the Opera*

b) *Cats*

c) *Les Misérables*

4 Who was 'the lady in the tutti-frutti hat'?

a) Josephine Baker

b) Carmen Miranda

c) Edith Piaf

5 Which musical was adapted from *Pygmalion*, a play by George Bernard Shaw?

a) *My Fair Lady*

b) *Carousel*

c) *Kiss me Kate*

6 What is the name of the *Simpsons* character based on Mary Poppins?

a) Fairy Strawbins

b) Geri Toppings

c) Sherri Bobbins

7 In which musical did the actors all perform wearing roller skates?

a) *Starlight Express*

b) *A Chorus Line*

c) *Jesus Christ Superstar*

8 Who wrote the lyrics for a musical version of *Sweeney Todd* for the stage?

a) Tim Rice

b) Stephen Sondheim

c) Rodgers and Hammerstein

9 Which musical's songs are adapted from poetry by T. S. Eliot?

a) *Rent*

b) *Godspell*

c) *Cats*

10 Which musical features a plant that feeds on human blood?

a) *Little Shop of Horrors*

b) *Rocky Horror Picture Show*

c) *Avenue Q*

A

1 a
2 b
3 c
4 b
5 a
6 c
7 a
8 b
9 c
10 a

Q ENTERTAINERS

1 In which decade did Bruce Forsyth make his television debut?

a) 1930s

b) 1940s

c) 1950s

2 What was George Formby's profession before he became a music hall star?

a) Bus conductor

b) Window cleaner

c) Jockey

3 Which of the following did not appear on the Morecambe & Wise Show?

a) Harold Wilson

b) Gene Kelly

c) Elton John

4 Who presented *Wipeout*, *Bonkers!* and *Family Fortunes*?

a) Henry Kelly

b) Bob Monkhouse

c) Les Dennis

5 Why was Noel Edmonds' *The Late, Late Breakfast Show* cancelled?

a) A contestant died during rehearsals for one of the stunts

b) Edmonds' salary demands were dismissed as 'ludicrous' by the BBC director-general

c) An audience member exposed himself during a live broadcast

6 **Which light entertainer had a number one hit with 'I Pretend' in 1968?**

a) Cilla Black

b) Des O'Connor

c) Lulu

7 **Lulu married which Bee Gee?**

a) Maurice

b) Robin

c) Barry

8 **Which TV show was hosted by Gordon Burns?**

a) *Scrapheap Challenge*

b) *The Krypton Factor*

c) *You Bet!*

9 **Who is entertainer Leslie Crowther's son-in-law?**

a) Jeremy Paxman

b) Phil Lynott

c) Pierce Brosnan

10 **Whose first solo single was a cover of a George Michael song?**

a) James Blunt

b) Robbie Williams

c) Craig David

A

1 a
2 c
3 b
4 b
5 a
6 b
7 a
8 b
9 b
10 b

HORROR

1 What is the name of the character killed in the infamous shower scene in Hitchcock's 1960 film *Psycho*?

a) Melanie Daniels

b) Marion Crane

c) Sarah Arbogast

2 Which film has spawned the most sequels?

a) *Scream*

b) *Friday the 13th*

c) *A Nightmare on Elm Street*

3 Which M. Night Shyamalan film features mysterious crop-circles?

a) *The Village*

b) *Lady in the Water*

c) *Signs*

4 What is the disease that infects the British population in *28 Days Later*?

a) Rage virus

b) Flesh-eating plague

c) A mutated cure for cancer

5 What is the name of the Satanic child in the 1976 movie *The Omen*?

a) Dorian

b) Julian

c) Damien

ENTERTAINMENT

6 **In *Jaws*, who is the first victim?**

a) Alex Kintner

b) Chrissie Watkins

c) Martin Brody's son

7 **In which European city is Nicolas Roeg's 1973 film *Don't Look Now* largely set?**

a) Paris

b) Prague

c) Venice

8 **Who directed the 1968 film *Night of the Living Dead*?**

a) George A. Romero

b) Wes Craven

c) Tobe Hooper

9 **In which state was *The Blair Witch Project* set?**

a) Maine

b) Maryland

c) Minnesota

10 **Who wrote the score to the film *Halloween*?**

a) Ennio Morricone

b) John Williams

c) John Carpenter

A

1 b

2 b

3 c

4 a

5 c

6 b

7 c

8 a

9 b

10 c

ENTERTAINMENT

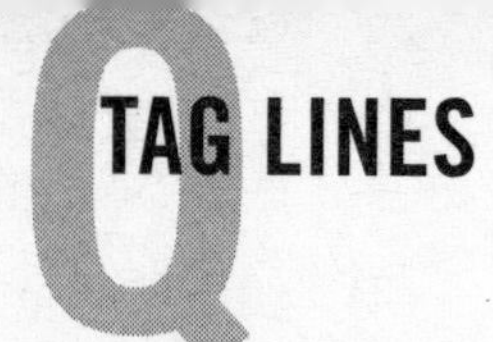

TAG LINES

Match the following tag lines to their films.

1 'Be afraid. Be very afraid.'

a) *Alien*

b) *The Exorcist*

c) *The Fly*

2 'His whole life was a million-to-one shot.'

a) *Rocky*

b) *Forrest Gump*

c) *8 Mile*

3 'Sit back, relax, enjoy the fright.'

a) *Final Destination*

b) *Snakes on a Plane*

c) *Alive*

4 'Does for rock and roll what *The Sound of Music* did for hills.'

a) *Empire Records*

b) *School of Rock*

c) *This is . . . Spinal Tap*

5 'How did they ever make a movie of . . .'

a) *Salo*

b) *Lolita*

c) *A Clockwork Orange*

A

1 c

2 a

3 b

4 c

5 b

GEOGRAPHY

AFRICA

THE AMERICAS

ASIA

OCEANIA

THE UK

THE POLES

HUMAN GEOGRAPHY

EUROPE

LAKES, RIVERS, SEAS AND OCEANS

LONDON

RECORD-BREAKING STRUCTURES

PLACES

NATURAL DISASTERS

CAPITAL CITIES

ISLANDS

EXPLORERS

MOUNTAINS AND VOLCANOES

AFRICA

1 What is the largest country in Africa by surface area?

a) Algeria

b) Angola

c) Sudan

2 Which country is bordered by Tanzania, Mozambique and Zambia?

a) Zimbabwe

b) Malawi

c) Botswana

3 In which country is Africa's most northerly point?

a) Morocco

b) Algeria

c) Tunisia

4 Mount Kilimanjaro, Africa's tallest mountain, is found in which country?

a) Kenya

b) Uganda

c) Tanzania

5 Which city was formerly known as Salisbury?

a) Kampala

b) Ouagadougou

c) Harare

6 Which country's capital, Malabo, is situated on an island 40km from the coast of Cameroon?

a) Equatorial Guinea

b) Togo

c) Gabon

7 Which of the following countries is entirely surrounded by South Africa?

a) Namibia

b) Lesotho

c) Angola

8 Which African country was founded in 1847 by freed American slaves?

a) Libya

b) Liberia

c) Burkina Faso

9 Complete the sequence: Gabon, Republic of Congo, Democratic Republic of Congo, Uganda, Kenya, ___________?

a) Mozambique

b) Ethiopia

c) Somalia

10 Which country shares its name with its capital?

a) Guinea

b) Mali

c) Djibouti

A

1 c
2 b
3 c
4 c
5 c
6 a
7 b
8 b
9 c
10 c

Q THE AMERICAS

1 What is the capital city of Canada?

a) Ottawa

b) Quebec

c) Toronto

2 Which are the only two landlocked countries in South America?

a) Bolivia and Uruguay

b) Paraguay and Bolivia

c) Venezuela and Bolivia

3 From which country did the USA purchase Alaska for $7.2m in 1867?

a) United Kingdom

b) Canada

c) Russia

4 Easter Island, with its mysterious statues, belongs to which South American country?

a) Argentina

b) Chile

c) Peru

5 In which American state is the Grand Canyon?

a) Colorado

b) New Mexico

c) Arizona

6 In which South American country are the Angel Falls, the longest free fall of water in the world?

a) Venezuela

b) Suriname

c) Brazil

7 Which of the following is not a place in the USA?

a) Norfolk

b) London

c) Bury

8 What bird features on the flag of Mexico?

a) A condor

b) An eagle

c) A hummingbird

9 Springfield is the capital of which state of the USA?

a) Illinois

b) Iowa

c) Idaho

10 Which river in Texas forms part of the border between the USA and Mexico?

a) Rio Grande

b) Mississippi

c) Colorado

A

1 a

2 b

3 c

4 b

5 c

6 a

7 c

8 b

9 a

10 a

ASIA

1 What is the largest inland sea in the world?

a) Aral Sea

b) Caspian Sea

c) Black Sea

2 Which mountain range contains nine of the ten world's highest peaks?

a) The Himalayas

b) The Urals

c) The Pamirs

3 Which is the largest of the following former Soviet republics?

a) Turkmenistan

b) Kazakhstan

c) Uzbekistan

4 Which country was formerly known as Siam?

a) Indonesia

b) Malaysia

c) Thailand

5 The Great Wall of China runs along part of the border between China and which country?

a) Mongolia

b) Vietnam

c) Russia

6 Which river runs through China, Myanmar, Thailand, Laos, Cambodia and Vietnam?

a) Mekong

b) Pearl

c) Red

7 In which modern country is the ancient city of Bukhara?

a) Uzbekistan

b) Turkmenistan

c) Iran

8 Which is Japan's largest island?

a) Hokkaido

b) Kyushu

c) Honshu

9 Which European country ruled Macau until 1999?

a) France

b) Belgium

c) Portugal

10 Which country consists of 17,504 islands?

a) The Philippines

b) Indonesia

c) The Maldives

A

1 b
2 a
3 b
4 c
5 a
6 a
7 a
8 c
9 c
10 b

Q OCEANIA

1 What percentage of Australian plant and animal life is unique to the country?

a) 40

b) 60

c) 80

2 Which is the largest state in Australia?

a) Western Australia

b) Queensland

c) South Australia

3 Which world capital is closest to the Australian city of Darwin?

a) Sydney

b) Wellington

c) Dili

4 What is the only country in the world to designate sign-language an official state language?

a) Australia

b) New Zealand

c) Tonga

5 In which year were the last convicts shipped from Britain to Australia?

a) 1858

b) 1868

c) 1878

6 **Which body of water separates Australia and Tasmania?**

a) Bass Strait

b) Turbot Strait

c) Plaice Strait

---

7 **Who, or what, is the Fremantle Doctor?**

a) Australian fast-bowler Jeff Thomson, whose line and length used to 'stitch up' opposing batsmen

b) A cooling sea breeze apparent on the coast of Western Australia

c) A species of Australian acacia plant known for its effective treatment of eczema

---

8 **How many people per square kilometre are there estimated to be in Australia?**

a) 3

b) 30

c) 300

---

9 **What is the aboriginal name of Ayers Rock?**

a) Uhuru

b) Uluru

c) Toowoomba

---

10 **Taumatawhakatangihangakoauauotameteaturipukakapikimaunga horonukupokaiwhenakita natahu in New Zealand is one of the longest place names in the world. What does it mean?**

a) The summit where Tamatea, the man with the big knees, the climber of mountains, the land swallower who travelled about, played his flute to his loved one

b) The soaring peak of the south where the song of the Waitangi bird can be heard

c) Taumata's hill, next to the hollow of the white hazel, near to the rapid whirlpool and the mouth of the never-ending red caves

A

1 c

2 a

3 a

4 b

5 b

6 a

7 b

8 a

9 b

10 a

THE UK

1 Which range of hills is often referred to as 'the backbone of England'?

a) The Chilterns

b) The Cheviots

c) The Pennines

2 What is the Scottish term for a sea estuary?

a) An inch

b) A strath

c) A firth

3 What is the highest point in Northern Ireland?

a) Slieve Donard in the Mountains of Mourne

b) Mossey's Hill above Gortin, County Tyrone

c) Trostan in County Antrim

4 Which three Scottish mainland counties border England?

a) Berwickshire, Roxburghshire and Dumfriesshire

b) Berwickshire, Selkirkshire and Kirkcubrightshire

c) Roxburghshire, Wigtonshire and Dumfriesshire

5 Which English city is associated with the legend of Lady Godiva?

a) Coventry

b) Gloucester

c) Chester

6 **A man born in the county of Kent is called either 'a Kentish man' or 'a man of Kent' but what determines which term is used?**

a) Which side of the river Medway he was born

b) Whether a man was born on the Kent Weald or not

c) Whether or not he was born on the Isle of Sheppey

7 **Which of these counties was not one of the original six in Northern Ireland?**

a) Armagh

b) Omagh

c) Tyrone

8 **What is the name of the Manx parliament?**

a) Tynwald

b) Althingi

c) Stortinget

9 **What is the English name for the city that Welsh-speakers call Abertawe?**

a) Swansea

b) St Davids

c) Cardiff

10 **Where in Edinburgh is there an unfinished replica of the Parthenon?**

a) On Arthur's Seat

b) On Calton Hill

c) In the National Museum of Scotland

A

1 c
2 c
3 a
4 a
5 a
6 a
7 c
8 a
9 a
10 b

THE POLES

1 What is the internet domain name for Antarctica?

a) .ant

b) .aq

c) .brrr

2 The Vostok research station in Antarctica holds the record for the coldest temperature recorded on Earth. But how cold was it?

a) –57.2°C

b) –78.6°C

c) –89.2°C

3 Which two countries claim the same area of Antarctica as Britain?

a) Chile and Argentina

b) France and Norway

c) Australia and New Zealand

4 In which year was the first Lonely Planet guidebook to Antarctica published?

a) 1960

b) 1985

c) 1996

5 At which pole(s) can you find polar bears?

a) The North

b) The South

c) Both

6 How many countries have territories inside the Arctic Circle?

a) 3

b) 5

c) 8

7 Which country planted a flag on the Arctic seabed in 2007 as part of a claim for sovereignty?

a) Russia

b) Denmark

c) Canada

8 What species of penguin – native to Antarctica – were featured in the Oscar-winning film *March of the Penguins*?

a) Adelie

b) Emperor

c) Chinstrap

9 What was the name of the Antarctic ice-shelf, 3,250km^2 in area, which collapsed in 2002?

a) Amundsen A

b) Larsen B

c) Shackleton C

10 Approximately what percentage of the world's fresh water is frozen in Antarctica?

a) 30

b) 50

c) 70

A

1 b
2 c
3 a
4 c
5 a
6 c
7 a
8 b
9 b
10 c

Q HUMAN GEOGRAPHY

1 What is Africa's most populous country?

a) Egypt

b) Nigeria

c) South Africa

2 In which of the following countries would someone have the highest life expectancy?

a) Norway

b) Austria

c) Andorra

3 According to the World Health Organisation, which country's population are the most diligent users of contraception?

a) China

b) France

c) Canada

4 Who published *The End of Poverty* in 2005, which argued that eradicating global poverty was possible by 2025?

a) Paul Wolfowitz

b) Jeffrey Sachs

c) Gordon Brown

5 In Burundi, it is 10 per cent, in Croatia it is 56 per cent and in Qatar it is 95 per cent. What is being measured?

a) The number of the adult population that are literate

b) The proportion of people living in urban areas

c) The Muslim population of a country

6 According to the UN, what percentage of the world's population now lives in cities?

a) 25

b) 50

c) 75

7 In a worldwide survey by *The Economist*, which city was voted the best to live in for five consecutive years from 2003?

a) Sydney

b) Brussels

c) Vancouver

8 What geopolitical concept was coined by Friedrich Ratzel in 1897?

a) Collectivisation

b) Genocide

c) Lebensraum

9 Which country attracted the most tourists in 2006 according to the World Tourism Organisation?

a) United States

b) France

c) China

10 Which philosopher and political economist ambitiously declared 'the end of history' following the end of the Cold War?

a) Francis Fukuyama

b) Milton Friedman

c) Arthur Schlesinger Jr

A

1 b

2 c

3 a

4 b

5 b

6 b

7 c

8 c

9 b

10 a

EUROPE

1 **Which country has borders with Bulgaria, Serbia, Hungary, Ukraine and Moldova?**

a) Macedonia

b) Slovakia

c) Romania

2 **Which country owns the Kaliningrad enclave, a strip of land sandwiched between Lithuania and Poland?**

a) Belarus

b) Russia

c) Ukraine

3 **Which of these countries is the smallest by land area?**

a) Malta

b) Luxembourg

c) Andorra

4 **What is the capital of Albania?**

a) Sarajevo

b) Skopje

c) Tirana

5 **In which of the following countries is the euro not the unit of currency?**

a) Greece

b) Norway

c) Finland

6 **Which of the following cities does not stand on the River Danube?**

a) Bucharest

b) Belgrade

c) Budapest

7 **Ajaccio is the capital of which European territory?**

a) Corsica

b) Crete

c) Sicily

8 **Which poet swam across the Hellespont, a strait separating the Balkans from Asia Minor?**

a) Percy Bysshe Shelley

b) Lord Byron

c) William Blake

9 **In which country is Romansch one of four official languages?**

a) Switzerland

b) Italy

c) Croatia

10 **What percentage of Turkey is in Europe?**

a) 3 per cent

b) 13 per cent

c) 30 per cent

A

1	c
2	b
3	a
4	c
5	b
6	a
7	a
8	b
9	a
10	a

LAKES, RIVERS, SEAS AND OCEANS

GEOGRAPHY

1 Which is the longest lake in England?

a) Windermere

b) Ullswater

c) Ness

2 Which river runs at the bottom of the Grand Canyon?

a) Rio Grande

b) Snake

c) Colorado

3 Which lake is the source of the White Nile?

a) Lake Chad

b) Lake Victoria

c) Lake Tanganyika

4 Which is the largest in area of these Great Lakes?

a) Lake Superior

b) Lake Michigan

c) Lake Huron

5 Which two countries are separated by the Strait of Otranto?

a) Italy and Albania

b) Greece and Albania

c) Italy and Greece

6 **Into which body of water does the River Ganges empty?**

a) The Bay of Bengal

b) The Indian Ocean

c) The Coral Sea

7 **What is unusual about the Caspian Sea?**

a) It is really a salt-water lake

b) It contains no salt

c) It has no tributary rivers

8 **Which is the deepest lake in the world?**

a) Lake Titicaca

b) Lake Baikal

c) Lake Tanganyika

9 **Where is the Sargasso Sea?**

a) North Atlantic Ocean

b) Indian Ocean

c) Arctic Ocean

10 **What makes the Red Sea red?**

a) The red clay that forms its bed

b) Dead algae

c) Reflection of light on its surface

A

1 a
2 c
3 b
4 a
5 a
6 a
7 a
8 b
9 a
10 b

LONDON

1 **In which street did the Great Fire of London start in 1666?**

a) Fleet Street

b) Pudding Lane

c) Poultry Grove

2 **In which London square are there statues of both Winston Churchill and Abraham Lincoln?**

a) Trafalgar Square

b) St John's Square

c) Parliament Square

3 **Which London church is known as 'The Actors' Church' because of its long association with theatrical people?**

a) St Anne's, Soho

b) St Martin-in-the-Fields

c) St Paul's, Covent Garden

4 **Which of the following is not a London borough?**

a) Waltham Forest

b) Hillingdon

c) Spelthorne

5 **Which of the following has a commemorative blue plaque on their London home?**

a) John Nash, creator of Regent Street and Regent's Park

b) Harry Beck, designer of the London Underground map

c) Alfred Hitchcock, film director who shot many films in London

6 What was the second bridge to be built across the Thames, after London Bridge in 1176?

a) Putney

b) Westminster

c) Blackfriars

7 What are 'The Magnificent Seven', located throughout London?

a) Markets

b) Monuments

c) Cemeteries

8 Which museum had its own (now disused) tube station?

a) The V&A

b) The National Gallery

c) The British Museum

9 Which of the following tube stations takes its name from a pub that used to be on the site?

a) Angel

b) Royal Oak

c) Barbican

10 Who wrote: 'I had been in London innumerable times, and yet till that day I had never noticed one of the worst things about London – the fact it costs money even to sit down'?

a) John Bunyan

b) George Orwell

c) Thomas de Quincey

A

1 b
2 c
3 c
4 c
5 c
6 a
7 c
8 c
9 a
10 b

Q RECORD-BREAKING STRUCTURES

1 For how many years was the Empire State Building in New York the world's tallest inhabited building?

a) 32

b) 43

c) 65

2 Sears Tower – the tallest building in the USA since its completion in 1973 – is in which state?

a) California

b) Texas

c) Illinois

3 Which film featured a climax at the then newly opened Petronas Towers in Malaysia?

a) *The 51st State*

b) *Entrapment*

c) *Sin City*

4 In what year was the Golden Gate Bridge over San Francisco Bay completed?

a) 1917

b) 1937

c) 1957

5 Which river is regulated by the Three Gorges Dam?

a) Yangtze

b) Tigris

c) Euphrates

6 **Which European church is tallest?**

a) Cologne Cathedral

b) Basilica of St Peter, Vatican City

c) Notre-Dame de Paris

7 **How many miles long is the Channel Tunnel linking the UK and France?**

a) 22

b) 31

c) 40

8 **The longest railway line in the world, the Trans-Siberian Railway, runs from Moscow to where?**

a) Almaty

b) Vladivostok

c) Yakutsk

9 **On which line is the longest tunnel on the London underground?**

a) Northern

b) Central

c) Piccadilly

10 **The world's longest suspension bridge is found in which country?**

a) China

b) Japan

c) USA

A

1 b

2 c

3 b

4 b

5 a

6 c

7 b

8 b

9 a

10 b

PLACES

GEOGRAPHY

1 **Where is Cape Wrath?**

a) Scotland

b) Canada

c) South America

2 **Which Manhattan street runs from Washington Square Park to the Harlem River?**

a) Wall Street

b) Fifth Avenue

c) Broadway

3 **In which city can you find the Topkapi Palace?**

a) Delhi

b) Istanbul

c) Beijing

4 **In which city are gates called 'bars' and streets called 'gates'?**

a) Liverpool

b) Bath

c) York

5 **Which Canadian province has Regina as its state capital?**

a) Manitoba

b) Nova Scotia

c) Saskatchewan

6 **Which city was the birthplace of the poet and playwright Christopher Marlowe?**

a) Canterbury

b) Rochester

c) Norwich

7 **Which two cities are connected by the Suez Canal?**

a) Port Said and Suez

b) Port Said and Cairo

c) Suez and Cairo

8 **The Dogger Bank is a hazard to shipping in which body of water?**

a) The English Channel

b) The North Sea

c) The Irish Sea

9 **Which of the following countries lies on the equator?**

a) Gabon

b) Rwanda

c) Mali

10 **Which two countries are connected by the Khyber Pass?**

a) Afghanistan and India

b) Afghanistan and Pakistan

c) India and Pakistan

A

1	a
2	b
3	b
4	c
5	c
6	a
7	a
8	b
9	a
10	b

Q NATURAL DISASTERS

1 The most deadly earthquake in history is thought to have happened in Shansi, China, in 1556. How many people were killed?

a) 230,000

b) 510,000

c) 830,000

2 Which film features Dennis Quaid as a paleoclimatologist charged with saving the world from the catastrophic effects of climate change?

a) *The Day After Tomorrow*

b) *The Core*

c) *The Abyss*

3 What was the name of the hurricane that devastated New Orleans in 2005?

a) Rita

b) Katrina

c) Wilma

4 What does the Mercalli scale measure?

a) Earthquake intensity

b) Volcanic activity

c) Wind speed

5 On average, how often does an earthquake hit the UK?

a) Every four years

b) Every four months

c) Every four days

6 **Which country has the most tornadoes by land area?**

a) Thailand

b) USA

c) United Kingdom

7 **Which country is below the hole in the ozone layer?**

a) Antarctica

b) China

c) USA

8 **What is located on Svalbard in case of global natural disaster?**

a) Emergency instructions for survivors

b) A vault containing millions of seeds to replenish crops

c) An underground bunker reserved for world leaders

9 **On the European avalanche risk table, what does a black and yellow chequered flag indicate?**

a) Low risk

b) Medium to high risk

c) Extremely high risk

10 **What is the literal translation of tsunami?**

a) Harbour wave

b) Water crash

c) Sea volcano

A

1 c
2 a
3 b
4 a
5 c
6 c
7 a
8 b
9 b
10 a

Q CAPITAL CITIES

1 What is the highest capital city in the world?

a) Quito, Ecuador

b) La Paz, Bolivia

c) Kathmandu, Nepal

2 Which capital city is furthest away from any other?

a) Wellington, New Zealand

b) Suva, Fiji

c) Manila, the Philippines

3 Which of these purpose-built capitals is the youngest?

a) Abuja, Nigeria

b) Brasilia, Brazil

c) New Delhi, India

4 Which of these countries has a capital which is not its largest city?

a) Argentina

b) Mexico

c) Brazil

5 When translated into English, which two countries have capitals pronounced the same way?

a) Senegal and Bangladesh

b) Zimbabwe and Tanzania

c) Cuba and the Philippines

6 What connects the capitals of Mauritius, Papua New Guinea and Trinidad and Tobago?

a) Each was badly damaged by flooding during the 1990s

b) Each has the prefix 'Port'

c) Each has been the setting for a James Bond novel

7 When the capitals of the world are listed alphabetically, which country's is last?

a) Armenia

b) Cameroon

c) Croatia

8 The name of which capital city means 'new flower'?

a) Addis Ababa

b) Dar es Salaam

c) Ouagadougou

9 Which capital city was divided by a partition running down Ledra Street for 44 years?

a) Berlin

b) Nicosia

c) Jerusalem

10 What is the most easterly capital in South America?

a) Montevideo

b) Buenos Aires

c) Brasilia

A

1 b
2 a
3 a
4 c
5 a
6 b
7 c
8 a
9 b
10 c

ISLANDS

1 What was the name of the fictional island in the film *Jaws*?

a) Angel Island

b) Amity Island

c) Atlantic Island

2 To which country does the island of Phuket belong?

a) Myanmar

b) Thailand

c) Malaysia

3 Which poet wrote the lines 'No man is an island, entire of itself'?

a) Edmund Spenser

b) Alexander Pope

c) John Donne

4 The Isle of Sheppey is part of which English county?

a) Dorset

b) Kent

c) Sussex

5 In which ocean is the island of Sao Tome?

a) Atlantic

b) Indian

c) Pacific

6 Which of the Scilly Islands is known for its beautiful sub-tropical gardens?

a) St Mary's

b) St Martin's

c) Tresco

7 In which group of islands would you find Yell and Nesting?

a) The Faroe Islands

b) The Shetland Islands

c) The Orkney Islands

8 Which country is building a series of artificial islands known as the Palm Islands?

a) Bahrain

b) United Arab Emirates

c) Saudi Arabia

9 What is the most highly populated island in the world?

a) Great Britain

b) Honshu, Japan

c) Java, Indonesia

10 Which country administers the Galapagos Islands?

a) Ecuador

b) Chile

c) Venezuela

A

1 b

2 b

3 c

4 b

5 a

6 c

7 b

8 b

9 c

10 a

EXPLORERS

1 What nationality was Christopher Columbus?

a) Spanish

b) Portuguese

c) Italian

2 Which continent was John Franklin attempting to map when he and his crew perished in 1847?

a) North America

b) Africa

c) Australasia

3 What was the name of the ship in which Francis Drake circumnavigated the world in 1577–80?

a) The Mary Rose

b) The Discovery

c) The Golden Hind

4 What was Captain Scott's middle name?

a) Tercel

b) Falcon

c) Whippet

5 Which continent were Robert O'Hara Burke and William John Wills attempting to cross from south to north and back when they died in 1861?

a) Australia

b) Antarctica

c) Africa

6 Which 19th-century British explorer not only made dangerous journeys in Africa but also translated the Kama Sutra?

a) David Livingstone

b) Mungo Park

c) Richard Burton

7 How old was Yuri Gagarin when he died in a plane crash?

a) 24

b) 34

c) 54

8 Which explorer, after shrugging off double heart bypass surgery, ran seven marathons in seven days in 2003?

a) Ranulph Fiennes

b) Bruce Parry

c) David Hempleman-Adams

9 Who, in 2002, became the first person to circumnavigate the globe alone in a hot air balloon?

a) Richard Branson

b) Steve Fosset

c) Jeannette Piccard

10 Who was the first man to reach the South Pole?

a) William Edward Parry

b) Ernest Shackleton

c) Roald Amundsen

A

1 c
2 a
3 c
4 b
5 a
6 c
7 b
8 a
9 b
10 c

Q

MOUNTAINS AND VOLCANOES

1 What is the longest mountain range in the world?

a) The Andes

b) The Himalayas

c) The Rockies

2 In which country is the volcano Popocatepetl?

a) Mexico

b) Peru

c) Bolivia

3 The second highest mountain in the world, K2 or Godwin Austen, is on the border between which two countries?

a) Nepal and China

b) Bhutan and Nepal

c) Pakistan and China

4 Which volcano was responsible for the greatest volcanic explosion ever recorded?

a) Krakatoa

b) Stromboli

c) Tambora

5 In which decade was the first ascent of Everest completed?

a) 1930s

b) 1950s

c) 1970s

A

1 a

2 a

3 c

4 c

5 b

HISTORY

AMERICAN HISTORY

THE ANCIENT WORLD

ARCHAEOLOGY

HISTORY OF THE BRITISH ISLES

BRITISH ROYALTY

WORLD WARS

ROYAL DYNASTIES

CRIME AND PUNISHMENT

MEDIEVAL TIMES

WORLD HISTORY

WARS AND BATTLES

TUDORS AND STUARTS

VICTORIANA

20TH CENTURY

RULERS

Q AMERICAN HISTORY

1 Along with Iran and Iraq, which other country was named by President George W. Bush as part of the 'axis of evil'?

a) Russia

b) North Korea

c) Bolivia

2 Which British general surrendered at Yorktown in October 1781, effectively ending the War of Independence?

a) Howe

b) Wolfe

c) Cornwallis

3 Where was President Abraham Lincoln when he was shot and fatally wounded in 1865?

a) At the White House

b) In his barber's chair

c) In a box at Ford's Theatre, Washington

4 Which American city was known as Yerba Buena until it was claimed by the USA in 1848?

a) Los Angeles

b) San Francisco

c) Las Vegas

5 In which city were the peace accords which ended the Vietnam War signed?

a) Madrid

b) Oslo

c) Paris

6 Who revealed himself as the Watergate informant 'Deep Throat' in 2005?

a) Former advisor to Nixon, John Ehrlichman

b) White House chief counsel Fred Fielding

c) FBI agent Mark Felt

7 Who was president at the time of the Wall Street Crash in 1929?

a) Calvin Coolidge

b) Woodrow Wilson

c) Herbert Hoover

8 Who was the first woman to run for president of the USA?

a) Victoria Claflin Woodhull

b) Harriet Beecher Stowe

c) Eleanor Roosevelt

9 In which city was Martin Luther King Jr. assassinated in 1968?

a) Dallas

b) Chicago

c) Memphis

10 Who was the first person to sign the Declaration of Independence in 1776?

a) John Hancock

b) Benjamin Franklin

c) George Washington

A

1 b

2 c

3 c

4 b

5 c

6 c

7 c

8 a

9 c

10 a

THE ANCIENT WORLD

Q

1 The city of Troy is thought to have been located in which modern-day country?

a) Greece

b) Turkey

c) Syria

2 In which ancient empire was the city of Nineveh?

a) Assyrian

b) Egyptian

c) Persian

3 Who were the Aztecs conquered by?

a) The Spanish

b) The French

c) The English

4 What was the name of the sister of Alexander the Great?

a) Olympias

b) Roxane

c) Cleopatra

5 Which Egyptian pharaoh was married to Nefertiti?

a) Akhenaten

b) Tutenkhamen

c) Ramses II

6 Which of the following is the closest translation of the word pharaoh?

a) Great leader

b) Great priest

c) Great house

7 From which century do the Qin Shi Huang terracotta warriors and horses of China date?

a) 1st century AD

b) 3rd century AD

c) 3rd century BC

8 In which ancient culture did the myths of Gilgamesh originate?

a) Egyptian

b) Sumerian

c) Persian

9 To which of the Olympian gods was the Parthenon dedicated?

a) Athena

b) Zeus

c) Hera

10 What was unusual about the Roman Incitatus, whom Caligula attempted to get elected between 37 and 41 AD?

a) She would have been the first woman elected to public office

b) He would have been the first plebeian consul

c) He was a horse

A

1 b

2 a

3 a

4 b

5 a

6 c

7 c

8 b

9 a

10 c

ARCHAEOLOGY

1 Who sold the Elgin Marbles, now in the British Museum, to Lord Elgin in the early nineteenth century?

a) Greece

b) The Ottoman Empire

c) Iraq

2 Where is the city of Machu Picchu?

a) Ecuador

b) Peru

c) Venezuela

3 Why is Pompeii significant to archaeologists?

a) They believe that Julius Caesar's remains are buried there

b) A volcano erupted and preserved the whole town under ash

c) It is the site where the first Roman roads were built

4 Why were the terracotta warriors, found in Xi'an, China, built?

a) To protect the emperor in the afterlife

b) To plan the tactics of the real army

c) To be placed on top of the city walls to deter invaders

5 When the ancient Egyptians mummified the bodies of their pharaohs, how did they remove the brains?

a) Through the nose

b) Through the mouth

c) Through the ears

6 What was discovered in caves at Altamira in Spain in 1879?

a) Prehistoric paintings

b) Neanderthal skeletons

c) Preserved mammoths

7 What was found at Sutton Hoo, in Suffolk?

a) A Ròman amphitheatre

b) The oldest preserved settlement in existence

c) A large Anglo-Saxon burial site

8 When was the first part of Stonehenge built?

a) 1,000 years ago

b) 2,000 years ago

c) 5,000 years ago

9 Cadmea was the central fortress of which ancient Greek city?

a) Corinth

b) Sparta

c) Thebes

10 What are Grime's Graves, found in Norfolk?

a) Rocks where ships were often wrecked

b) Prehistoric flint mines

c) The site of a mass grave of deserting soldiers

1 b

2 b

3 b

5 a

6 a

7 c

8 c

9 c

10 b

Q HISTORY OF THE BRITISH ISLES

1 Who is believed to be the first Celtic race to arrive in Britain?

a) The Beaker folk

b) The Goidels

c) The Picts

2 In which British city did the Peterloo Massacre of 1819 take place?

a) Birmingham

b) Liverpool

c) Manchester

3 What disaster occurred in London in 1665?

a) The Great Fire of London

b) The burning of the Savoy Palace

c) The start of the Great Plague

4 What tax was levied by British governments between 1696 and 1851?

a) Income tax

b) Salt tax

c) Window tax

5 When was the slave trade abolished in Britain?

a) 1757

b) 1807

c) 1857

6 What were the repercussions of the 1605 Gunpowder Plot for Catholics?

a) They were banned by law from gathering in groups of more than three

b) They were made to swear allegiance to the king individually

c) They were not allowed to vote in elections until 1829

7 Which city was the capital of England before London, from the late 9th to the early 11th centuries?

a) Winchester

b) Cirencester

c) York

8 Which was the first country to form a union with England?

a) Scotland

b) Wales

c) Ireland

9 What relation does Jersey have to the rest of the UK?

a) It is part of the United Kingdom

b) It is a British crown dependency

c) It is a British overseas territory

10 Who became the first prime minister in 1721?

a) Henry Pelham

b) William Pitt

c) Sir Robert Walpole

A

1	b
2	c
3	c
4	c
5	b
6	c
7	a
8	b
9	b
10	c

BRITISH ROYALTY

1 Who was the first monarch of the House of Hanover?

a) Edward VII

b) Victoria

c) George I

2 Which English monarch allegedly had a lover called Piers Gaveston?

a) Richard I

b) Elizabeth I

c) Edward II

3 What is the surname of the descendants of Queen Elizabeth II?

a) Windsor

b) Mountbatten-Windsor

c) Saxe-Coburg and Gotha

4 Who holds the title of Princess Royal?

a) The wife of the Prince of Wales

b) The monarch's youngest sister

c) The monarch's eldest daughter

5 Which of the following is not true?

a) Sturgeons, whales and dolphins in UK waters are 'fishes Royal' and are the property of the Crown

b) Advocating the abolition of the monarchy in print is punishable by life imprisonment

c) The husband of a female monarch is awarded equal status, rights and privileges

6 Which monarch was on the throne before the interregnum of 1649?

a) Charles I

b) Charles II

c) James II

7 Who was the son of Henry VII who married Catherine of Aragon and died in 1502?

a) Arthur

b) Edward

c) Henry

8 What prevented Wallis Simpson from becoming queen after her marriage to Edward VIII, leading to his abdication?

a) She was a Catholic

b) She was a divorcee

c) She was an American

9 Who was the first ruler of England, Scotland and Ireland together?

a) Richard II

b) Elizabeth I

c) James I

10 Which dukedom is not held by the sovereign's eldest son from the moment of his birth or the sovereign's accession?

a) Cornwall

b) Rothesay

c) Gloucester

A

1 c
2 c
3 b
4 c
5 c
6 a
7 a
8 b
9 c
10 c

WORLD WARS

1 How much land did the Allies gain at the Battle of the Somme?

a) 5 miles

b) 30 miles

c) None; they lost 10 miles

2 Which American general was nicknamed 'Old Blood and Guts'?

a) Patton

b) McArthur

c) Eisenhower

3 The Triple Entente alliance of the First World War was made up of Britain, France and which other country?

a) Belgium

b) Italy

c) Russia

4 What was the real name of the German air ace known as the 'Red Baron'?

a) Von Bülow

b) Von Falkenhayn

c) Von Richthofen

5 Which of these countries was occupied by Germany in the Second World War?

a) Iceland

b) Sweden

c) Norway

6 Who is pointing his finger in the 'Your Country Needs You' recruitment poster of the First World War?

a) Prime Minister David Lloyd-George

b) Lord Horatio Kitchener

c) Field Marshal Douglas Haig

7 Which passenger ship was sunk by a German U-boat in May 1915?

a) Mauretania

b) Titanic

c) Lusitania

8 In which city was Archduke Franz Ferdinand assassinated in June 1914, thus setting in motion events that culminated in the outbreak of war?

a) Belgrade

b) Sarajevo

c) Split

9 In the Second World War, which South American country declared war on Germany less than six weeks before the end of hostilities in Europe?

a) Argentina

b) Bolivia

c) Peru

10 When did Adolf Hitler become chancellor of Germany?

a) 1928

b) 1934

c) 1938

A

1	a
2	a
3	c
4	c
5	c
6	b
7	c
8	b
9	a
10	b

Q ROYAL DYNASTIES

1 Which European country was ruled by monarchs of the House of Braganza?

a) Spain

b) Portugal

c) Greece

2 Who, ruling between 1329–1371, was the second monarch of the Scottish House of Bruce?

a) Robert I

b) Robert II

c) David II

3 Which of the following was not a genuine daughter of Tsar Nicholas II, assassinated in 1918?

a) Grand Duchess Olga

b) Grand Duchess Maria

c) Grand Duchess Inna

4 Which one of Queen Victoria's daughters married the German Emperor Friedrich III?

a) Princess Victoria

b) Princess Alice

c) Princess Beatrice

5 Why did George V succeed to the throne instead of his elder brother?

a) His elder brother abdicated

b) His elder brother predeceased his father, Edward VII

c) His elder brother was declared insane

6 What is the name of the royal house of King Carl XVI Gustaf of Sweden?

a) Bernadotte

b) Västerbotten

c) Saxe-Coburg and Gotha

7 What relation is Viscount Severn to Elizabeth II?

a) Her grandson

b) Her nephew

c) Her cousin

8 As the husband of Mary I, which king of Spain was also king consort of England?

a) Philip IV

b) Philip III

c) Philip II

9 How was Lady Jane Grey, who reigned for nine days in 1553, related to Henry VIII?

a) She was his cousin

b) She was his great-niece

c) She was his aunt

10 How many children did Queen Victoria have?

a) Five daughters, four sons

b) Five sons, four daughters

c) Five sons, five daughters

A

1	b
2	c
3	c
4	a
5	b
6	a
7	a
8	c
9	b
10	a

Q CRIME AND PUNISHMENT

1 **The son of which American folk hero was kidnapped and murdered in the 1930s?**

a) Babe Ruth

b) Charles Lindbergh

c) Douglas Fairbanks

2 **Which notorious murderer lived at 10 Rillington Place?**

a) Dr. Crippen

b) John Christie

c) Dennis Nilsen

3 **The wife of which film director was murdered by Charles Manson's followers, known as 'the Family'?**

a) Roman Polanski

b) Martin Scorsese

c) Milos Forman

4 **Which artist caused an outrage in 1997 when his painting of Moors murderer Myra Hindley went on display?**

a) Damien Hirst

b) Simon Patterson

c) Marcus Harvey

5 **The gruesome assassination of which African leader was recorded on videotape and shown around the world in 1990?**

a) Samuel Doe

b) Milton Obote

c) Patrice Lumumba

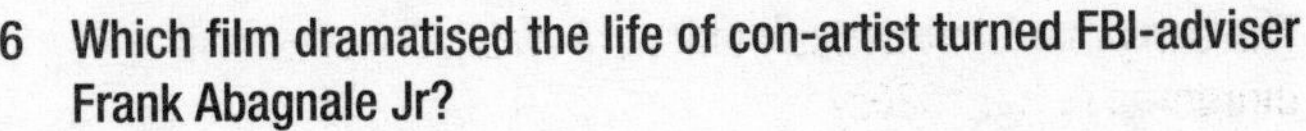

6 **Which film dramatised the life of con-artist turned FBI-adviser Frank Abagnale Jr?**

a) *Ordinary Decent Criminal*

b) *Catch Me If You Can*

c) *The Score*

7 **In her book *Portrait of a Killer*, which painter does Patricia Cornwell accuse of being Jack the Ripper?**

a) Edward Burne-Jones

b) Walter Sickert

c) Thomas Wainewright

8 **Anthony Babington was hung, drawn and quartered for plotting the assassination of which British monarch?**

a) Richard III

b) Elizabeth I

c) Charles II

9 **Which literary classic describes the real-life murder of Herbert Clutter and his family by Richard Hickock and Perry Smith?**

a) *To Kill a Mockingbird*

b) *The Executioner's Song*

c) *In Cold Blood*

10 **Who was assassinated by Gavrilo Princip?**

a) Martin Luther King

b) Leon Trotsky

c) Franz Ferdinand

A

1 b
2 b
3 a
4 c
5 a
6 b
7 b
8 b
9 c
10 c

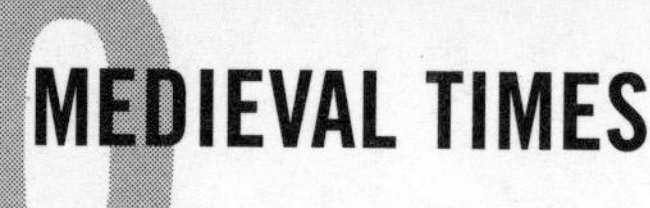

MEDIEVAL TIMES

1 What was the Domesday Book?

a) A population survey

b) A land and property census

c) A means of predicting judgement day

2 In a medieval castle what was the 'garderobe'?

a) A ladies' dressing room

b) Toilet

c) Lord's private quarters

3 Which of the following countries did not go to war with England between 1250–1350 AD?

a) Wales

b) France

c) Spain

4 Where was the Magna Carta signed by King John?

a) York

b) Winchester

c) Runnymede

5 What was William II known as?

a) Rufus the Red

b) The Black Prince

c) The King in Yellow

6 Which of the following medieval laws is still in place?

a) It is illegal to enter parliament wearing a suit of armour

b) It is legal to shoot a Welshman with a crossbow in Chester after sunset

c) Piracy on the high seas is subject to the death penalty

7 In medieval armour, what did a vambrace protect?

a) The arm

b) The neck

c) The thigh

8 What was the highest office in the Christian military order of the Knights Templar?

a) The Seneschal

b) The Grand Master

c) The Ultimate Vizier

9 What were tithes?

a) Gatehouses in castles

b) Rakes used in farming

c) Taxes set by the church

10 What symbol appeared on Richard I's shield?

a) Three lions

b) An eagle

c) A white rose

A

1 b

2 b

3 c

4 c

5 a

6 a

7 a

8 b

9 c

10 a

Q WORLD HISTORY

1 Of which country was Antonio de Oliveira Salazar dictator from 1932 to 1968?

a) Chile

b) Brazil

c) Portugal

2 Which of the following countries never had a colony on the North American mainland?

a) Germany

b) The Netherlands

c) Sweden

3 What was the codename given to Hitler's planned invasion of Britain in 1940?

a) Operation Barbarossa

b) Operation Sea Lion

c) Operation Dolphin

4 Which of these South American countries was named in honour of the man who drew up its first constitution?

a) Ecuador

b) Venezuela

c) Bolivia

5 Where was the first permanent English settlement in North America, founded in 1607?

a) Cupar's Cove, Newfoundland

b) Jamestown, Virginia

c) Plymouth, Massachusetts

6 In the 1850s, why was Edward Hargraves awarded £10,000 by the government of New South Wales, Australia?

a) He captured the outlaw Ned Kelly

b) He was the first to find gold in the state

c) He had been wrongfully transported to Australia 30 years earlier

7 Where did the Mau Mau rebellion take place in the 1950s?

a) Kenya

b) Cambodia

c) Tahiti

8 Which country witnessed an 'orange revolution' between 2004–5?

a) Belarus

b) Ukraine

c) Estonia

9 What was the first African country to gain independence from a European power after World War II?

a) Sudan

b) Egypt

c) Libya

10 The capital of which country is named after explorer and colonialist Pierre de Brazza?

a) Republic of Congo

b) Cote d'Ivoire

c) Cameroon

A

1 c
2 a
3 b
4 c
5 b
6 b
7 a
8 b
9 c
10 a

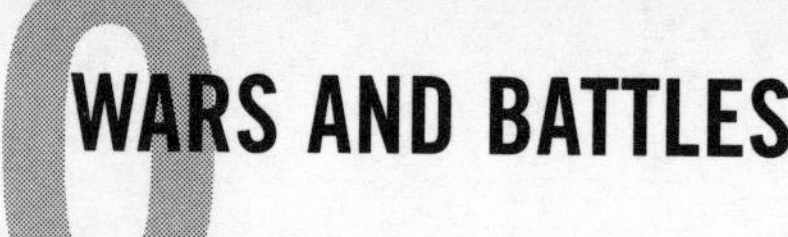

WARS AND BATTLES

1 Which of the following was not a real war in Europe?

a) Seven Years' War

b) Twenty Years' War

c) Hundred Years' War

2 Which was the last land battle fought in mainland Great Britain?

a) Battle of Culloden

b) Battle of the Boyne

c) Battle of Naseby

3 Who was the last English king to die in combat?

a) Richard III

b) Edward IV

c) Henry V

4 Which Scottish leader was defeated at the Battle of Falkirk in 1298?

a) Robert the Bruce

b) John Balliol

c) William Wallace

5 In which war was the chemical defoliant 'Agent Orange' first used?

a) Second World War

b) Korean War

c) Vietnam War

6 Where did the battle of Jutland take place?

a) Land

b) Sea

c) Air

---

7 At which battle in 1066 did King Harold defeat an invading force from Norway, just a few weeks before he fought the invading Normans at the Battle of Hastings and lost?

a) Battle of Towton

b) Battle of Maldon

c) Battle of Stamford Bridge

---

8 In which battle did the famed 'Charge of the Light Brigade' take place?

a) Battle of Alma

b) Battle of Balaclava

c) Battle of Inkerman

---

9 Which two countries fought in the Opium Wars?

a) England and China

b) India and Afghanistan

c) China and Japan

---

10 A series of confrontations between the UK and Iceland in the 1950s and 70s over fishing rights in the North Atlantic ocean were known as what?

a) The Cold Wars

b) The Cod Wars

c) The Ice Wars

A

1 b
2 a
3 a
4 c
5 c
6 b
7 c
8 b
9 a
10 b

Q TUDORS AND STUARTS

1 What did women use to brighten eyes in Elizabeth I's reign?

a) Sulphur

b) Mercury

c) Deadly nightshade

2 Which monarch lost England's last territory in France?

a) Elizabeth I

b) Mary I

c) Charles I

3 How is Edward VI believed to have died at the age of 15?

a) Tuberculosis

b) Plague

c) Cholera

4 What was banned under Oliver Cromwell's government?

a) Music

b) Theatre

c) Books

5 Which of Henry VIII's wives gave birth to Edward VI?

a) Catherine Howard

b) Jane Seymour

c) Catherine Parr

6 Where was Charles I executed?

a) Outside Banqueting House

b) The Tower of London

c) Westminster Palace Yard

---

7 How did the third wife of Henry VIII die?

a) She was executed

b) She died in childbirth

c) She died due to old age

---

8 Under which monarch was the Act of Union with Scotland passed?

a) Mary II

b) James II

c) Anne

---

9 What was the name of Oliver Cromwell's son who briefly succeeded him as Lord Protector?

a) Henry

b) Charles

c) Richard

---

10 Which statesman's secret marriage to Elizabeth Throckmorton, Elizabeth I's lady-in-waiting, resulted in his exile from court?

a) Robert Devereux, Earl of Essex

b) Sir Walter Raleigh

c) Robert Dudley, Earl of Leicester

A

1 c

2 b

3 a

4 b

5 b

6 a

7 b

8 c

9 c

10 b

VICTORIANA

1 **During Victoria's reign the official mourning period for the death of a husband was two to three years. What was it for the death of a wife?**

a) Five years

b) One year

c) Three months

2 **Who first argued for 'the greatest happiness for the greatest number'?**

a) Jeremy Bentham

b) Thomas Malthus

c) John Stuart Mill

3 **What was 'Captain Swing' famous for?**

a) He was captain of Britain's largest ship in the Crimean War

b) He led riots against low wages and unemployment

c) It was the popular nickname for Oscar Wilde

4 **What name was given to events in London in 1858?**

a) The Great Stink

b) The Great Reek

c) The Great Stench

5 **On world maps, what colour represented countries that were part of the British Empire?**

a) Blue

b) Yellow

c) Pink

6 **Which of the following was never a demand made by the Chartists?**

a) Secret ballots

b) Votes for women

c) Payment for members of parliament

7 **How long was the typical factory working day in the Victorian era?**

a) 8 hours

b) 12 hours

c) 15 hours

8 **What happened to the Tolpuddle Martyrs?**

a) They were transported to Australia

b) They were executed

c) They were shot by police at a protest

9 **Who designed the Crystal Palace, venue for the 1851 Great Exhibition?**

a) Joseph Paxton

b) Isambard Kingdom Brunel

c) Joseph Bazalgette

10 **Why has the Ten Bells pub in East London become an unlikely tourist attraction?**

a) It was known to be frequented by several of Jack the Ripper's victims

b) A hole has been preserved in the ceiling from a train crash in 1881

c) It was the site of the death of Prince Albert, who collapsed outside

1 c
2 a
3 b
4 a
5 c
6 b
7 c
8 a
9 a
10 a

Q 20TH CENTURY

1 In 1907, who was the first woman to receive the Order of Merit?

a) Elizabeth Garrett Anderson

b) Florence Nightingale

c) Marie Curie

2 In which colonial outpost was the so-called 'Happy Valley' found?

a) Kenya

b) India

c) South Africa

3 In which year did the contraceptive pill first become available on the NHS?

a) 1951

b) 1961

c) 1971

4 In which Northern Irish city did the Bloody Sunday march take place?

a) Armagh

b) Londonderry

c) Belfast

5 To which journalist did Princess Diana grant her 1995 interview for *Panorama*?

a) Trevor McDonald

b) Nicholas Witchell

c) Martin Bashir

6 **Which of the following is a 20th-century invention?**

a) Coca-cola

b) Teabags

c) Contact lenses

7 **What did the letters MAD stand for in the Cold War?**

a) Mutually Assured Destruction

b) Massive Atomic Deployment

c) Meet American Demands

8 **What did Franklin D. Roosevelt name his programme of economic recovery during the Great Depression in the USA?**

a) The New Deal

b) The Raw Deal

c) The Real Deal

9 **Which was the first black African state to gain independence, in 1957?**

a) Nigeria

b) Somalia

c) Ghana

10 **When did the October Revolution take place in Russia?**

a) 1917

b) 1926

c) 1905

A

1 b
2 a
3 b
4 a
5 c
6 b
7 a
8 a
9 c
10 a

RULERS

1 What is the name of the present Japanese emperor?

a) Hirohito

b) Yoshihito

c) Akihito

2 Who ordered the building of St Basil's Cathedral in Moscow?

a) Catherine the Great

b) Ivan the Terrible

c) Peter the Great

3 Which Communist ruler composed the *July Theses*?

a) Fidel Castro

b) Nicolae Ceausescu

c) Pol Pot

4 Which of these monarchs reigned the longest?

a) King Louis XIV of France

b) Queen Victoria of Great Britain

c) Emperor Franz-Josef of Austria

5 Which ruler was responsible for the destruction of the temple at Jerusalem in 588 BC?

a) Nebuchadnezzar II

b) Xerxes

c) Alexander the Great

A

1 c

2 b

3 b

4 a

5 a

LANGUAGE AND LITERATURE

AMERICAN LITERATURE

FICTIONAL CHARACTERS AND PLACES

CELEBRITY AUTOBIOGRAPHY

SEX IN LITERATURE

FIRST LINES

CHILDREN'S CLASSICS

BESTSELLERS

THE NOVEL

WORLD LITERATURE

POETRY

WORD ORIGINS

WORD MEANINGS

NAME THAT POEM

SHAKESPEARE

PLAYWRIGHTS

NOMS DES PLUME

Q AMERICAN LITERATURE

1 Ernest Hemingway wrote that 'all modern American literature comes from one book.' Which book?

a) *Huckleberry Finn* by Mark Twain

b) *Moby Dick* by Herman Melville

c) *The Scarlet Letter* by Nathaniel Hawthorne

2 Which author set many of his works in the fictional Yoknapatawpha county?

a) William Faulkner

b) Saul Bellow

c) John Irving

3 What is the name of the family of prodigies and geniuses that features in many of J. D. Salinger's short stories?

a) Glass

b) Holden

c) Caulfield

4 In F. Scott Fitzgerald's *The Great Gatsby*, where does Nick Carraway live?

a) Orange County

b) West Egg

c) Ocean Beach

5 John Kennedy Toole wrote two novels. *The Neon Bible* was one, what was the other?

a) *The Shipping News*

b) *A Confederacy of Dunces*

c) *The Hours*

6 What was the name of Bret Easton Ellis' *American Psycho*?

a) Sean Bateman

b) Richard Bateman

c) Patrick Bateman

7 Whose poetry anthologies include *North and South* and *Questions of Travel*?

a) Robert Lowell

b) Elizabeth Bishop

c) Allen Tate

8 What is the name of the novel by Jeffrey Eugenides that won the Pulitzer Prize for Fiction in 2003?

a) *The Little Friend*

b) *The Corrections*

c) *Middlesex*

9 Which writer spent two years living in isolation by Walden Pond?

a) Ralph Emerson

b) Henry Thoreau

c) Walt Whitman

10 Whose first novel was published in 1974 and adapted into a film in 1976 starring Sissy Spacek?

a) Stephen King

b) Dean Koontz

c) James Ellroy

1 a

2 a

3 a

4 b

5 b

6 c

7 b

8 c

9 b

10 a

FICTIONAL CHARACTERS AND PLACES

1 **Which writer created an imaginary land at the centre of the Earth's core called Pellucidar?**

a) Edgar Rice Burroughs

b) Edgar Allan Poe

c) Edgar Wallace

2 **Which school did fictional fat boy Billy Bunter attend?**

a) Blackfriars

b) Whitefriars

c) Greyfriars

3 **What is the surname of Emma in Jane Austen's novel of that name?**

a) Woodhouse

b) Dashwood

c) Bennett

4 **Who wrote a series of novels set on a desert planet called Arrakis?**

a) Ray Bradbury

b) Isaac Asimov

c) Frank Herbert

5 **What was the name of the land of giants visited by Gulliver in Jonathan Swift's *Gulliver's Travels*?**

a) Laputa

b) Brobdingnag

c) Gargantua

6 **In which novel does a pivotal incident take place in the Malabar Caves?**

a) *Lord of the Flies* by William Golding

b) *Midnight's Children* by Salman Rushdie

c) *A Passage to India* by E. M. Forster

7 **Which author's protagonists include Mitchell McDeere, Darby Shaw and Nicholas Easter?**

a) James Patterson

b) Dick Francis

c) John Grisham

8 **Which novel is set in Hampden College, a fictional university in Vermont?**

a) *The Secret History* by Donna Tartt

b) *The Corrections* by Jonathan Franzen

c) *Wonder Boys* by Michael Chabon

9 **What is the name of Tom Ripley's French wife?**

a) Helena

b) Héloïse

c) Hortense

10 **What is the name of the hotel occupied by the Torrance family in Stephen King's *The Shining*?**

a) The Hotel New Hampshire

b) The Overlook Hotel

c) Hotel Trianon

A

1 a
2 c
3 a
4 c
5 b
6 c
7 c
8 a
9 b
10 b

Q CELEBRITY AUTOBIOGRAPHY

1 Which of the following celebrities allegedly received the highest advance for their ghost-written autobiography?

a) Russell Brand

b) Gordon Ramsay

c) Gary Barlow

2 Whose autobiography was 'sloppy, self-indulgent and often eye-crossingly dull' according to a review by the *New York Times*?

a) Al Gore

b) Bill Clinton

c) Hillary Clinton

3 Whose autobiography opens with the line 'Ding dong! Was that the doorbell? You can never be too sure'?

a) Billy Connolly

b) Ricky Tomlinson

c) Peter Kay

4 Which of the following published their autobiography at the age of 15?

a) Charlotte Church

b) Billie Piper

c) Daniel Radcliffe

5 Hunter Davies wrote a biography of William Wordsworth, whose autobiography did he ghost-write?

a) Katie Price

b) Wayne Rooney

c) Victoria Beckham

6 **Whose autobiography was called *Life in the Jungle*?**

a) Ray Mears

b) David Gest

c) Michael Heseltine

7 **Which eminent historian was duped by the so-called Hitler Diaries in 1983?**

a) Robin Lane Fox

b) Simon Sebag-Montefiore

c) Hugh Trevor-Roper

8 **If Ulrika Jonsson was *Honest* and Sharon Osbourne *Extreme*, what was Boy George?**

a) *Straight*

b) *Out*

c) *Proud*

9 **Whose memoirs of their childhood was titled *Moab is My Washpot*?**

a) Hugh Grant

b) Stephen Fry

c) Boris Johnson

10 **Which member of the Red Hot Chili Peppers published *Scar Tissue*?**

a) Anthony Kiedis

b) Flea

c) John Frusciante

A

1 c
2 b
3 c
4 a
5 b
6 c
7 c
8 a
9 b
10 a

Q SEX IN LITERATURE

1 What was the subtitle of *The Joy of Sex* in 1973?

a) 'A Gourmet Guide'

b) 'A Blow-by-Blow Account'

c) 'Positioning for Beginners'

2 Which Tom Wolfe novel was the recipient of the *Literary Review*'s Bad Sex Award?

a) *The Bonfire of the Vanities*

b) *A Man in Full*

c) *I Am Charlotte Simmons*

3 Which Philip Roth novel is a monologue on sexual frustration?

a) *Portnoy's Complaint*

b) *When She Was Good*

c) *Everyman*

4 Who was Lady Chatterley's lover?

a) Clay Boone

b) Oliver Mellors

c) Rupert Burkin

5 Which erotic novel was written by John Cleland?

a) *A Spy in the House of Love*

b) *Fanny Hill*

c) *The Autobiography of a Flea*

6 **Which poet wrote the lines: 'License my roving hands, and let them go/Behind, before, above, between, below/Oh my America, my new found land/My kingdom, safeliest with one man manned'?**

a) John Wilmot, Earl of Rochester

b) John Clare

c) John Donne

7 ***Memories of My Melancholy Whores* is a novella by which writer?**

a) Carlos Fuentes

b) Gabriel Garcia Marquez

c) Julio Cortazar

8 **In Marquis de Sade's book, how many days of Sodom were there?**

a) 12

b) 120

c) 1,200

9 **Stanley Kubrick's *Eyes Wide Shut* was based on which short novel?**

a) *The Story of the Eye* by Georges Bataille

b) *Dream Story* by Arthur Schnitzler

c) *Tropic of Cancer* by Henry Miller

10 **What did Casanova call his memoirs?**

a) *The Story of My Life*

b) *Women I Have Loved*

c) *The Naked Sword*

A

1 a

2 c

3 a

4 b

5 b

6 c

7 b

8 b

9 b

10 a

Q FIRST LINES

1 'If you really want to hear about it, the first thing you'll probably want to know is where I was born . . . and all that David Copperfield kind of crap, but I don't feel like going into it, if you want to know the truth.'

a) *Portnoy's Complaint*

b) *The Invisible Man*

c) *The Catcher in the Rye*

2 'It was a bright cold day in April, and the clocks were striking thirteen.'

a) *Nineteen Eighty-Four*

b) *Brave New World*

c) *The Chrysalids*

3 'riverrun, past Eve and Adam's, from swerve of shore to bend of bay, brings us by a commodius vicus of recirculation back to Howth Castle and Environs'

a) *A Clockwork Orange*

b) *The Waves*

c) *Finnegans Wake*

4 'There was a boy called Eustace Clarence Scrubb, and he almost deserved it.'

a) *Charlie and the Chocolate Factory*

b) *The Voyage of the Dawn Treader*

c) *Five Children and It*

5 'This is the saddest story I have ever heard.'

a) *Never Let Me Go*

b) *Memoirs of a Geisha*

c) *The Good Soldier*

LANGUAGE AND LITIERATURE

6 'It was a dark and stormy night and the rain fell in torrents – except at occasional intervals.'

a) *Paul Clifford*

b) *Reaper Man*

c) *Frankenstein*

7 'The beginning is simple to mark.'

a) *Atonement*

b) *On Chesil Beach*

c) *Enduring Love*

8 'It was the afternoon of my eighty-first birthday, and I was in bed with my catamite when Ali announced that the archbishop had come to see me.'

a) *The Satanic Verses*

b) *Earthly Powers*

c) *A Suitable Boy*

9 'Happy families are all alike; every unhappy family is unhappy in its own way.'

a) *Persuasion*

b) *Madame Bovary*

c) *Anna Karenina*

10 'There was no possibility of taking a walk that day.'

a) *Jane Eyre*

b) *Middlemarch*

c) *Cranford*

1 c
2 a
3 c
4 b
5 c
6 a
7 c
8 b
9 c
10 a

CHILDREN'S CLASSICS

1 Who created the character Tracy Beaker?

a) Jacqueline Wilson

b) Judy Blume

c) Robin Klein

2 Which character in children's fiction was created by Jean de Brunhoff?

a) Tintin

b) Babar the Elephant

c) Matilda

3 How is Theodor S. Geisel better known?

a) Hergé

b) Captain W. E. Johns

c) Dr Seuss

4 Who wrote *A Little Princess* and *The Secret Garden*?

a) Edith Nesbit

b) Frances Hodgson Burnett

c) Enid Blyton

5 In the stories of Beatrix Potter, what kind of animal is Mr Tod?

a) A fox

b) A badger

c) A toad

6 In *The Lion, The Witch and The Wardrobe*, the arrival of which character heralds the end of the winter?

a) Mr Tumnus the Fawn

b) Father Christmas

c) Aslan the Lion

7 Who wrote the play *Toad of Toad Hall*, an adaptation of Kenneth Grahame's *The Wind in the Willows*?

a) A. A. Milne

b) Enid Blyton

c) C. S. Lewis

8 In *Treasure Island*, who is the one-legged pirate?

a) Bluebeard

b) Blackbeard

c) Long John Silver

9 Who catalogues *A Series of Unfortunate Events* in the lives of the Baudelaire children?

a) Anthony Horowitz

b) Eoin Colfer

c) Lemony Snicket

10 Which book by Roald Dahl contains the characters Mike Teavee and Violet Beauregarde?

a) The Twits

b) Charlie and the Chocolate Factory

c) The BFG

A

1	a
2	b
3	c
4	b
5	a
6	b
7	a
8	c
9	c
10	b

Q BESTSELLERS

1 Which of the following writers worked as an attorney before becoming a writer?

a) John Grisham

b) Dan Brown

c) Thomas Harris

2 Who was author of romance novels Mary Westmacott also known as?

a) Ruth Rendell

b) P. D. James

c) Agatha Christie

3 Whose offspring are James, Albus and Lily?

a) Harry Potter and Ginevra Weasley

b) Elizabeth Bennet and Fitzwilliam Darcy

c) Rex Harrison and Scarlett O'Hara

4 Which author wrote *Circle of Friends*, which was adapted into a 1995 film starring Minnie Driver?

a) Joanna Trollope

b) Barbara Taylor Bradford

c) Maeve Binchy

5 Who was the target of an assassination attempt in Frederick Forsyth's *The Day of the Jackal*?

a) John F. Kennedy

b) Charles de Gaulle

c) Winston Churchill

6 Which of the following is not a Mills and Boon imprint?

a) Historical

b) Medical

c) Gastronomical

7 Who wrote the *Rutshire Chronicles*?

a) Thomas Hardy

b) Elizabeth Gaskell

c) Jilly Cooper

8 In which newspaper did Bridget Jones' column originally appear?

a) *The Guardian*

b) *The Times*

c) *The Independent*

9 Dava Sobel's *Longitude* described the career of which English scientist?

a) John Harrison

b) Michael Faraday

c) Robert Hooke

10 What is the shared surname of the children in Enid Blyton's *Famous Five* series?

a) Tiffin

b) Kirrin

c) Griffin

1 a
2 c
3 a
4 c
5 b
6 c
7 c
8 c
9 a
10 b

THE NOVEL

1 Which of the following has a sequel written by a different author?

a) *Gone with the Wind*

b) *Little Women*

c) *Villette*

2 Which novel did Charles Dickens leave unfinished at his death?

a) *Dombey and Son*

b) *Our Mutual Friend*

c) *The Mystery of Edwin Drood*

3 In which novel is the hero so incompetent at telling his own story that he fails to get himself born until the third volume?

a) *Tristram Shandy*

b) *Joseph Andrews*

c) *Tom Jones*

4 The central characters of which Jane Austen novel live at Barton Cottage?

a) *Emma*

b) *Sense and Sensibility*

c) *Persuasion*

5 Which novelist's autobiographical protagonist is known throughout his novels as Sal Paradise, Jack Duluoz, Ray Smith and Leo Percepied?

a) Richard Brautigan

b) Jack Kerouac

c) Tom Wolfe

6 Which of the following novels won the Booker of Bookers prize?

a) Kazuo Ishiguro's *The Remains of the Day*

b) Margaret Atwood's *The Blind Assassin*

c) Salman Rushdie's *Midnight's Children*

7 Which classic novel has the alternative title of *The Modern Prometheus*?

a) Mary Shelley's *Frankenstein*

b) R. L. Stevenson's *Dr. Jekyll and Mr. Hyde*

c) Bram Stoker's *Dracula*

8 Which novel was inspired by the real-life adventures of Alexander Selkirk?

a) *Rob Roy*

b) *Kidnapped*

c) *Robinson Crusoe*

9 In which novel does a character called Billy Pilgrim survive the fire-bombing of Dresden in World War II?

a) Kurt Vonnegut's *Slaughterhouse-5*

b) Joseph Heller's *Catch-22*

c) John O'Hara's *Butterfield 8*

10 Who wrote an unfinished novel called *Sanditon*?

a) Jane Austen

b) George Eliot

c) Charlotte Bronte

1 a
2 c
3 a
4 b
5 b
6 c
7 a
8 c
9 a
10 a

Q WORLD LITERATURE

1 Who was the author of *Madame Bovary*?

a) Honoré de Balzac

b) Guy de Maupassant

c) Gustave Flaubert

2 Chinua Achebe, author of *Things Fall Apart*, is from which African country?

a) South Africa

b) Sudan

c) Nigeria

3 Which German novelist won the Nobel Prize for Literature in 1999?

a) Günter Grass

b) Thomas Mann

c) Heinrich Böll

4 What nationality is Orhan Pamuk?

a) Armenian

b) Turkish

c) Cypriot

5 In *Les Misérables*, what is the name of the central character?

a) Jean Valjean

b) Javert

c) Gavroche

6 **Fyodor Dostoyevsky's work is generally considered a precursor to which philosophical movement?**

a) Deconstruction

b) Existentialism

c) Postmodernism

7 **Who wrote the short story 'Funes the Memorious', about a man who remembers everything?**

a) Jorge Luis Borges

b) Mario Vargas Llosa

c) Gabriel Garcia Marquez

8 **In which picaresque novel is the protagonist tutored by Dr Pangloss, flogged in the army, injured in the 1755 Lisbon earthquake and accompanied by a Dutchman called Martin?**

a) *Don Juan*

b) *Candide*

c) *Emile*

9 **Who wrote *A Modest Proposal*, a satirical pamphlet which proposed eating babies as the solution to eighteenth-century poverty in Ireland?**

a) Jonathan Swift

b) Jean-Jacques Rousseau

c) Thomas Paine

10 **In Dante's *Inferno*, which sin is found in the ninth, and innermost, circle of hell?**

a) Lust

b) Treachery

c) Heresy

A

1 c

2 c

3 a

4 b

5 a

6 b

7 a

8 b

9 a

10 b

POETRY

1 Who wrote in praise of older women: 'No spring, nor summer beauty hath such grace/As I have seen in one autumnal face'?

a) Walter Raleigh

b) John Donne

c) Alexander Pushkin

2 Which 20th-century poet's autobiography is entitled *Summoned by Bells*?

a) John Betjeman

b) Wilfred Owen

c) W. H. Auden

3 In *The Pied Piper of Hamelin* what kind of creatures did the piper spirit away?

a) Rats and mice

b) Rats and children

c) Rats and the Town Council

4 Which of the following poets has not translated *Beowulf*?

a) Seamus Heaney

b) Simon Armitage

c) Andrew Motion

5 In 1995 the poem *If* was voted the nation's favourite poem. Who was the author?

a) Alfred Lord Tennyson

b) Rudyard Kipling

c) Robert Browning

LANGUAGE AND LITIERATURE

6 What was Philip Larkin' 'Annus Mirabilis', when sex began 'Between the end of the Chatterley ban/And The Beatles' first LP'?

a) 1958

b) 1963

c) 1967

7 Who wrote the poems which are used in the lyrics for the Andrew Lloyd Webber musical *Cats*?

a) Ted Hughes

b) T. S. Eliot

c) W. B. Yeats

8 Who wrote the following haiku: 'The apparition of these faces in a crowd;/Petals on a wet, black bough'?

a) T. S. Eliot

b) Ezra Pound

c) Wyndham Lewis

9 Which Caribbean writer's major poetic work is the epic *Omeros*, which is based on Homer's *Iliad* and *Odyssey*?

a) Derek Walcott

b) Grace Nichols

c) John Agard

10 Who was the author of the lament for a dead lover *Stop All the Clocks*, used in the film *Four Weddings and a Funeral*?

a) Louis MacNeice

b) W. H. Auden

c) John Betjeman

A

1 b
2 a
3 b
4 c
5 b
6 b
7 b
8 b
9 a
10 b

Q WORD ORIGINS

1 From which language do we get the word 'bungalow'?

a) Bengali

b) Portuguese

c) Gujarati

2 'Plebs' were the common people of which ancient society?

a) Greece

b) Rome

c) Gaul

3 The term 'jeans' derives from the French name for which Italian city?

a) Bari

b) Turin

c) Genoa

4 The word 'canopy' derives from the Greek term for what?

a) Shade

b) Shadow

c) Mosquito

5 What is the meaning of the Dutch word *ezel*, the origin of the English word 'easel'?

a) Donkey

b) Crutch

c) Triangle

6 **The word 'barbecue' is the derived from the language used by the inhabitants of which island?**

a) Jamaica

b) Australia

c) Haiti

7 **From which language does the word 'cathedral' derive?**

a) Hebrew

b) Latin

c) Greek

8 **Franz Anton Mesmer, a trance-inducing doctor from whom the word 'mesmerise' is derived, was from which country?**

a) Austria

b) Germany

c) Switzerland

9 **The literal meaning of which word, in its old French original version, was 'fine thing of a woman'?**

a) Blush

b) Prude

c) Tart

10 **Which settlers in the USA were the original 'Yankees'?**

a) Spanish

b) English

c) Dutch

A

1 a
2 b
3 c
4 c
5 a
6 c
7 c
8 a
9 c
10 c

Q WORD MEANINGS

1 Which of the following is not a definition of the word 'augur'?

a) A screw-like device for moving material and/or making holes

b) To predict some future event or trend from signs or omens

c) A greenish-black mineral found in igneous rocks

2 What is the correct meaning of the verb 'coruscate'?

a) To censure strongly, denounce or chafe

b) To emit flashes of light or to exhibit sparkling virtuosity

c) To undervalue oneself and one's abilities

3 To what animal does the adjective 'hircine' refer?

a) Deer

b) Sheep

c) Goat

4 What does it mean if something is described as a 'cakewalk'?

a) It is an easy accomplishment

b) It is an unproductive course of action

c) It is an unexpected bonus

5 Which was never a name for a dictionary?

a) Alphography

b) Lexicon

c) Abcedariaum

6 What is a 'wayzgoose'?

a) The largest turkey at a farm

b) The works outing of a printing house

c) A signpost marking the route of a footpath

7 If something is described as 'helminthoid', what shape is it?

a) Shield-shaped

b) Worm-shaped

c) Arrow-shape

8 What is a 'quango'?

a) A horse-like mammal native to southern Africa

b) A long pole used for propelling a boat

c) An organisation that financed by government but acts independently of it

9 A 'campanologist' is an enthusiast of what?

a) Bell-ringing

b) Tents

c) Musical shows

10 A 'fitchew' is an archaic name for which animal?

a) Pine marten

b) Badger

c) Polecat

A

1 c

2 b

3 c

4 a

5 a

6 b

7 b

8 c

9 a

10 c

Q NAME THAT POEM

1 Which poem opens with the line 'Had we but world enough and time'?

a) 'The Passionate Shepherd to his Love' by Christopher Marlowe

b) 'To His Coy Mistress' by Andrew Marvell

c) 'To the Virgins, to Make Much of Time' by Robert Herrick

2 Which poem by T. S. Eliot features the refrain 'In the room the women come and go/Talking of Michelangelo'?

a) 'The Love Song of J. Alfred Prufrock'

b) 'The Hollow Men'

c) 'The Waste Land'

3 Who wrote the lines: 'When I am an old woman, I shall wear purple/With a red hat which doesn't go, and doesn't suit me.'

a) Stevie Smith

b) Jenny Joseph

c) Muriel Spark

4 Who is the author of these lines 'Be nice to yu turkeys dis christmas/Cos' turkeys just wanna hav fun'?

a) Spike Milligan

b) Benjamin Zephaniah

c) Roger McGough

5 Which poem by Wilfred Owen begins: 'What passing-bells for these who die as cattle?/Only the monstrous anger of the guns/On the stuttering rifles' rapid rattle/Can patter out their hasty orisons'?

a) 'Dulce et Decorum Est'

b) 'Anthem for Doomed Youth'

c) 'Strange Meeting'

6 Which of John Keats' odes features the lines: When old age shall this generation waste/Thou shalt remain, in midst of other woe/Than ours, a friend to man, to whom thou say'st/'Beauty is truth, truth beauty' – that is all/Ye know on earth, and all ye need know'?

a) 'Ode on a Grecian Urn'

b) 'Ode to a Nightingale'

c) 'Ode on Melancholy'

7 In which city did William Blake observe a 'mark in every face I meet/Marks of weakness, marks of woe'?

a) London

b) Manchester

c) Sheffield

8 Which poem features the death of an albatross?

a) 'Sea Fever' by John Masefield

b) 'Dover Beach' by Matthew Arnold

c) 'The Rime of the Ancient Mariner' by Samuel Taylor Coleridge

9 Which poem opens with the line 'The Curfew tolls the knell of parting day'?

a) 'Elegy Written in a Country Churchyard' by Thomas Gray

b) 'On his Blindness' by John Milton

c) 'Composed upon Westminster Bridge, Sept 3, 1802' by William Wordsworth

10 Which poem concludes: 'And we are here as on a darkling plain/Swept with confused alarms of struggle and flight/Where ignorant armies clash by night'?

a) 'Dover Beach' by Matthew Arnold

b) 'As Kingfishers Catch Fire' by Gerald Manley Hopkins

c) 'The Cry of the Children' by Elizabeth Barrett Browning

A

1	b
2	a
3	b
4	b
5	b
6	a
7	a
8	c
9	a
10	a

Q SHAKESPEARE

1 Which play begins in Venice and then moves to Cyprus?

a) *As You Like It*

b) *Othello*

c) *Merchant of Venice*

2 To whom are Shakespeare's sonnets dedicated?

a) His wife, Ann Hathaway

b) The King, James I

c) An anonymous friend, Mr W. H.

3 Which Pre-Raphaelite artist painted Ophelia, inspired by the Shakespearean character?

a) Holman Hunt

b) Dante Gabriel Rossetti

c) John Everett Millais

4 Which play has the subtitle, 'Or What You Will'?

a) *Twelfth Night*

b) *The Tempest*

c) *Much Ado About Nothing*

5 In which play do the feuding lovers Beatrice and Benedick appear?

a) *Love's Labour's Lost*

b) *The Taming of the Shrew*

c) *Much Ado About Nothing*

6 From which Shakespeare play did Aldous Huxley take the title of his novel *Brave New World*?

a) *Hamlet*

b) *The Tempest*

c) *Othello*

7 How did a performance of *Henry VIII* destroy the original Globe theatre?

a) A cannon used for special effects set fire to the thatched roof

b) The unflattering depiction of Elizabeth I caused a riot among the crowd

c) The play's commercial failure led to the sale of the theatre's grounds

8 Which of the following is not one of King Lear's daughters?

a) Rosalind

b) Regan

c) Cordelia

9 Which Shakespeare play includes the famous stage direction, 'Exit, pursued by a bear'?

a) *The Tempest*

b) *All's Well That Ends Well*

c) *The Winter's Tale*

10 A character called Portia appears in *The Merchant of Venice* and which other Shakespeare play?

a) *Julius Caesar*

b) *Antony and Cleopatra*

c) *The Taming of the Shrew*

A

1 b
2 c
3 c
4 a
5 c
6 b
7 a
8 a
9 c
10 a

Q PLAYWRIGHTS

1 Which Greek tragedian wrote *Oedipus the King*?

a) Sophocles

b) Euripides

c) Aeschlyus

2 Which English monarch links Christopher Marlowe and Bertold Brecht?

a) Richard III

b) Edward II

c) Henry VIII

3 Fashion designer Nicole Farhi is married to which British playwright?

a) David Hare

b) Alan Ayckbourn

c) Tom Stoppard

4 Which playwright created his own alphabet?

a) George Bernard Shaw

b) Harold Pinter

c) Noel Coward

5 T. S. Eliot's *Murder in the Cathedral* concerned the death of which archbishop?

a) Thomas Cranmer

b) Thomas Beckett

c) Thomas Langton

LANGUAGE AND LITIERATURE

6 Which playwright disowned his daughter Oona, after she married the much-older Charlie Chaplin?

a) Arthur Miller

b) Eugene O'Neill

c) Edward Albee

7 According to a collection published by Oxford University Press, which play did Thomas Middleton help Shakespeare to write?

a) *Titus Andronicus*

b) *Timon of Athens*

c) *Troilus and Cressida*

8 Which play's three acts are titled 'Fun and Games', 'Walpurgisnacht' and 'The Exorcism'?

a) *Who's Afraid of Virginia Woolf?*

b) *A Streetcar Named Desire*

c) *Abigail's Party*

9 According to T. S. Eliot, which dramatist saw 'the skull beneath the skin'?

a) John Webster

b) Thomas Dekker

c) Ben Jonson

10 Which English playwright is married to the award-winning biographer Claire Tomalin?

a) Alan Ayckbourn

b) Michael Frayn

c) Edward Bond

1 a
2 b
3 a
4 a
5 b
6 b
7 b
8 a
9 a
10 b

Q NOMS DES PLUME

1 Daniel Handler's books are published under what name?

a) Lemony Snicket

b) Mark Twain

c) Dr Seuss

2 Which one of these pen names does not belong to a husband-and-wife duo?

a) Nicci French

b) Lewis Padgett

c) Ayn Rand

3 Which of these novelists uses their real name?

a) Agatha Christie

b) John le Carré

c) John Buchan

4 Which 19th-century novelist published sketches and essays under the pseudonym Michael Angelo Titmarsh?

a) Charles Dickens

b) W. M. Thackeray

c) Thomas Hardy

5 What was the name of the fake critic created by Sony to write favourable reviews of films released by its subsidiary Columbia Pictures?

a) David Manning

b) Peter Foster

c) John Turnbull

A

1 a

2 c

3 c

4 b

5 a

MUSIC

LYRICS

ALSO KNOWN AS

BEHIND THE MUSIC

CHART RECORDS

CLASSICAL MUSIC

MUSICAL DYNASTIES

ONE-HIT WONDERS

ROCK

POP

BLUES AND SOUL

JAZZ

FOLK AND COUNTRY

RAP AND HIP-HOP

ELECTRONICA

MUSIC AND FILM

OPERA

LYRICS

Identify the song from the following lyrics:

1 'Did I disappoint you/Or leave a bad taste in your mouth/You act like you never had love/And you want me to go without'

a) 'Baker Street' by Gerry Rafferty

b) 'Clocks' by Coldplay

c) 'One' by U2

2 'If you should ever leave me/Well life would still go on, believe me/The world could show nothing to me/So what good would living do me?'

a) 'God Only Knows' by The Beach Boys

b) 'She Loves You' by The Beatles

c) 'This Will Be Our Year' by The Zombies

3 'Your beauty is beyond compare/With flaming locks of auburn hair/With ivory skin and eyes of emerald green'

a) 'D.I.V.O.R.C.E.' by Tammy Wynette

b) 'Jolene' by Dolly Parton

c) 'Respect' by Otis Redding

4 'Baby, I have been here before/I know this room, I've walked this floor/I used to live alone before I knew you'

a) 'I Want You' by Bob Dylan

b) 'Hallelujah' by Leonard Cohen

c) 'Waterloo Sunset' by The Kinks

5 'I don't want to be your friend/I just want to be your lover'

a) 'Little Red Corvette' by Prince

b) 'You're My First, My Last, My Everything' by Barry White

c) 'House of Cards' by Radiohead

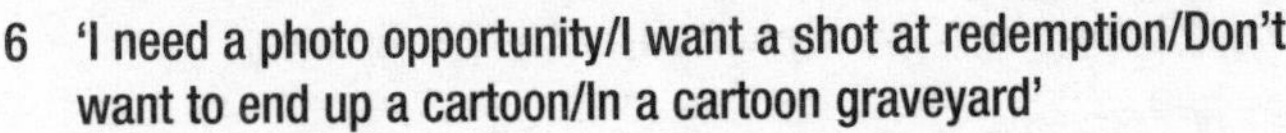

6 'I need a photo opportunity/I want a shot at redemption/Don't want to end up a cartoon/In a cartoon graveyard'

a) 'Lose Yourself' by Eminem

b) 'You Can Call Me Al' by Paul Simon

c) 'Pinball Wizard' by The Who

7 'Mars ain't the kind of place to raise your kids/In fact it's cold as hell/And there's no one there to raise them if you did/And all this science I don't understand'

a) 'Rocket Man' by Elton John

b) 'Life on Mars' by David Bowie

c) 'Venus as a Boy' by Bjork

8 'I gotta be cool, relax, get hip/Get on my tracks/Take a back seat, hitch-hike/And take a long ride on my motorbike'

a) 'Shake, Rattle and Roll' by Bill Haley and the Comets

b) 'Whole Lotta Shakin' Going On' by Jerry Lee Lewis

c) 'Crazy Little Thing Called Love' by Queen

9 'Between the eyes of love I call your name/Behind the guarded walls I used to go/Upon a summer wind there's a certain melody/Takes me back to the place that I know'

a) 'On the Beach' by Neil Young

b) 'On the Beach' by Chris Rea

c) 'On the Beach' by The Faces

10 'If there's a bustle in your hedgerow/Don't be alarmed now/It's just a spring clean for the May Queen'

a) 'Stairway to Heaven' by Led Zeppelin

b) 'Whiter Shade of Pale' by Procol Harum

c) 'Mull of Kintyre' by Wings

A

1 c
2 a
3 b
4 b
5 c
6 b
7 a
8 c
9 b
10 a

ALSO KNOWN AS

1 Which band was originally known as The Pendletones?

a) The Beach Boys

b) The Mamas and the Papas

c) The Byrds

2 Vincent Damon Furnier is the birth name of which US rock star?

a) Axl Rose

b) Alice Cooper

c) Neil Young

3 Who began their career as On a Sunday?

a) Blur

b) Pulp

c) Radiohead

4 Whose real name is Michael Balzary?

a) The Edge (of U2)

b) Flea (of Red Hot Chili Peppers)

c) Daddy G (of Massive Attack)

5 Who is missing from rock supergroup the Traveling Wilburys: Bob Dylan, George Harrison, Jeff Lynne, Tom Petty and __________?

a) Johnny Cash

b) Roy Orbison

c) Neil Young

6 Who has recorded under the names Pizzaman, Freak Power and the Mighty Dub Katz?

a) Armand van Helden

b) Norman Cook

c) Moby

7 How is Shawn Carter better known?

a) 50 Cent

b) R. Kelly

c) Jay-Z

8 Which group featured members of Santana, the Steve Miller Band and the Tubes?

a) Bad Company

b) Derek and the Dominoes

c) Journey

9 Which member of Bruce Springsteen's E Street Band appeared on The Sopranos as Silvio Dante?

a) Nils Lofgren

b) Clarence Clemons

c) Steven Van Zandt

10 Who is Don Van Vliet better known as?

a) Captain Beefheart

b) Frank Zappa

c) Syd Barrett

A

1	a
2	b
3	c
4	b
5	b
6	b
7	c
8	c
9	c
10	a

Q BEHIND THE MUSIC

1 Which band was managed by Andrew Loog Oldham?

a) The Rolling Stones

b) The Who

c) Led Zeppelin

2 Which producer links the Righteous Brothers, the Ronettes and the Crystals?

a) Berry Gordy

b) Phil Spector

c) Ike Turner

3 Which band's PopMart tour featured a 100ft golden arch, a lemon mirrorball and a martini stick on stage?

a) REM

b) U2

c) XTC

4 In which district of London can the Abbey Road studios be found?

a) Battersea

b) Notting Hill

c) St John's Wood

5 What was the name of John Peel's first British radio show, broadcast on pirate station Radio London?

a) *The Perfumed Garden*

b) *The Hallowed Sanctuary*

c) *The Norfolk Hour*

6 Who played legendary music journalist Lester Bangs in the film *Almost Famous*?

a) John Cusack

b) Philip Seymour Hoffman

c) William H. Macy

7 Which of these lead singers is the shortest, at 5ft 5.3in?

a) Bono

b) Thom Yorke

c) Iggy Pop

8 Who wrote the song 'I Will Always Love You', a hit for Whitney Houston in 1992?

a) Dolly Parton

b) Reba McEntire

c) Emmylou Harris

9 What do singer/songwriters Joni Mitchell and Neil Young have in common?

a) Both are lactose intolerant

b) Both contracted polio as children

c) Both collect classic American cars

10 Which 1960s pop star died at a house once owned by A. A. Milne, the creator of Winnie the Pooh?

a) Jimi Hendrix

b) Janis Joplin

c) Brian Jones

A

1 a

2 b

3 b

4 c

5 a

6 b

7 b

8 a

9 b

10 c

CHART RECORDS

1 What was Blondie's first UK No. 1?

a) 'The Tide Is High'

b) 'Heart of Glass'

c) 'Hanging on the Telephone'

2 Who is the only artist to have had a No.1 as a solo artist as well as a member of a duo, trio, quartet, quintet and sextet?

a) Rod Stewart

b) Michael Jackson

c) Paul McCartney

3 What was Abba's last UK No.1, released in 1980?

a) 'Take a Chance on Me'

b) 'Knowing Me, Knowing You'

c) 'Super Trouper'

4 What was the only Smiths LP to reach the top of the album charts?

a) *Strangeways, Here We Come*

b) *Meat is Murder*

c) *The Queen is Dead*

5 Who was the subject of the original version of 'Candle in the Wind', Elton John's re-recording of which, after Princess Diana's death, became the biggest-selling single in the UK?

a) Janis Joplin

b) Judy Garland

c) Marilyn Monroe

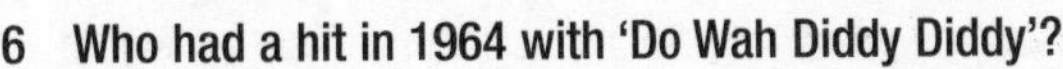

6 **Who had a hit in 1964 with 'Do Wah Diddy Diddy'?**

a) Herman's Hermits

b) Manfred Mann

c) Dave Dee, Dozy, Beaky, Mick and Tich

7 **Which single became the 1,000th to top the UK charts in 2005?**

a) 'Goodies' by Ciara

b) 'One Night' by Elvis Presley

c) 'Like Toy Soldiers' by Eminem

8 **Which album has spent the longest – 477 weeks – on the UK chart?**

a) *Bat Out of Hell* by Meat Loaf

b) *Rumours* by Fleetwood Mac

c) *Tubular Bells* by Mike Oldfield

9 **Which single spent the longest at No.1 in the UK singles chart during the 1990s?**

a) 'Believe' by Cher

b) 'Love is All Around' by Wet Wet Wet

c) '(Everything I Do) I Do It For You' by Bryan Adams

10 **What is the biggest-selling single never to top the UK chart?**

a) 'Angels' by Robbie Williams

b) 'Blue Monday' by New Order

c) 'Last Christmas' by Wham!

A

1	b
2	c
3	c
4	b
5	c
6	b
7	b
8	b
9	c
10	c

Q CLASSICAL MUSIC

1 Beethoven used the words of which poet for the 'Ode to Joy' in his 9th Symphony?

a) Goethe

b) Heine

c) Schiller

2 How many movements did Schubert complete in his Symphony No. 8 in B Minor, known as the *Unfinished Symphony*?

a) 1

b) 2

c) 3

3 In Gustav Holst's 'The Planets Suite' which planet is described as the 'bringer of jollity'?

a) Saturn

b) Jupiter

c) Neptune

4 How is Beethoven's Piano Sonata No. 14 in C-sharp Minor Opus 27, No. 2 better known?

a) The Moonlight Sonata

b) The Appassionata Sonata

c) The Waldstein Sonata

5 Which well-known composition includes pieces called 'In the Hall of the Mountain King' and 'Anitra's Dance?

a) Prokofiev's 'Peter and the Wolf' Suite

b) Mussorgsky's 'Pictures at an Exhibition'

c) Grieg's 'Peer Gynt Suite'

6 What does the word glagolitic mean in Leos Janacek's *Glagolitic Mass*?

a) It is the Czech word for 'spoken'

b) It is the name of the old Slavic alphabet

c) It is a reference to a symmetric nine-movement composition

7 For which eccentric habit was pianist Glenn Gould not famed?

a) Humming while he played

b) Wearing winter clothing and gloves while he played

c) Insisting on having his feet in a sandbox while he played

8 Which of the following collaborations between film directors and composers did not take place?

a) Sergei Prokofiev and Sergei Eisenstein

b) Michael Nyman and Peter Greenaway

c) Alfred Hitchcock and Ennio Morricone

9 Which piece of music was played at the funerals of both Franklin Roosevelt and Princess Diana, and in 2001 at a ceremony at the World Trade Centre?

a) Samuel Barber's Adagio for Strings

b) 'Dido's Lament' from Henry Purcell's *Dido and Aeneas*

c) Adagietto from Gustav's Mahler's 5th Symphony

10 How was Igor Stravinsky's *The Rite of Spring* received when it premiered in 1913 in Paris?

a) It was celebrated as a new way of appreciating rhythmic structure

b) It caused a riot and the police were called to restore order

c) Stravinsky was offered a directorship at the Théâtre des Champs-Élysées

1 c

2 b

3 b

4 a

5 c

6 b

7 c

8 c

9 a

10 b

Q MUSICAL DYNASTIES

1 **Who is Norah Jones' father?**

a) Lee 'Scratch' Perry

b) Ravi Shankar

c) Ali Farka Toure

2 **How is Mike Love related to Brian, Dennis and Carl Wilson – the other original Beach Boys?**

a) Adopted brother

b) Cousin

c) Stepfather

3 **How many Jackson siblings had albums on the market in 1984?**

a) 3

b) 6

c) 9

4 **Which German musical dynasty is still involved in the organisation of the annual Bayreuth Festival, conceived by their famous ancestor?**

a) The Strausses

b) The Bachs

c) The Wagners

5 **US indie band The Wallflowers are fronted by Jakob, but who is his famous father?**

a) Robbie Robertson

b) Bruce Springsteen

c) Bob Dylan

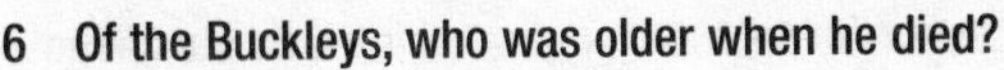

6 **Of the Buckleys, who was older when he died?**

a) Tim Buckley

b) Jeff Buckley

c) Neither, they were the same age

7 **What links Brandon Flowers of The Killers, minimalist rock band Low and the Osmonds?**

a) They share a great-grandfather

b) They are all Mormons

c) They have all made cameo appearances in a Woody Allen film

8 **Folk singer Eliza Carthy is the daughter of Martin Carthy, also a folk musician – who is her equally musical mother?**

a) Norma Waterson

b) Kate McGarrigle

c) Joan Armatrading

9 **Which musical family composed the songs 'Dinner at Eight', 'You Never Phone', 'A Father and a Son' and 'Pretty Little Martha' about their relationships with each other?**

a) The Wainwrights

b) The Nolans

c) The Carters

10 **Which group featured the most sisters?**

a) Cleopatra

b) Sister Sledge

c) All Saints

A

1 b

2 b

3 c

4 c

5 c

6 b

7 b

8 a

9 a

10 b

Q ONE-HIT WONDERS

1 Mr Oizo's 'Flat Beat', No.1 in 1999, originated in an ad campaign for what product?

a) Levi's jeans

b) Nokia mobile phones

c) Budweiser beer

2 Which comedy duo had a No.1 in 1991 with 'The Stonk'?

a) Smashie and Nicey

b) Hale and Pace

c) Cannon and Ball

3 Nizlopi's one and only chart hit was a paean to which vehicle?

a) Milkfloat

b) JCB

c) VW Campervan

4 Who boasted of being 'the one and only' in 1991?

a) Rick Astley

b) Chesney Hawkes

c) Jason Donovan

5 Jazzy Jeff and the French Prince, Tori Amos and Korean rappers Dynamic Duo have all covered which one-hit wonder?

a) Anita Ward's 'Ring My Bell'

b) Phyllis Nelson's 'Move Closer'

c) Ricky Valance's 'Tell Laura I Love Her'

6 'All Out of ______' was the sole Top 40 hit for Air Supply?

a) Love

b) Luck

c) Dough

7 'Just Say No' was a hit for the cast of which TV show?

a) *Byker Grove*

b) *Grange Hill*

c) *Press Gang*

8 Which former soap star had a one-hit wonder in 1990 with 'Just This Side of Love'?

a) *Coronation Street*'s Adam Rickitt

b) *Emmerdale*'s Malandra Burrows

c) *Neighbours*' Stefan Dennis

9 What was the name of socialite Paris Hilton's one chart success?

a) 'Stars are Blind'

b) 'Born to Be Free'

c) 'Being Me'

10 Which Bob Dylan's song was re-recorded for charity in the wake of the Dunblane massacre?

a) 'Knockin' on Heaven's Door'

b) 'Blowin' in the Wind'

c) 'Like a Rolling Stone'

A

1 a
2 b
3 b
4 b
5 a
6 a
7 b
8 b
9 a
10 a

ROCK

1 What links the Collective Consciousness Society, Phil Lynott of Thin Lizzy, Paul Hardcastle and Vince Clarke of Erasure?

a) Each has been arrested for cannabis possession

b) Each has produced a theme tune for *Top of the Pops*

c) Each has collaborated with a football team on a World Cup song

2 Which Sun Records star's third wife was his 13-year-old first cousin?

a) BB King

b) Jerry Lee Lewis

c) Ike Turner

3 Which band was on stage when Meredith Hunter was murdered at the infamous Altamont Festival in 1969?

a) Rolling Stones

b) Grateful Dead

c) Jefferson Airplane

4 Bill Berry was the drummer in which band before retiring to become a farmer?

a) U2

b) Smashing Pumpkins

c) REM

5 Sean Penn's first film as a director – *The Indian Runner* – is based on which song by Bruce Springsteen?

a) 'Born in the USA'

b) 'Dancing in the Dark'

c) 'Highway Patrolman'

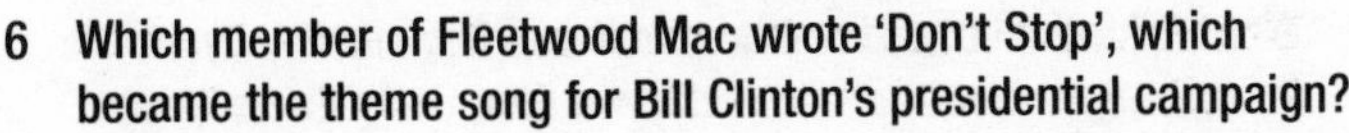

6 Which member of Fleetwood Mac wrote 'Don't Stop', which became the theme song for Bill Clinton's presidential campaign?

a) Stevie Nicks

b) Christine McVie

c) Lindsay Buckingham

7 Which band headlined the first Glastonbury Festival (then known as the Pilton Festival)?

a) T.Rex

b) The Sweet

c) Mott the Hoople

8 What record label was founded by Geoff Travis?

a) Parlophone

b) Rough Trade

c) Domino

9 Nick Cave's first band shares its name with which Harold Pinter play?

a) *The Birthday Party*

b) *Tea Party*

c) *Party Time*

10 Which album won the first Mercury Music Prize?

a) Primal Scream's *Screamadelica*

b) U2's *Achtung Baby*

c) Simply Red's *Stars*

1 b
2 b
3 a
4 c
5 c
6 b
7 a
8 b
9 a
10 a

POP

1 Which of the following was a member of Boyzone?

a) Stephen Gately

b) Mark Owen

c) Jason Orange

2 Who is Florian Cloud de Bounevialle O'Malley Armstrong?

a) Dido

b) Cher

c) Nico

3 Which Beatle wrote 'Yesterday'?

a) George Harrison

b) John Lennon

c) Paul McCartney

4 What song title links Britney Spears, Aerosmith and Patsy Cline?

a) 'Lucky'

b) 'Crazy'

c) 'Happy'

5 Whose history of pop music was called *Awopbopaloobop Alopbamboom*?

a) Nik Cohn

b) Tony Parsons

c) Julie Burchill

6 Which group recorded 'World In Motion' with the England football team for the 1990 World Cup?

a) Happy Mondays

b) The Farm

c) New Order

7 With which group did Lionel Richie sing before pursuing a successful 80s solo career?

a) The Manhattans

b) Chairmen of the Board

c) The Commodores

8 What is missing from Prince's 'When Doves Cry'?

a) A drum track

b) A bass line

c) A guitar solo

9 What is in the swimming pool on the cover of Oasis' *Be Here Now* album?

a) A Rolls Royce

b) Noel Gallagher's then-wife, Meg Mathews

c) £1m in banknotes

10 What was the name of Madonna's first single?

a) 'Holiday'

b) 'Burning Up'

c) 'Everybody'

A

1	a
2	a
3	c
4	b
5	a
6	c
7	c
8	b
9	a
10	c

BLUES AND SOUL

1 **In which US city was the Motown label founded?**

a) Detroit

b) Memphis

c) Atlanta

2 **The song 'Respect' – adapted into a feminist anthem by Aretha Franklin – was written by which musician?**

a) Mary Wells

b) Otis Redding

c) Wilson Pickett

3 **Which bluesman features on the cover of *Led Zeppelin II*?**

a) Blind Joe Reynolds

b) Blind Lemon Jefferson

c) Blind Willie Johnson

4 **Who shot dead Marvin Gaye?**

a) His father, Marvin Sr

b) The owner of his record label, Berry Gordy

c) His regular singing partner, Tammi Terrell

5 **Who performed with The Miracles?**

a) George Clinton

b) Martha Reeves

c) Smokey Robinson

6 Which blues musician was allegedly killed by a bottle of whiskey laced with pesticide?

a) Lead Belly

b) Robert Johnson

c) Sleepy John Estes

7 How is McKinley Morganfield better known?

a) Muddy Waters

b) Howlin' Wolf

c) Son House

8 Who recorded the classic 1971 album *There's a Riot Goin' On*?

a) Funkadelic

b) Sly and the Family Stone

c) Parliament

9 *The Cry of Love* was the last completed album by which artist?

a) Ray Charles

b) Jimi Hendrix

c) Sam Cooke

10 Which soul standard was originally recorded by Dionne Warwick and has since been covered by Cliff Richard, the Beach Boys and Seal?

a) 'Walk On By'

b) 'I Just Don't Know What to Do With Myself'

c) 'You've Lost That Lovin' Feeling'

A

1	a
2	b
3	c
4	a
5	c
6	b
7	a
8	b
9	b
10	a

JAZZ

1 **Which musician's plane disappeared in bad weather whilst travelling to entertain troops in France during the Second World War?**

a) Duke Ellington

b) Artie Shaw

c) Glenn Miller

2 **Whose most famous album was called *Kind of Blue*?**

a) Charlie Parker

b) Miles Davis

c) Dizzy Gillespie

3 **In which US state is the Newport Jazz Festival held?**

a) Pennsylvania

b) New Jersey

c) Rhode Island

4 **What nationality was guitarist Django Reinhardt?**

a) Belgian

b) Dutch

c) German

5 **Which legendary female vocalist began her career with the Chick Webb Orchestra?**

a) Billie Holiday

b) Ella Fitzgerald

c) Sarah Vaughan

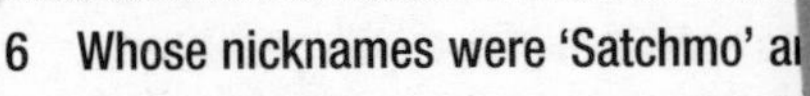

6 Whose nicknames were 'Satchmo' a ?

a) Hoagy Carmichael

b) Fats Waller

c) Louis Armstrong

7 Who was the first jazz artist to receive the Pulitzer Prize for Music?

a) Wynton Marsalis

b) Pat Metheny

c) Keith Jarrett

8 What was Thelonious Monk's middle name?

a) Planet

b) Sphere

c) Globe

9 From which Rodgers and Hart musical is jazz standard 'My Funny Valentine' taken?

a) *A Connecticut Jankee*

b) *Babes in Arms*

c) *Jumbo*

10 Which of these is not a composition by Duke Ellington?

a) 'It Don't Mean a Thing (If It Ain't Got That Swing)'

b) 'Just Squeeze Me (But Please Don't Tease Me)'

c) '(I've Got) Beginner's Luck'

A

1 c
2 b
3 c
4 a
5 b
6 c
7 a
8 b
9 b
10 c

Q FOLK AND COUNTRY

1 Which folk musician used to sport a sticker on his guitar that read 'This machine kills fascists'?

a) Woody Guthrie

b) Pete Seeger

c) Phil Ochs

2 Which folk group had an international hit with 'Blowin' in the Wind', written by the then-unknown Bob Dylan?

a) The Hollies

b) Peter, Paul and Mary

c) The Turtles

3 The 1980 Oscar-winning biopic *The Coal Miner's Daughter* is based on the life of which country singer?

a) Loretta Lynn

b) Patsy Cline

c) Tammy Wynette

4 What happened to Gram Parsons' body after his death from a drug overdose in 1973?

a) It was preserved for display in the offices of his family's citrus fruit empire in Winter Haven, Florida

b) It was stolen from Los Angeles airport by two of his friends who attempted an amateur cremation in the Joshua Tree National Park

c) The third finger on his left hand was eaten by the pathologist's pet terrier in the mortuary

5 What is Garth Brooks' real first name?

a) Trojan

b) Trevor

c) Troyal

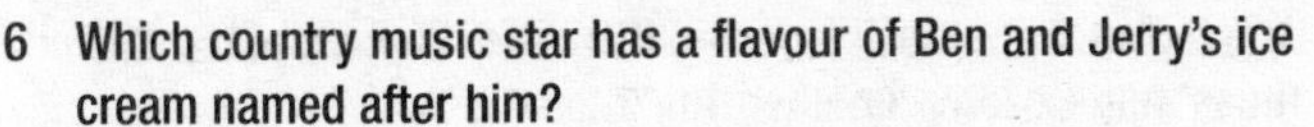

6 **Which country music star has a flavour of Ben and Jerry's ice cream named after him?**

a) Willie Nelson

b) Kris Kristofferson

c) Waylon Jennings

---

7 **What was the name of the disastrous musical based on the life of Johnny Cash that lasted just one month on Broadway?**

a) *The Man in Black*

b) *Cry Cry Cry*

c) *Ring of Fire*

---

8 **Which band's *Rum, Sodomy and the Lash* album featured cover art inspired by Théodore Géricault's painting *The Raft of the Medusa*?**

a) The Chieftains

b) The Pogues

c) The Dubliners

---

9 **Which band organises the annual Cropredy Festival in Oxfordshire?**

a) Clannad

b) Steeleye Span

c) Fairport Convention

---

10 **Which Irish folk band endured the ignominy of a last-place finish at the 2007 Eurovision Song Contest?**

a) Four Men and a Dog

b) Dervish

c) Lunasa

A

1 a

2 b

3 a

4 b

5 c

6 a

7 c

8 b

9 c

10 b

RAP AND HIP-HOP

1 **Which pioneering track sampled Blondie's 'Rapture', Chic's 'Good Times' and Queen's 'Another One Bites the Dust'?**

a) 'The Adventures of Grandmaster Flash on the Wheels of Steel'

b) 'Rapper's Delight'

c) 'U Can't Touch This'

2 **Which hip-hop group's albums include *Things Fall Apart*, *Phrenology* and *The Tipping Point*?**

a) The Roots

b) The Sugarhill Gang

c) De La Soul

3 **Which rapper's LP *The Black Album* was illegally mixed with The Beatles' *The White Album* to create *The Grey Album*, which caused EMI to take out an injunction against its release?**

a) Timbaland

b) Jay-Z

c) Common

4 **Mystikal, 2Hats and Maggot belong to which rap collective?**

a) So Solid Crew

b) Blazin' Squad

c) Goldie Lookin' Chain

5 **'He has created a sense of what is possible. He has sent a voltage around a generation. He has done this not just through his subversive attitude by also his verbal energy.' Who is the poet Seamus Heaney describing?**

a) Eminem

b) Pharrell Williams

c) Kanye West

6 **'There's the sense of the envelope not merely being pushed, but being waggled furiously in the faces of the slack, the lame and the inspiration-free.' What landmark hip-hop track is *NME* describing?**

a) Rhianna's 'Umbrella'

b) Outkast's 'Hey Ya'

c) 50 Cent's 'In The Club'

7 **Which British rapper has not won the Mercury Music Prize?**

a) Dizzee Rascal

b) Ms Dynamite

c) The Streets

8 **Which rap star was shot dead in September 1996?**

a) Tupac Shakur

b) Biggie Smalls

c) Sean Combs

9 **'Ain't Nuthin' But A _ Thang' – which letter is missing from Dr. Dre's 1993 hit?**

a) B

b) G

c) T

10 **How are Kelvin Mercer, David Jude Jolicoeur and Vincent Mason better known?**

a) A Tribe Called Quest

b) De La Soul

c) Run DMC

A

1	a
2	a
3	b
4	c
5	a
6	b
7	c
8	a
9	b
10	b

Q ELECTRONICA

1 Why was Wendy Carlos' *Switched-On Bach* a notable record?

a) It was the first popular use of the Moog synthesiser

b) Mike Oldfield acknowledged it as his inspiration for *Tubular Bells*

c) It was playing on Mark David Chapman's stereo on the morning he shot John Lennon

2 Whose single 'Computer Love' was sampled by Coldplay?

a) Neu!

b) Kraftwerk

c) Can

3 Which band's 1994 album *Music for the Jilted Generation* openly protested against the Criminal Justice and Public Order Act which outlawed outdoor raves?

a) The Crystal Method

b) The Prodigy

c) The Chemical Brothers

4 What links Aphex Twin's 'Come to Daddy', Bjork's 'All Is Full of Love' and 'Frozen' by Madonna?

a) All contain pro-Tibetan messages when played backwards

b) Each contains a sample from 'Voodoo Ray' by A Guy Called Gerald

c) The video for each song was shot by maverick director Chris Cunningham

5 Thomas Bangalter, who created Stardust's house classic 'Music Sounds Better With You' is also a member of which French act?

a) Daft Punk

b) Air

c) Justice

6 **From which TV show did Moby sample incidental music for his breakthrough hit 'Go'?**

a) *The Rockford Files*

b) *Twin Peaks*

c) *NYPD Blue*

7 **'I know that I've imagined love before/And how it could be with you/Really hurt me baby, really cut me baby/How can you have a day without a night?' What's the song?**

a) 'Don't Leave' by Faithless

b) 'Unfinished Sympathy' by Massive Attack

c) 'Missing' by Everything But The Girl

8 **Which Ibiza club inspired Energy 52 to name a trance anthem after it?**

a) Amnesia

b) Pacha

c) Café del Mar

9 **Which British DJ wrote the theme tune to *Big Brother*?**

a) Dave Pearce

b) Paul Oakenfold

c) Judge Jules

10 **Who achieved a number one hit with a remix of Tori Amos' 'Professional Widow'?**

a) Armand van Helden

b) Paul van Dyk

c) Armand van Buren

A

1 a

2 b

3 b

4 c

5 a

6 b

7 b

8 c

9 b

10 a

MUSIC AND FILM

1 Which rock star appeared in *Merry Christmas Mr Lawrence*, *Absolute Beginners* and *The Last Temptation of Christ*?

a) Tom Waits

b) David Bowie

c) Peter Frampton

2 After stripping down to his boxer shorts for a Levi's advert in 1985, which actor began a short-lived musical career?

a) Nick Kamen

b) Nik Kershaw

c) Nick Lowe

3 Who wrote the film scores for both Hitchcock's *North by Northwest* and Scorsese's *Taxi Driver*?

a) Bernard Herrmann

b) Henry Mancini

c) John Barry

4 Which song links Bob Dylan's debut album and the film *O Brother Where Art Thou*?

a) 'In the Jailhouse Now'

b) 'Man of Constant Sorrow'

c) 'You Are My Sunshine'

5 Who sang the theme song for the 1987 Bond movie *The Living Daylights*?

a) A-Ha

b) Duran Duran

c) Sheena Easton

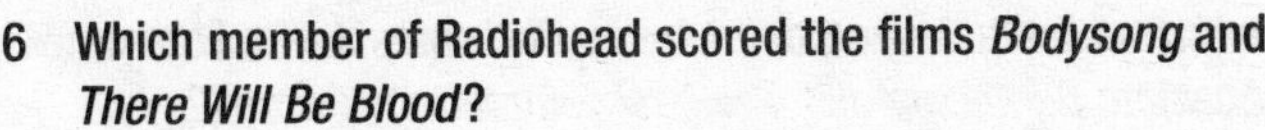

6 Which member of Radiohead scored the films *Bodysong* and *There Will Be Blood*?

a) Thom Yorke

b) Jonny Greenwood

c) Ed O'Brien

7 Who were Dirk, Barry, Stig and Ron?

a) The Rutles

b) Spinal Tap

c) The Commitments

8 What was the name of Eminem's semi-autobiographical character in the film *8 Mile*?

a) O'Hare

b) Weasel

c) B-Rabbit

9 Who has been played on screen by both Steve Coogan and Craig Parkinson?

a) Shaun Ryder

b) Ian Curtis

c) Tony Wilson

10 What is the biggest-selling film soundtrack of all time?

a) *Saturday Night Fever*

b) *Purple Rain*

c) *The Bodyguard*

A

1 b
2 a
3 a
4 b
5 a
6 b
7 a
8 c
9 c
10 c

MUSIC

OPERA

1 In which of the following operas does the character of Figaro not appear?

a) The Marriage of Figaro

b) The Barber of Seville

c) Don Giovanni

2 Who wrote the opera *Turandot*?

a) Giacomo Puccini

b) Giuseppe Verdi

c) Georges Bizet

3 In Bizet's Carmen what does Escamillo do for a living?

a) He is a salesman

b) He is a tavern landlord

c) He is a bullfighter

4 Where does Wagner's *Tristan and Isolde* take place?

a) Cornwall

b) Munich

c) Strasbourg

5 In which Puccini opera do friends ply their landlord with drinks in order to avoid paying the rent?

a) *Tosca*

b) *La Boheme*

c) *Madame Butterfly*

A

1 c

2 a

3 c

4 a

5 b

THE NATURAL WORLD

PLANTS AND FLOWERS

SWARMS, FLOCKS AND HERDS

BRITISH FLORA AND FAUNA

ENDANGERED AND EXTINCT

BIRDS

DINOSAURS AND ANCIENT ANIMALS

UNDERWATER LIFE

MAMMALS

AMPHIBIANS

FICTIONAL ANIMALS

CREEPY CRAWLIES

REPTILES

TREES

RECORD BREAKERS

Q PLANTS AND FLOWERS

1 What is remarkable about the Asian plant called the Rafflesia?

a) Its roots stretch hundreds of yards underground

b) It has the world's largest flower

c) It only flowers once every five years

2 Which flower is a symbol of imperial power in Japan?

a) Chrysanthemum

b) Lily

c) Rose

3 What is a prickly pear?

a) A fern

b) A cactus

c) A fruit

4 From which plant is atropine derived?

a) Foxglove

b) Belladonna

c) Henbane

5 In which of the following parts of a plant is the pollen found?

a) Anther

b) Calyx

c) Sepal

THE NATURAL WORLD

6 **Which of the following flowers is named after an 18th-century French explorer?**

a) Begonia

b) Bougainvillea

c) Zinnia

7 **What colour is the flower edelweiss?**

a) Yellow

b) White

c) Red

8 **For how long do the flowers of the Queen of the Night cactus bloom?**

a) 2 hours

b) 12 hours

c) 24 hours

9 **Approximately how many species of angiosperms, or flowering plants, are there in the world?**

a) 25,000

b) 110,000

c) 230,000

10 **In which plant is the poison solanine found?**

a) Potato plant

b) Nettle

c) Purple foxglove

1 b
2 a
3 b
4 b
5 a
6 b
7 b
8 a
9 c
10 a

SWARMS, FLOCKS AND HERDS

What is the collective noun for the following?

1 A group of beavers

a) A colony

b) An empire

c) An outpost

2 A group of eagles

a) A consternation

b) A confederation

c) A convocation

3 A group of ravens

a) An insult

b) An unkindness

c) A cruelty

4 A group of rhinoceroses

a) A crash

b) A wallow

c) A boast

5 A group of owls

a) A house

b) An assembly

c) A parliament

6 A group of leopards

a) A bound

b) A leap

c) A hurdle

7 A group of camels

a) A caravan

b) A convoy

c) A cavalcade

8 A group of turkeys

a) A tile

b) A beam

c) A rafter

9 A group of toads

a) A knot

b) A blot

c) A squat

10 A group of hedgehogs

a) An assortment

b) A selection

c) An array

1 a
2 c
3 b
4 a
5 c
6 b
7 a
8 c
9 a
10 c

Q BRITISH FLORA AND FAUNA

1 The coasts of Britain are home to half of the world's population of which mammal?

a) European wildcat

b) Grey seal

c) Atlantic puffin

2 What part of a toadstool is the 'pileus'?

a) Cap

b) Stalk

c) Roots

3 Which of the following is a British butterfly?

a) Camberwell beauty

b) Peckham painted lady

c) Greenwich admiral

4 Which animal lives in a 'holt'?

a) Badger

b) Fox

c) Otter

5 By what name is the protected plant *Cynoglossum germanicum* better known?

a) Green hound's tongue

b) Dickie's bladder fern

c) Stinking goosefoot

6 **A garland of which native British flower has been traditionally used as a migraine remedy?**

a) Lavender

b) Elder

c) Feverfew

---

7 **Which common mammal was introduced to Britain in the 12th century as a valuable source of meat and skins?**

a) Otter

b) Goat

c) Rabbit

---

8 **Which of the following animals hibernates?**

a) Mole

b) Hedgehog

c) Rabbit

---

9 **What are 'spraints'?**

a) the droppings of an otter

b) the tracks of a badger

c) the feet of a fox

---

10 **Which British tree's bark and leaves contain the basis for acetylsalicylic acid, more commonly known as aspirin?**

a) Aspen

b) Willow

c) Blackthorn

A

1 b
2 a
3 a
4 c
5 a
6 c
7 c
8 b
9 a
10 b

Q ENDANGERED AND EXTINCT

1 The shortest recorded interval between discovery and extinction relates to the Stephen's Island wren – what caused the species to become extinct?

a) A small meteor completely destroyed the birds' habitat

b) A single cat killed the entire population

c) An oil spill decimated the birds' only nesting site

2 Of the nine known subspecies of tiger, how many are already extinct?

a) 0

b) 3

c) 5

3 Of almost 10,000 known species of birds, how many are endangered?

a) 200+

b) 700+

c) 1,200+

4 Which of the following animals is not extinct?

a) Przewalski's horse

b) California grizzly bear

c) Quagga

5 On which continent has there been the most mammal extinctions over the past 200 years?

a) Australasia

b) South America

c) Africa

6 The World Conservation Union's directory of threatened species is known as what?

a) The Black List

b) The Red List

c) The White List

7 The baiji, a species of dolphin, was declared extinct in 2007; its only habitat was in which river?

a) The Indus

b) The Amazon

c) The Yangtze

8 Commonly known as the Tasmanian tiger and declared extinct in 1986, what was the name of the largest known carnivorous marsupial of modern times?

a) Lupacine

b) Vulpacine

c) Thylacine

9 Approximately when did the woolly mammoth become extinct?

a) 12,000 years ago

b) 4,000 years ago

c) 1,000 years ago

10 Where was the last dodo seen in the 17th century?

a) Mauritius

b) Madagascar

c) New Guinea

A

1 b
2 b
3 c
4 a
5 a
6 b
7 c
8 c
9 b
10 a

BIRDS

1 **What is the wingspan of the great bustard, the world's heaviest flying bird?**

a) 1.8m

b) 2.5m

c) 3.6m

2 **What is the name of the world's smallest bird?**

a) Mosquito hummingbird

b) Pygmy hummingbird

c) Bee hummingbird

3 **Which of the following is the name of an American diving bird?**

a) The blue-footed booby

b) The blue-footed loon

c) The blue-footed dolt

4 **Which of the following is the only bird that hunts by sense of smell?**

a) Lyre bird

b) Kiwi

c) Emu

5 **In which continent would you find budgerigars in their natural habitat?**

a) Australia

b) Asia

c) South America

6 **What sound does a flamingo make?**

a) It honks like a goose

b) It makes no sound

c) It has a clear, piercing scream

7 **Ruppell's griffon flies higher than any other bird – what is the greatest height above sea level that one has been seen?**

a) 6,658m

b) 9,467m

c) 11,278m

8 **What is the state bird of Florida?**

a) Pelican

b) Mockingbird

c) Roadrunner

9 **To which family of birds does the quail belong?**

a) Coot

b) Partridge

c) Dove

10 **What species was the oldest bird recorded in Britain, at the age of 52?**

a) Mute swan

b) Golden eagle

c) Manx Shearwater

1 b
2 c
3 a
4 b
5 a
6 a
7 c
8 b
9 b
10 c

DINOSAURS AND ANCIENT ANIMALS

1 What does the name 'dinosaur' mean?

a) Great monster

b) Terrible lizard

c) Fire dragon

2 At up to 100 tonnes, what is the heaviest dinosaur to have been discovered to date?

a) Seismosaurus

b) Diplodocus

c) Argentinosaurus

3 What is the scientific name for fossilised dinosaur droppings?

a) Cacoliths

b) Scatolites

c) Coprolites

4 Roughly how many species of dinosaur have been identified?

a) 300

b) 700

c) 1,200

5 For how long did dinosaurs roam the Earth before they became extinct?

a) 165 million years

b) 85 million years

c) 255 million years

6 What name was given to the 30-year feud that developed between two pre-eminent palaeontologists of the 19th century, Edward Drinker Cope and Othniel Charles Marsh?

a) Dino Wars

b) Bone Wars

c) Jaws Wars

7 Which of the following is not a genuine dinosaur classification?

a) Utahraptor spielbergi

b) Arthurdactylus conandoylensis

c) Bienosaurus attenbororex

8 How big was the brain of the 9m long stegosaurus?

a) The size of a walnut

b) The size of a peanut

c) The size of a coconut

9 Where would archaeopteryx have been found?

a) In the sea

b) On land

c) In the air

10 This marine reptile was the largest aquatic predator ever, at over 25m in length; what was it called?

a) Ichthyosaur

b) Liopleurodon

c) Placodont

A

1 b
2 c
3 c
4 b
5 a
6 b
7 c
8 a
9 c
10 b

Q UNDERWATER LIFE

1 **The black marlin's eggs are just 1mm in diameter; how many can it lay at a single spawning?**

a) 29 million

b) 103 million

c) 226 million

2 **The *Arctica islandica* clam is the world's longest-lived creature, and is known to reach what age?**

a) 257 years

b) 405 years

c) 601 years

3 **After the blue whale, what is the largest marine mammal?**

a) Fin whale

b) Sperm whale

c) Humpback whale

4 **The blue blood of an octopus is pumped around its body by how many hearts?**

a) One

b) Two

c) Three

5 **What are young eels called?**

a) Elvers

b) Elmets

c) Eldreds

6 **What is the top speed of the sailfish, the fastest creature in the sea?**

a) 41 mph

b) 55 mph

c) 68 mph

7 **Which of the following is a kind of fish capable of wriggling on to land to transfer from one pool to another?**

a) Climbing perch

b) Shuffling tench

c) Walking loach

8 **What is the greatest depth at which fish have been found?**

a) 2,900m

b) 8,300m

c) 13,800m

9 **Which of the following statements is true of the sand tiger shark?**

a) Its embryonic young are cannibalistic

b) It can live to be over 90 years old

c) It is known to swim upside down to confuse its prey

10 **What is the name of the fish, first seen alive in 1938, that was thought to have become extinct 65 million years ago?**

a) Cheiracanthus

b) Congorhynchus

c) Coelacanth

1 c
2 b
3 a
4 c
5 a
6 c
7 a
8 b
9 a
10 c

Q MAMMALS

1 **What is commonly held to be the most intelligent mammal, after humans?**

a) Chimpanzee

b) Gorilla

c) Orang-utan

2 **What is the name for a female cat which is breeding?**

a) Dame

b) Queen

c) Empress

3 **Which of the following bat species, measuring less than a bumblebee at 2.9cm, is the smallest mammal on earth?**

a) Southern blossom bat

b) Pipistrelle bat

c) Kitti's hog-nosed bat

4 **What is the most common group or order of mammals, with over 2,000 known species?**

a) Insectivores

b) Rodents

c) Primates

5 **Which of the following mammals is the sole species classified as belonging to the order of tubulidentata?**

a) Aardvark

b) Opossum

c) Duck-billed platypus

6 In which of the following continents are bears not found?

a) Africa

b) Europe

c) Australia

7 How much weight does a newborn blue whale gain every day?

a) 90kg

b) 10kg

c) 40kg

8 Which of the following mammals has not yet been shown to use tools?

a) Sea otter

b) Chimpanzee

c) Killer whale

9 How do rabbits maximise the nutrients available from their diet?

a) They cannibalise the weaker members of their litter

b) They re-ingest their own faeces

c) They eat only the youngest available plants

10 Which animal has the shortest weaning period of any mammal – sometimes as little as four days?

a) Arabian camel

b) Hooded seal

c) Pygmy possum

A

1	a
2	b
3	c
4	b
5	a
6	c
7	a
8	c
9	b
10	b

Q AMPHIBIANS

1 What is the name of the world's largest known frog, measuring up to 87cm and weighing as much as 3.6kg?

a) The goliath frog

b) The gargantuan frog

c) The behemoth frog

2 The Chinese giant salamander is the largest amphibian in the world and is purported to be capable of growing to what length?

a) 100cm

b) 180cm

c) 270cm

3 Which order of amphibians uses only internal insemination as a means of reproduction?

a) Frogs

b) Salamanders

c) Caecilians

4 Along with reptiles and fish, amphibians are 'cold-blooded' – otherwise known as what?

a) Ectothermic

b) Endothermic

c) Emothermic

5 The Colombian golden arrow-poison frog is the world's most poisonous amphibian; one adult contains enough toxic poison in its skin to kill how many humans?

a) 10

b) 100

c) 1,000

6 Which of the following is true of the species Darwin's frog?

a) It is named for its resemblance to Charles Darwin, with an apparent bushy beard

b) The male of the species raises its young in its vocal sac

c) Female Darwin's frogs only become fertile in the final year of their lives

7 What is the UK's rarest newt species?

a) Palmate newt

b) Great crested newt

c) Smooth newt

8 Caecilians are the only land-living animal to have exhibited what unusual parenting behaviour?

a) The mother allows its young to peel off and eat its skin

b) The father severs its own tail and feeds it to his young

c) The parents kill the weakest offspring and feed them to the remainder

9 What is thought to be the loudest amphibian found in Europe?

a) European spadefoot toad

b) European fire-bellied toad

c) Natterjack toad

10 The Mexican axolotl salamander retains its larval features, such as a tadpole-like dorsal fin and feathery external gills, throughout its adult life – what is this condition called?

a) Neoteny

b) Nuevoplasis

c) Neupsois

A

1 a
2 b
3 c
4 a
5 a
6 b
7 b
8 a
9 c
10 a

Q FICTIONAL ANIMALS

Who are the following fictional animals and in what do they appear?

1 Nana

a) The wolf that is Mowgli's foster-mother in *The Jungle Book*

b) The dog in *The Incredible Journey*

c) The Darling family dog in *Peter Pan*

2 Elvis

a) Sonny Crockett's pet alligator in *Miami Vice*

b) Joey and Chandler's pet duck in *Friends*

c) Margot and Jerry's pet cockatoo in *The Good Life*

3 King Louie

a) The ape king in the Disney film of *The Jungle Book*

b) The orang-utan in the Clint Eastwood movie *Every Which Way But Loose*

c) The ape in C. S. Lewis' *The Last Battle*

4 Aloysius Snuffleupagus

a) The elephant prince from the books by Jean de Brunhoff

b) The woolly mammoth in *Sesame Street*

c) Bart Simpson's pet elephant in *The Simpsons*

5 Feathers McGraw

a) An unhatched chick egg in *Garfield and Friends*

b) Donald Duck's uncle in Disney's *Duck Tales*

c) A penguin in Wallace and Gromit's *The Wrong Trousers*

6 Hedwig

a) A snowy owl in the *Harry Potter* series of novels by J. K. Rowling

b) Legolas's horse in J. R. R. Tolkien's *The Lord of the Rings*

c) Lord Asriel's snow leopard daemon in Philip Pullman's *His Dark Materials* trilogy

7 Napoleon

a) Doc Brown's dog in *Back to the Future*

b) A pig in George Orwell's *Animal Farm*

c) A cat in Stephen King's *Pet Sematary*

8 Ziz

a) A giant bird from Jewish mythology

b) A feathered serpent from Aztec mythology

c) One of Achilles' two immortal horses from Greek mythology

9 Rikki-Tikki-Tavi

a) The snake in the Sherlock Holmes story 'The Speckled Band'

b) A mongoose in a story by Rudyard Kipling

c) Hiawatha's hunting dog in Henry Longfellow's poem

10 Montmorency

a) The leader of the stoats and weasels in *The Wind in the Willows*

b) The dog in Jerome K. Jerome's *Three Men in a Boat*

c) The caterpillar in *Alice in Wonderland*

A

1 c
2 a
3 a
4 b
5 c
6 a
7 b
8 a
9 b
10 b

Q CREEPY CRAWLIES

1 The bite of which insect causes the disease known as Lyme disease?

a) Tsetse fly

b) Mosquito

c) Deer tick

2 With approximately 370,000 known species, what is the most common order of insects?

a) Lepidoptera – those with scaly wings, such as butterflies and moths

b) Hymenoptera – those with membrane wings, such as ants and bees

c) Coleoptera – those with hard wings, such as beetles

3 What is the less colloquial name for the Daddy Long Legs?

a) Mayfly

b) Cranefly

c) Horsefly

4 How many hearts does an earthworm have?

a) 1

b) 3

c) 10

5 Where are the organs of hearing on a locust?

a) Legs

b) Abdomen

c) Antennae

6 What is the world's biggest spider, with a body as long as 9cm and a leg span of up to 28cm?

a) Goliath spider

b) Hercules spider

c) Samson spider

7 How many species of aphid have been identified?

a) 40

b) 400

c) 4,000

8 Which of the following facts is true of scorpions?

a) They commit suicide by stinging themselves to death when surrounded by fire

b) They glow fluorescent under ultraviolet light

c) Of 2,000 different species, over 150 are capable of killing a human

9 What is the name of the substance which makes up the exoskeletons of insects?

a) Chitin

b) Keratin

c) Riboflavin

10 The white witch moth is thought to possess the greatest wingspan of any insect in the world – it can reach what size?

a) 30cm

b) 46cm

c) 72cm

A

1	c
2	c
3	b
4	c
5	b
6	a
7	c
8	b
9	a
10	a

Q REPTILES

1 How many species of snake are native to the British Isles?

a) Four

b) Three

c) Two

2 Where is the only place in the world you can find the lizard-like tuatara?

a) Mexico

b) Japan

c) New Zealand

3 The flowerpot blindsnake is the only snake to reproduce without being fertilised by the male's sperm – what is this process called?

a) Parthenogenesis

b) Solomentasis

c) Unigestasis

4 Which of the following is a member of the crocodile family?

a) Taiman

b) Coatimundi

c) Gharial

5 What, at up to 10m, is the longest land animal is the world?

a) Anaconda

b) Reticulated python

c) Boa constrictor

6 Slow worms look superficially like snakes – what distinguishing feature can be used to identify them?

a) Slow worms have a three-pronged tongue

b) Slow worms have four small but visible protrusions where legs would be

c) Slow worms have eyelids

7 Galapagos giant tortoises are the longest-lived of all vertebrates – the oldest on record lived to what age?

a) 129

b) 152

c) 176

8 Which order of reptiles are the closest living relatives of birds?

a) Crocodilia (alligators, crocodiles etc)

b) Squamata (lizards, snakes etc)

c) Chelonia (turtles, tortoises etc)

9 What is a fear of reptiles known as?

a) Batrachophobia

b) Herpetophobia

c) Ophidiophobia

10 What is the world's largest turtle?

a) Leatherback turtle

b) Loggerhead sea turtle

c) Green turtle

A

1 b
2 c
3 a
4 c
5 b
6 c
7 c
8 a
9 b
10 a

TREES

1 A Koala bear eats the leaves from which tree?

a) Gum tree

b) Paperbark tree

c) Eucalyptus tree

2 From which small tree do sloe berries come?

a) Hawthorn

b) Whitethorn

c) Blackthorn

3 From what does the Sequoia, the world's largest tree, take its name?

a) The Aztec word for 'giant'

b) A Cherokee Indian leader

c) A god in Native American mythology

4 Great Basin bristlecone pines are among the longest-lived trees on Earth – approximately when was the oldest specimen still living today germinated?

a) 2,832 BC

b) 1,237 BC

c) 478 BC

5 A fully grown British oak can produce how many acorns in a good year?

a) 10,000

b) 50,000

c) 200,000

6 **Which of the following is not a genuine tree?**

a) Balsa

b) Bamboo

c) Bay

7 **From which tree was the English longbow traditionally made?**

a) Yew

b) Ash

c) Birch

8 **Which of the following is a deciduous rather than an evergreen tree?**

a) Scots Pine

b) Juniper

c) Aspen

9 **What is the study of trees known as?**

a) Dendrology

b) Agrostology

c) Pomology

10 **Which of the following tree's sap is not used to make syrup?**

a) Birch

b) Pine

c) Maple

A

1 c

2 c

3 b

4 a

5 b

6 b

7 a

8 c

9 a

10 b

RECORD BREAKERS

1 What is the largest rodent in the world?

a) Agouti

b) Capybara

c) Coypu

2 What is the world's longest animal?

a) Bootlace worm

b) Blue whale

c) Arctic giant jellyfish

3 What is the name given to the tallest tree in the world, a coast redwood in California that measures over 115m?

a) General Sherman

b) Hyperion

c) Massive Mutsy

4 The male of what fish is thought to be the smallest vertebrate in the world, at around 6.5mm?

a) *Schindleria brevipinguis* (a species of infantfish)

b) *Paedocypris progenetica* (a species of carp)

c) *Photocorynus spiniceps* (a species of anglerfish)

5 Reaching speeds of up to 217mph, when diving, which bird is the fastest animal on Earth?

a) Golden eagle

b) Spine-tailed swift

c) Peregrine falcon

A

1	b
2	a
3	b
4	c
5	c

BELIEFS

SACRED TEXTS

SAINTS AND SINNERS

RELIGIOUS PRACTICES

EASTERN RELIGIONS

GODS AND GODDESSES

GREEK MYTHOLOGY

CHRISTIANITY

ISLAM

JUDAISM

'ISMS'

MYTHS AND LEGENDS

FEASTS AND FESTIVALS

RELIGIOUS LEADERS

GREAT THINKERS

19TH AND 20TH CENTURY PHILOSOPHERS

WISE WORDS

BELIEFS

1 Before he founded the Church of Scientology, what career had L. Ron Hubbard pursued?

a) Encyclopaedia salesman

b) Science fiction writer

c) Priest

2 Which religious group was founded by George Fox?

a) The Methodists

b) The Quakers

c) The Seventh Day Adventists

3 How are members of the Church of Jesus Christ of Latter Day Saints better known?

a) Mormons

b) Christian Scientists

c) Jehovah's Witnesses

4 In which city did John Calvin establish a theocratic state in the 16th century?

a) Geneva

b) Zurich

c) Toulouse

5 Which of these is not one of the 'five Ks' of Sikhism?

a) A sword

b) A bracelet

c) A coin

6 What is unusual about the Naqshbandi order of Islam?

a) Its followers believe in silent remembrance of God

b) They do not fast for Ramadan

c) They do not face Mecca to pray

7 Which year marks the return of Christ, according to Jehovah's Witnesses?

a) 1914

b) 2000

c) 2028

8 Where do the central beliefs of Candomblé originate from?

a) Africa

b) Asia

c) North America

9 Which of the following do Mormons believe?

a) That humans are reincarnated in an endless cycle

b) That humans cease to exist after they die

c) That humans exist before their lives on Earth as spirit children

10 What is Maundy Thursday the anniversary of, according to Christianity?

a) The first day of Jesus' 40-day fast

b) The Last Supper

c) The death of Jesus

A

1 b
2 b
3 a
4 a
5 c
6 a
7 a
8 a
9 c
10 b

Q SACRED TEXTS

1 Which of the following is a name for the first five books of the Old Testament?

a) Pentateuch

b) Pentapolis

c) Pentarchy

2 Which Old Testament prophet gives his name to someone who habitually foretells doom and disaster?

a) Jeremiah

b) Jonah

c) Job

3 According to John's Gospel, what was Jesus' first miracle?

a) Feeding of the five thousand

b) Walking on the waters of Lake Galilee

c) Turning water into wine at the wedding in Cana

4 What is the term for the study of sacred texts?

a) Speleology

b) Hierographology

c) Steganography

5 What was the name of the child God gave to Eve in place of the murdered Abel?

a) Micah

b) Jacob

c) Seth

6 What is not contained within the *Talmud*, the Jewish scripture?

a) Rituals and fast days

b) Civic and religious laws

c) A list of every male descendant of Moses for 2,000 years

7 The four *Vedas* are the primary sacred texts for which religion?

a) Hinduism

b) Buddhism

c) Sikhism

8 How do Sikhs show their respect to the *Guru Granth Sahib*, their sacred text and eternal Guru?

a) It is kept under a spotlight in the centre of the Gurudwara

b) It is never touched with bare hands

c) It is placed on a raised platform and fanned during a service

9 In Genesis, for what is Nimrod most famed?

a) He is a great hunter

b) He is an expert chariot driver

c) He has a beautiful singing voice

10 Who discovered the first Dead Sea Scrolls in 1947?

a) A British couple on holiday

b) A team of American archaeologists

c) A Bedouin goat-herder

A

1 a
2 a
3 c
4 b
5 c
6 c
7 a
8 c
9 a
10 c

Q SAINTS AND SINNERS

1 Which saint's day falls on Boxing Day?

a) St Andrew

b) St Stephen

c) St Wenceslas

2 For what crime was Al Capone jailed in 1931?

a) Murder

b) Tax evasion

c) Gun running

3 Which animal is usually associated with St Mark?

a) A winged leopard

b) A winged horse

c) A winged lion

4 What was the name of Dr Crippen's mistress, with whom he fled Britain after murdering his wife?

a) Ethel Le Neve

b) Edith Thompson

c) Belle Elmore

5 Which two Anglican bishops were martyred near Balliol College, Oxford in 1555?

a) Cranmer and Fisher

b) Ridley and Latimer

c) Cranmer and Ridley

6 Whom did the anarchist Leon Czogolsz assassinate in 1901?

a) US president William McKinley

b) King Umberto I of Italy

c) Empress Elizabeth of Austria

7 Who is the patron saint of music?

a) St Christopher

b) St Cecilia

c) St Catherine

8 Which of the following was one of the legitimate business that the Kray twins ran to hide their criminal activities?

a) A nightclub in Knightsbridge

b) A betting shop in Bethnal Green

c) A grocery store in Finsbury Park

9 Who is the patron saint of travellers?

a) St Brendan

b) St Paul

c) St Christopher

10 Which book did Mark David Chapman leave in a hotel room as 'his statement' before shooting John Lennon?

a) The Bible

b) *The Beatles Anthology*

c) *The Catcher in the Rye*

A

1 b
2 b
3 c
4 a
5 b
6 a
7 b
8 a
9 c
10 c

Q RELIGIOUS PRACTICES

1 According to the Roman Catholic Church, what do the bread and wine given at Holy Communion represent?

a) The last supper eaten by Christ

b) Christ's feeding of the 5,000

c) The body and blood of Christ

2 When did it become possible for women to be ordained as priests in the Church of England?

a) 1962

b) 1994

c) 2006

3 What are the Tefillin, used in Judaism?

a) Square leather boxes containing biblical verses that are used in prayer

b) Candlesticks placed on dining tables at mealtimes on the Sabbath

c) Men who supervise the manufacture of kosher food

4 What is the continually lit lamp in a synagogue a reminder of?

a) The synagogue as a place of sanctuary

b) The continually lit menorah in the Temple of Jerusalem

c) The constant presence of God

5 According to the *Mahabharata*, what is the greatest duty for Hindus?

a) Praying to images of deities

b) Visiting temples

c) The repetition of mantras

6 What animal is considered sacred by Hindus?

a) Cow

b) Lamb

c) Elephant

7 What middle name or surname is commonly adopted by male Sikhs?

a) Singh

b) Rama

c) Kaur

8 Which of the following is forbidden in Sikhism?

a) Eating meat

b) Wearing jewellery

c) Cutting hair

9 How many Pillars of Islam are there?

a) Three

b) Five

c) Seven

10 Which of the following is considered to be a religious obligation for Muslims?

a) Giving away a fixed portion of personal income

b) Converting as many non-Muslims as possible

c) Dedicating at least two hours a day to the family

A

1 c
2 b
3 a
4 b
5 c
6 a
7 a
8 c
9 b
10 a

Q EASTERN RELIGIONS

1 Which of the following is not one of the Four Noble Truths of Buddhism?

a) The cause of suffering is craving

b) Existence is characterised by suffering

c) Suffering enables one to acquire merit

2 Which Eastern religion features the concept of 'wu-wei'?

a) Shintoism

b) Taoism

c) Buddhism

3 What are the modern followers of Zoroastrianism called?

a) Parsees

b) Jains

c) Sikhs

4 In which Indian city is the Sikh Golden Temple?

a) Agra

b) Amritsar

c) Delhi

5 Which of the following sacred writings are the oldest among Hindu literature?

a) *Upanishads*

b) *Bhagavad Gita*

c) *Vedas*

6 Which of the following rivers is named after a Hindu goddess?

a) Ganges

b) Brahmaputra

c) Indus

7 What decoration does the Hindu goddess Kali usually wear about her neck?

a) A necklace of fire

b) A garland of skulls

c) A wreath of flowers

8 What is the final factor of enlightenment in the teachings of Buddha?

a) Awareness

b) Tranquillity

c) Equanimity

9 Which Hindu god is said to be the preserver of the universe?

a) Brahma

b) Vishnu

c) Indra

10 Which of these do followers of Jainism believe?

a) The universe is an illusion

b) There are no gods that will respond to prayer

c) Reincarnation does not exist

A

1 c

2 b

3 a

4 b

5 c

6 a

7 b

8 c

9 b

10 b

Q GODS AND GODDESSES

1 Which of the following was the Greek goddess of victory?

a) Nike

b) Adidas

c) Reebok

2 In Norse mythology who was the god of mischief, and son of the giantess Laufey?

a) Baldur

b) Loki

c) Siegfried

3 Who is the goddess of death in Hindu myth?

a) Shiva

b) Durga

c) Kali

4 In which religion do the letters YHVH represent God?

a) Islam

b) Judaism

c) Zoroastrianism

5 What is the name of the elephant-headed god in Hindu mythology?

a) Hanuman

b) Ganesha

c) Shiva

6 Which jackal-headed god of ancient Egypt was believed to be responsible for weighing the souls of the dead?

a) Osiris

b) Anubis

c) Horus

7 Which Egyptian goddess is often depicted in the shape of a cat?

a) Isis

b) Hathor

c) Bast

8 Who were the *Dii Consentes*?

a) The principal Roman gods

b) The rulers of the Incan underworld

c) Greek gods that were identical twins

9 Who was the messenger of the Roman gods?

a) Vulcan

b) Apollo

c) Mercury

10 Which of the following months is named after a Roman god?

a) January

b) September

c) July

A

1	a
2	b
3	c
4	b
5	b
6	b
7	c
8	a
9	c
10	a

Q GREEK MYTHOLOGY

1 Who was the wife of Orpheus?

a) Persephone

b) Andromeda

c) Eurydice

2 Who was the Roman equivalent of the Greek god of the underworld, Hades?

a) Pluto

b) Apollo

c) Mercury

3 Which of the following was not one of Jason's Argonauts?

a) Heracles

b) Odysseus

c) Theseus

4 What did the ruler of the Titans do to avoid being overthrown?

a) He imprisoned his opponents

b) He hid, disguised as a goat, on Mount Olympus

c) He ate his children

5 Who was the first mortal woman?

a) Persephone

b) Penelope

c) Pandora

6 Which of the following was not one of the foods of the gods?

a) Ambrosia

b) Nectar

c) Manna

7 Who was transformed into a spider after losing a weaving contest with the goddess Minerva?

a) Ariadne

b) Arachne

c) Atalanta

8 She is known as Helen of Troy, but where did she come from originally?

a) Athens

b) Arcadia

c) Sparta

9 How did Odysseus escape a Cyclops?

a) He clung to the underside of a sheep

b) He tricked the Cyclops into drinking too much

c) He sacrificed some of his own men

10 What kind of monster was the Hydra?

a) A woman with snakes for hair

b) A serpent-like beast that grew two heads for each one that was severed

c) A snake that turned people to stone upon sight

A

1 c
2 a
3 b
4 c
5 c
6 c
7 b
8 c
9 a
10 b

Q CHRISTIANITY

1 What significant event happened at Pentecost?

a) The ritual purification of Mary after giving birth

b) The descent of the Holy Spirit

c) The baptism of Jesus by St John the Baptist

2 In the Catholic church, which of these sacraments can be administered to a believer only once?

a) Marriage

b) Confirmation

c) Communion

3 Which branch of Christianity is also known as the Religious Society of Friends?

a) Quakers

b) The Amish

c) Christadelphians

4 What language was the Old Testament originally written in?

a) Hebrew

b) Arabic

c) English

5 The Ecumenical Patriarch of Constantinople is the senior figure in which branch of Christianity?

a) Methodist

b) Baptist

c) Eastern Orthodox

6 **Which version of the Bible is used in the Church of England?**

a) The King James Bible

b) The Douay-Rheims Bible

c) The Saint John's Bible

7 **Apart from Canterbury, which city has an archbishop?**

a) York

b) Winchester

c) Durham

8 **What announces the successful election of a new Pope?**

a) A procession of torches through the Vatican

b) White smoke sent through the chimney of the Sistine Chapel

c) A special bell rung in St Peter's Square

9 **When was the Great Schism that divided the church into Western and Eastern branches?**

a) 1054

b) 1287

c) 1538

10 **Where does the phase 'to condemn with book, bell and candle' come from?**

a) The tenth plague of Egypt that killed first-born children

b) Judas' betrayal of Jesus

c) Excommunication from the Roman Catholic church

A

1 b

2 b

3 a

4 a

5 c

6 a

7 a

8 b

9 a

10 c

ISLAM

1 What is a Sura?

a) One of the sayings of the prophet

b) A chapter of the Qur'an

c) A Muslim mystic

2 What is the name of a pulpit in a mosque?

a) Minbar

b) Muezzin

c) Mihrab

3 Which of the following is a prophet mentioned in the Qur'an?

a) Malachi

b) Noah

c) Matthew

4 What was the name of the daughter of the Prophet Muhammad?

a) Fatima

b) Khadija

c) Hafsa

5 Which angel passed the Qur'an down from heaven to Muhammad?

a) Azrael

b) Mikael

c) Gabriel

6 What is a hafiz?

a) One who has memorised the Qur'an

b) One who teaches in a Muslim school

c) One who has been on pilgrimage

7 What Country is Mecca in?

a) Syria

b) Jordan

c) Saudi Arabia

8 What is the literal translation of the word jihad?

a) Holy war

b) Struggle

c) The path

9 What is the name of the veil used to cover the face?

a) Niqab

b) Hijab

c) Jilbab

10 In which century was Muhammad born?

a) 12th century AD

b) 9th century AD

c) 6th century AD

A

1 b

2 a

3 b

4 a

5 c

6 a

7 c

8 b

9 a

10 c

JUDAISM

1 When does the Jewish Sabbath begin?

a) Sunset on Friday

b) Dawn on Saturday

c) Midday on Saturday

2 Which Jewish festival means, in translation, 'the head of the year'?

a) Yom Kippur

b) Rosh Hashanah

c) Bar Mitzvah

3 What does the word 'kosher' mean?

a) Traditional

b) Fit or proper

c) Bloodless

4 Which of the following Jewish names derives from a word for 'priest'?

a) Bloom

b) Levy

c) Cohen

5 Which foods must not be eaten at the same meal?

a) Fish and poultry

b) Milk and meat

c) Sugar and salt

6 What is the Kabbalah?

a) A set of Jewish prayer beads

b) A word for the expected Jewish messiah

c) A system of Jewish mystical beliefs

7 What title does a Jewish girl receive at the age of 12?

a) Bar Mitzvah

b) Brit Milah

c) Bat Mitzvah

8 What is the Ark?

a) A cupboard in a synagogue containing the Torah scrolls

b) A festival remembering Noah and the flood

c) A mythic lost temple outside Jerusalem

9 What does the Passover celebrate or commemorate?

a) The exodus of the Jews from Egypt

b) The start of a new year

c) The building of the temple in Jerusalem

10 What is a menorah?

a) A star of David

b) A seven-branched candlestick

c) A skullcap

A

1 a
2 b
3 b
4 c
5 b
6 c
7 c
8 a
9 a
10 b

'ISMS'

With which 'isms' would you most associate the following people?

1 Edmund Burke

a) Conservatism

b) Amoralism

c) Relativism

2 Jacques Derrida

a) Authoritarianism

b) Totalitarianism

c) Deconstructionism

3 Jean-Paul Sartre

a) Surrealism

b) Logical Positivism

c) Existentialism

4 David Hume

a) Scepticism

b) Social Darwinism

c) Postmodernism

5 Lao-tse Tzu

a) Confucianism

b) Buddhism

c) Taoism

6 Mikhail Bakunin

a) Anarchism

b) Post-impressionism

c) Catholicism

7 Milton Friedman

a) Socialism

b) Monetarism

c) Keynesianism

8 Andre Breton

a) Impressionism

b) Cubism

c) Surrealism

9 Simone de Beauvoir

a) Existentialism

b) Deism

c) Idealism

10 John Locke

a) Determinism

b) Utilitarianism

c) Empiricism

A

1 a
2 c
3 c
4 a
5 c
6 a
7 b
8 c
9 a
10 c

MYTHS AND LEGENDS

1 According to folklore, where in England are pixies most likely to be found?

a) Warwickshire

b) Norfolk

c) Cornwall

2 What happens to the eponymous hero in the Middle English poem *Sir Orfeo*?

a) He rescues his wife from the fairy kingdom

b) He accepts a challenge from a green knight

c) He completes twelve impossible tasks to win his bride

3 How did Beowulf mortally wound Grendel?

a) By beheading him with a sword

b) By pulling his arm off at the shoulder

c) By poisoning his mead

4 In Celtic mythology, who was Gogmagog?

a) The man who killed the last dragon in England

b) A giant, one of the original inhabitants of the British Isles

c) A god who was worshipped at the summer solstice

5 Where did heroes killed in battle go according to Norse myth?

a) Heorot

b) Elysium

c) Valhalla

6 How was Midas punished for insulting the god Apollo?

a) Apollo gave him the ears of an ass

b) Everything he touched turned to stone

c) He was forced to sing for eternity

7 In Arthurian legend, who was the child of a nun and a demon?

a) Lancelot

b) Guinevere

c) Merlin

8 Which country's mythology features Azi Dahaka, a dragon that was created to eat the universe?

a) Egypt

b) Iran

c) China

9 What remained in Pandora's Box after it had been opened?

a) Love

b) Pity

c) Hope

10 In Arthurian legend, what is the name of Sir Lancelot's castle?

a) Siege Perilous

b) Camelot

c) Joyous Gard

A

1	c
2	a
3	b
4	b
5	c
6	a
7	c
8	b
9	c
10	c

Q FEASTS AND FESTIVALS

1 The nine-night festival Navaratri is celebrated in which religion?

a) Islam

b) Hinduism

c) Sikhism

2 What is traditionally eaten to break fasting in Ramadan?

a) Sweets

b) Lamb

c) A date

3 Where is a radish festival celebrated?

a) Mexico

b) Kazakhstan

c) Indonesia

4 Whose return is celebrated by Diwali?

a) Shiva and Lakshmi

b) Rama and Sita

c) Brahma and Vishnu

5 What does the Epiphany celebrate in the Christian church?

a) The last appearance of Jesus on Earth

b) The Last Supper

c) The Magi visiting Jesus

6 How does the Bahai 'nineteen-day feast' get its name?

a) It lasts for 19 days

b) It takes place every 19 days

c) It celebrates 19 days of fasting by the Bab

7 Where does Halloween originate from?

a) The Incan month of Ayamarca

b) The Mexican Day of the Dead

c) The ancient Celtic festival of Samhain

8 How did the Notting Hill Carnival begin?

a) It developed from an 18th-century masquerade ball

b) Caribbean immigrants held spontaneous street parties upon their arrival in England

c) As a small party held in St Pancras town hall in 1959

9 The Feast of Tabernacles occurs in which religious calendar?

a) Jewish

b) Muslim

c) Buddhist

10 What does the Shinto Festival of Dolls celebrate?

a) Beginning of spring

b) Daughters in the family

c) New-born children

A

1 b
2 c
3 a
4 b
5 c
6 b
7 c
8 c
9 a
10 b

Q RELIGIOUS LEADERS

1 Which country was ruled by Haile Selassie, whom the Rastafari movement viewed as God incarnate?

a) Jamaica

b) Nigeria

c) Ethiopia

2 What led Mary Baker Eddy to form the Church of Christ, Scientist?

a) She was healed of an injury after reading the Bible

b) An angel was revealed to her in a vision while she was in surgery

c) She had developed a scientific theory for verses in the Old Testament

3 What was Gandhi's first name?

a) Mahatma

b) Mohandas

c) Mahadev

4 Which contemporary religious movement was founded by Li Hongzhi?

a) Unification Church

b) Falun Gong

c) Aum Shinrikyo

5 What was the name of the leader of the Russian Orthodox Church in Britain who died in 2003?

a) Metropolitan Anthony

b) Metropolitan Anatoly

c) Metropolitan Aloysius

6 **Where was the prophet Zoroaster (Zarathustra) born?**

a) India

b) Iran

c) Iraq

7 **What does the Dalai Lama traditionally govern?**

a) China

b) Thailand

c) Tibet

8 **Which religious order did Ignatius Loyola found?**

a) Cistercians

b) Jesuits

c) Trappists

9 **How did the founder of the Mormon religion, Joseph Smith, meet his death?**

a) By being shot and jumping from a window

b) By drowning in a freak flood

c) By burning in a fire at the first Mormon temple

10 **What was the name of the first caliph, chosen to rule Muslims after the death of Muhammad?**

a) Ali

b) Haroun al-Rashid

c) Abu-Bakr

A

1	c
2	a
3	b
4	b
5	a
6	b
7	c
8	b
9	a
10	c

Q GREAT THINKERS

1 Which philosopher and mathematician allegedly drowned one of his students for revealing the 'irrational' number π (pi) to the world?

a) Euclid

b) Pythagoras

c) Thales of Miletus

2 Which Greek philosopher was sentenced to death by taking the poison hemlock?

a) Parmenides

b) Socrates

c) Plato

3 What was unusual about the Diogenes the Cynic?

a) He would walk around backwards to try to reverse time

b) He would always keep one eye shut to remind him of his mortality

c) He lived in a barrel and believed that people should behave like dogs

4 Which philosopher was the tutor of Alexander the Great?

a) Anaximander

b) Pythagoras

c) Aristotle

5 Who invented the Parable of the Cave, which proposes that all humans are prisoners?

a) Plato

b) Aristotle

c) Socrates

6 Which of the following was not said by Confucius?

a) A man who stands on hill with his mouth open will wait a long time for roast duck to drop in

b) A fool marvels at rare things, but a wise man at common ones

c) Wisest is he who knows what he does not know

7 Which philosopher and cleric had an affair with a student and was castrated?

a) St Anselm

b) Peter Abelard

c) Bishop Berkeley

8 What is the name for St Thomas Aquinas' argument for the existence of God?

a) Cosmological

b) Ontological

c) Teleological

9 Who wrote *Leviathan*, a pessimistic account of human nature?

a) Thomas Hobbes

b) Gottfield Leibniz

c) David Hume

10 Who was the first to say that 'knowledge is power'?

a) Erasmus

b) Francis Bacon

c) Niccolò Machiavelli

A

1 b
2 b
3 c
4 c
5 a
6 c
7 b
8 a
9 a
10 b

Q 19TH- AND 20TH-CENTURY PHILOSOPHERS

1 Who argued that the human personality has three distinct aspects: the ego, the superego and the id?

a) Wilhelm Wundt

b) Carl Jung

c) Sigmund Freud

2 Which of the following was not a term created by 20th-century philosophers?

a) Phenomenology

b) Verificationism

c) Mysterology

3 Who is considered to be the founder of structuralism?

a) Julia Kristeva

b) Ferdinand de Saussure

c) Jacques Derrida

4 Which French philosopher wrote *Of Grammatology*?

a) Jean-Paul Sartre

b) Jacques Derrida

c) Julia Kristeva

5 Which philosophical movement was Ralph Waldo Emerson part of?

a) Transcendentalism

b) Utilitarianism

c) Pragmatism

6 **Which philosopher was shot dead by one of his students?**

a) Moritz Schlick

b) Michel Foucault

c) Karl Popper

7 **Which of the following is the title of a book by Friedrich Nietzsche?**

a) *The Gay Science*

b) *Moses and Monotheism*

c) *Madness and Civilization*

8 **Which philosopher murdered his wife?**

a) Rollo May

b) Hilary Putnam

c) Louis Althusser

9 **Who influenced the philosopher Jacques Lacan?**

a) Karl Marx

b) Sigmund Freud

c) Immanuel Kant

10 **Which philosopher suffered from mental illness in the last years of his life?**

a) Soren Kierkegaard

b) Georg Wilhelm Hegel

c) Friedrich Nietzsche

A

1 c
2 c
3 b
4 b
5 a
6 a
7 a
8 c
9 b
10 c

Q WISE WORDS

1 Who described religion as 'the opium of the people'?

a) Karl Marx

b) Jean-Paul Sartre

c) George Bernard Shaw

2 Which philosopher is responsible for the phrase *cogito ergo sum* ('I am thinking, therefore, I exist')?

a) Thomas Hobbes

b) René Descartes

c) Immanuel Kant

3 Who declared that 'God is dead'?

a) Georg F. Hegel

b) Friedrich Nietzsche

c) Bertrand Russell

4 The grammatically correct, but nonsensical, sentence 'Colourless green ideas sleep furiously' was written by who?

a) John Dewey

b) Jean Piaget

c) Noam Chomsky

5 Who wrote that 'The notion that human life is sacred, just because it is human life, is medieval'?

a) Peter Singer

b) Lawrence Kohlberg

c) B. F. Skinner

A

1 a

2 b

3 b

4 c

5 a

POLITICS

SCANDALS AND SLEAZE

BRITISH PARLIAMENT

BRITISH POLITICS

BRITISH PRIME MINISTERS

COUPS AND REBELLIONS

THE COLD WAR

DICTATORS

WILD PARTIES

EUROTRASH

FAMILY CONNECTIONS

POLITICAL QUOTATIONS

SPIES AND INTELLIGENCE

US PRESIDENTS

THE SCIENCE OF POLITICS

WORLD LEADERS

INTERNATIONAL ORGANISATIONS

SCANDALS AND SLEAZE

1 **To which film star was John Profumo married when his affair with showgirl Christine Keeler was discovered?**

a) Valerie Hobson

b) Celia Johnson

c) Honor Blackman

2 **Which French politician was revealed to have fathered a secret love child called Mazarine in 1994?**

a) Jacques Chirac

b) François Mitterand

c) Lionel Jospin

3 **Which British politician faked his own death and used the identity of a constituent to begin a new life in Australia with his secretary?**

a) Garry Allingham

b) Peter Baker

c) John Stonehouse

4 **How did former secretary of state for Wales, Ron Davies, explain his 'moment of madness' on Clapham Common?**

a) He was looking for badgers

b) He was walking his dog

c) He was metal-detecting

5 **Which MP was caught having an affair with Antonia de Sancha?**

a) Cecil Parkinson

b) Robin Cook

c) David Mellor

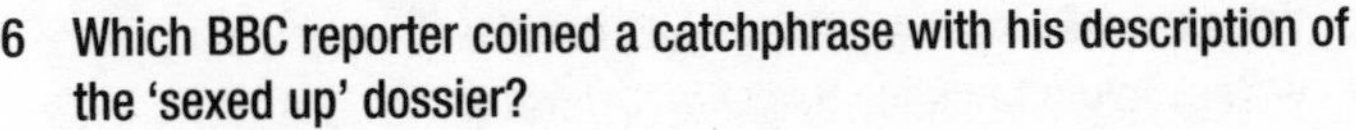

6 **Which BBC reporter coined a catchphrase with his description of the 'sexed up' dossier?**

a) Nick Robinson

b) Andrew Gilligan

c) John Humphrys

7 **From which British institution did Monica Lewinsky receive a Masters degree in social psychology?**

a) The School of Oriental and African Studies

b) University College London

c) The London School of Economics

8 **Which newspaper did MSP Tommy Sheridan win a defamation action against in 2006?**

a) *News of the World*

b) *Mail on Sunday*

c) *Sunday Mirror*

9 **Which US president was the subject of a biography by disgraced former MP Jonathan Aitken?**

a) Franklin Roosevelt

b) John F. Kennedy

c) Richard Nixon

10 **Which Labour PR officer infamously advised Stephen Byers that 9/11 was a good day to bury bad news?**

a) Jo Moore

b) Ruth Turner

c) Tracey Temple

A

1 a
2 b
3 c
4 a
5 c
6 b
7 c
8 a
9 c
10 a

Q BRITISH PARLIAMENT

1 **What were Old Sarum, Glatton and Bramber?**

a) The first three bars opened in the Palace of Westminster

b) 19th-century rotten boroughs

c) Hometowns of the last three Speakers of the House of Lords

2 **Who was the leader of the Conservative party at the beginning of the Second World War?**

a) Stanley Baldwin

b) Neville Chamberlain

c) David Lloyd George

3 **Which architect who designed the Scottish parliament building at Holyrood died before its completion in 2004?**

a) Enric Miralles

b) Benedetta Tagliabue

c) Carme Pinós

4 **Who was the first female speaker of the House of Commons?**

a) Bessie Braddock

b) Nancy Astor

c) Betty Boothroyd

5 **In which year was universal suffrage achieved in the UK?**

a) 1918

b) 1928

c) 1938

6 What is filibustering?

a) Forcing an MP to sit down through persistent heckling

b) Deliberately extending debate over a piece of legislation to delay its passage through parliament

c) When a group of MPs refuse to take part in a Commons debate

---

7 Who was the first Labour prime minister?

a) Clement Atlee

b) Harold Wilson

c) Ramsay MacDonald

---

8 How many British prime ministers were in office between 1900 and 2000?

a) 15

b) 20

c) 25

---

9 What form does a 'three-line whip' take?

a) It is an item in the weekly circular which is three lines in length

b) It is a written voting instruction issued to members which is underlined three times

c) It is a notice requiring members to vote at least three times in a particular week

---

10 Who was the last prime minister to have been a member of the House of Lords, prior to taking office?

a) Alec Douglas-Home

b) George Gordon

c) Ramsay MacDonald

A

1 b

2 b

3 a

4 c

5 b

6 b

7 c

8 b

9 b

10 a

Q BRITISH POLITICS

1 What was the name of the London restaurant where Tony and Gordon struck the infamous Blair-Brown pact?

a) Granta

b) Giganta

c) Granita

2 Why did Dr Ibrahim al-Marashi become embroiled in British politics in 2003?

a) He was arrested under the Terrorism Act for preaching extremist Islam in Finsbury Park mosque

b) His doctoral thesis was plagiarised by the British government to justify invading Iraq

c) He scaled the Houses of Parliament in a Batman costume to protest for Fathers 4 Justice

3 In which year was Margaret Thatcher first elected prime minister?

a) 1978

b) 1979

c) 1980

4 Who was the UK's first Muslim MP?

a) Shahid Malik

b) Sadiq Khan

c) Mohammad Sarwar

5 Who took the Enfield Southgate constituency from Michael Portillo in the 1997 general election?

a) Stephen Twigg

b) Diane Abbott

c) Chris Bryant

6 **In which year were the Liberal Democrats formed from the merger of the Liberal Party and the Social Democratic Party?**

a) 1978

b) 1983

c) 1988

7 **Who famously said of Michael Howard that 'There's something of the night about him'?**

a) Clare Short

b) Dennis Skinner

c) Ann Widdecombe

8 **For which union did John Prescott work as a full-time official before entering parliament?**

a) National Union of Miners

b) National Union of Seamen

c) National Union of Teachers

9 **Which holder of a Conservative safe seat did former BBC journalist Martin Bell defeat in Tatton in 1997 when he stood as an independent candidate?**

a) Jonathan Aitken

b) Neil Hamilton

c) Eric Pickles

10 **'Bush, and Blair, and the prime minister of Japan, and Silvio Berlusconi, these people are criminals, and they are responsible for mass murder in the world . . .' are the words of which MP?**

a) Hilary Benn

b) George Galloway

c) Clare Short

A

1 c
2 b
3 b
4 c
5 a
6 c
7 c
8 b
9 b
10 b

Q BRITISH PRIME MINISTERS

1 Who was the last Liberal prime minister of Great Britain?

a) David Lloyd George

b) Stanley Baldwin

c) Henry Campbell-Bannerman

2 Which of the following was prime minister during the American War of Independence?

a) Lord North

b) Lord Melbourne

c) Earl Grey

3 Which of the following was serving as prime minister at the age of 84?

a) William Gladstone

b) Lord Salisbury

c) Winston Churchill

4 Of the twelve prime ministers since 1945, how many have been graduates of Oxford University?

a) 3

b) 6

c) 8

5 Which of the following prime ministers was born outside Britain?

a) Andrew Bonar Law

b) Stanley Baldwin

c) Anthony Eden

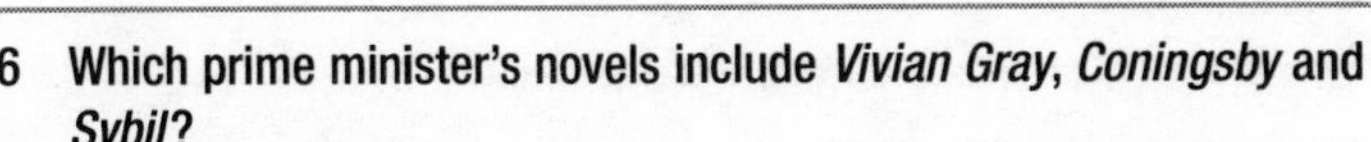

6 Which prime minister's novels include *Vivian Gray*, *Coningsby* and *Sybil*?

a) Benjamin Disraeli

b) Lord North

c) Herbert Asquith

7 Who was the only British prime minister to be assassinated?

a) Sir Robert Peel

b) Spencer Perceval

c) Lord Liverpool

8 Which prime minister served the shortest time in office, dying less than four months after being appointed?

a) Sir Robert Peel

b) George Canning

c) Viscount Goderich

9 Which future prime minister was forced to leave a heated public meeting about the Boer War disguised as a policeman?

a) Arthur Balfour

b) David Lloyd George

c) Winston Churchill

10 What was the name of the rock band in which Tony Blair played when he was at Oxford?

a) Ugly Rumours

b) Vile Bodies

c) Dirty Secrets

A

1	a
2	a
3	a
4	c
5	a
6	a
7	b
8	b
9	b
10	a

Q COUPS AND REBELLIONS

1 What is the literal meaning of *coup d'etat*?

a) Overthrow the establishment

b) A strike to the state

c) Pull out the rug

2 Which failed coup took place in England in 1605?

a) The Gunpowder Plot

b) The Popish Plot

c) The Glorious Revolution

3 In which city did Adolf Hitler attempt his Beer Hall Putsch in 1923?

a) Cologne

b) Munich

c) Berlin

4 The Congo Crisis of 1960 resulted in national independence for the Congo from which European country?

a) Great Britain

b) France

c) Belgium

5 In which year did Idi Amin gain control of Uganda through a military coup?

a) 1965

b) 1971

c) 1976

6 In which country did French mercenary Bob Denard – who died in 2007 – participate in four successful coups?

a) Seychelles

b) The Maldives

c) The Comoros

7 Who was overthrown and killed on the ides of March?

a) Julius Caesar

b) Mark Antony

c) Coriolanus

8 Which prime minister did Pervez Musharraf overthrow in Pakistan in 1999 with the help of the military?

a) Benazir Bhutto

b) Nawaz Sharif

c) Malik Meraj Khalid

9 In which country did Omar Hasan al-Bashir organise a successful coup d'etat in 1989?

a) Egypt

b) Algeria

c) Sudan

10 Which political leader is commonly believed to be represented by the character of Mr Jones in George Orwell's *Animal Farm*?

a) Nicholas II, Tsar of all the Russias

b) Joseph Stalin

c) Lenin

A

1 b

2 a

3 b

4 c

5 b

6 c

7 a

8 b

9 c

10 a

Q THE COLD WAR

1 **The 1947 Truman Doctrine, in which the US president pledged support to any country faced with communist insurgencies, was triggered by a conflict in which country?**

a) Greece

b) Yugoslavia

c) Malta

2 **In which year was the Berlin Wall erected?**

a) 1947

b) 1954

c) 1961

3 **The CIA's operation Ajax toppled the democratically elected government of which country in 1953?**

a) Iran

b) The Philippines

c) Guatemala

4 **Who was US president during the Cuban Missile Crisis?**

a) Dwight Eisenhower

b) Gerald Ford

c) John F. Kennedy

5 **In which country did the US-backed Contras battle for political power with the Soviet-sponsored Sandinistas?**

a) Panama

b) El Salvador

c) Nicaragua

6 **Which of the following was not blacklisted during the Red Scare in the USA?**

a) Charlie Chaplin

b) Cary Grant

c) Orson Welles

7 **Complete the sequence of general secretaries of the Communist Party of the Soviet Union: Stalin, Khrushchev, Brezhnev, ____________, Chernenko**

a) Andropov

b) Ivashko

c) Gorbachev

8 **Who directed the Cold War satire *Dr Strangelove*?**

a) Wolfgang Petersen

b) Stanley Kubrick

c) Roman Polanski

9 **Which war began in December 1979 and ended in February 1989?**

a) Soviet War in Afghanistan

b) Iran-Iraq War

c) Cambodian Civil War

10 **What is the literal meaning of 'glasnost'?**

a) Restructuring

b) Cooperation

c) Openness

1	a
2	c
3	a
4	c
5	c
6	b
7	a
8	b
9	a
10	c

Q DICTATORS

1 Which country did Mussolini invade in 1939?

a) Switzerland

b) Albania

c) Czechoslovakia

2 Who did Fidel Castro overthrow to gain power in Cuba?

a) Fulgencio Batista

b) Manuel Noriega

c) Omar Torrijos

3 In which country did president-for-life Saparmurat Niyazov rename the months of the year in 2002?

a) Tajikistan

b) Kazakhstan

c) Turkmenistan

4 Which South American country is named after the man who helped to establish its independence from Spain in 1825?

a) Colombia

b) Venezuela

c) Bolivia

5 Who declared himself 'Emperor of Central Africa' in December 1976?

a) Jean-Bédel Bokassa

b) David Dacko

c) André Kolingba

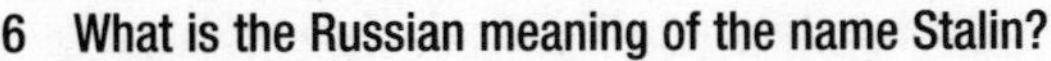

6 What is the Russian meaning of the name Stalin?

a) Unbreakable

b) Of steel

c) Of iron

7 In which European country did Kim Jong-Il attend university in the early 1970s?

a) Slovenia

b) Malta

c) Greece

8 Which Chilean president died during Augusto Pinochet's military coup of 1973?

a) Salvador Allende

b) Ricardo Escobar

c) Eduardo Montalva

9 Who was chosen as TIME Man of the Year in 1938?

a) Joseph Stalin

b) Winston Churchill

c) Adolf Hitler

10 China's Great Leap Forward was orchestrated by which leader?

a) Mao Zedong

b) Deng Xiaoping

c) Jiang Zemin

A

1 b
2 a
3 c
4 c
5 a
6 b
7 b
8 a
9 c
10 a

WILD PARTIES

1 What is the English meaning of Bertie Ahern's Fianna Fail party in Ireland?

a) Soldiers of Ireland

b) Soldiers of Fortune

c) Soldiers of God

2 What animal is the symbol of the US Republican party?

a) Toad

b) Elephant

c) Mountain lion

3 Which Italian political party was founded in 1993 by Silvio Berlusconi?

a) Forza Italia

b) National Alliance

c) Lega Nord

4 What is the name of Robert Mugabe's political party in Zimbabwe?

a) ZIMB-RM

b) ZANU-PF

c) MDC

5 Following the Sharpeville massacre of 1960 in South Africa, the African National Congress party formed a military wing. What was its translated name?

a) Spear of the Nation

b) Scourge of Corruption

c) Harbinger of Democracy

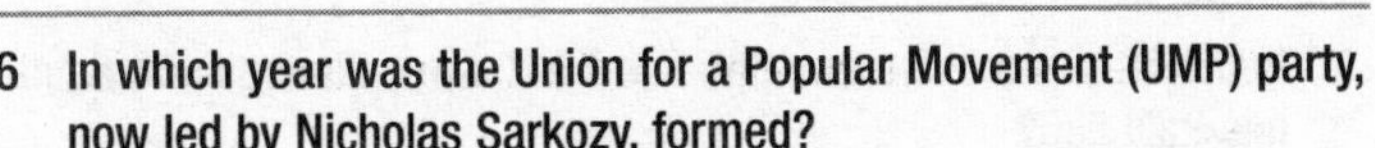

6 In which year was the Union for a Popular Movement (UMP) party, now led by Nicholas Sarkozy, formed?

a) 1802

b) 1902

c) 2002

7 In which country did the green party first contend in a national election?

a) The Netherlands

b) France

c) Germany

8 Which daytime television presenter formed the Veritas party in 2004?

a) Fern Britton

b) Jeremy Kyle

c) Robert Kilroy-Silk

9 What is the name of Thaksin Shinawatra's political party banned in Thailand?

a) Thais Love Thais

b) Thais For Thais

c) Thais Help Thais

10 Since 1950 how many leaders has the UK's Conservative party had?

a) 9

b) 10

c) 11

A

1 a

2 b

3 a

4 b

5 a

6 c

7 c

8 c

9 a

10 c

Q EUROTRASH

1 In the 52 years between 1945 and 2007, how many governments has Italy had?

a) 21

b) 41

c) 61

2 To what foodstuff did Finnish prime minister Matti Vanhanen favourably compare his ex-lover Susan Kuronen in 2007?

a) A chocolate mousse

b) A baked potato

c) A chicken leg

3 Which of the following is not believed to be a former lover of Carla Bruni-Sarkozy?

a) Mick Jagger

b) Eric Clapton

c) Pete Townshend

4 Which country boasts a Donald Duck party?

a) Switzerland

b) Spain

c) Sweden

5 What is the name of Vladimir Putin's wife?

a) Lyudmila

b) Natalia

c) Svetlana

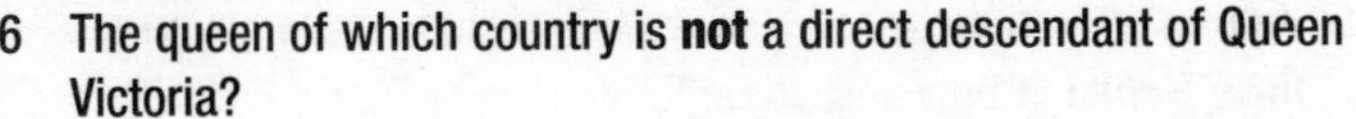

6 The queen of which country is not a direct descendant of Queen Victoria?

a) Norway

b) Spain

c) Denmark

7 Which country was without a government between June and December 2007, leading to speculation of a partition?

a) Belgium

b) Austria

c) Croatia

8 What is the official anthem of the European Union?

a) 'Ave Maria'

b) 'Ode to Joy'

c) 'Abide With Me'

9 Which two countries adopted the euro in 2008?

a) Ireland and the Czech Republic

b) Cyprus and Malta

c) Ukraine and Poland

10 Which of the following is not a member of the EU?

a) Sweden

b) Finland

c) Norway

1 c
2 b
3 c
4 c
5 a
6 a
7 a
8 b
9 b
10 c

Q FAMILY CONNECTIONS

1 Prior to Tony Blair, who was the last serving prime minister to have a child in Downing Street?

a) William Pitt the Younger

b) John Russell

c) Henry Campbell-Bannerman

2 What was the name of Indira Gandhi's son who eventually succeeded her as prime minister of India, before being assassinated in 1991?

a) Rahul

b) Rajiv

c) Kapil

3 The House of Saud rules which country?

a) Jordan

b) Syria

c) Saudi Arabia

4 What is the name of Fidel Castro's brother who succeeded him as prime minister of Cuba?

a) Raul

b) Luiz

c) Ruiz

5 Which of these African leaders is the son-in-law of Denis Sassou-Nguesso, president of the Republic of Congo

a) Joseph Kabila of DR Congo

b) Omar Bongo of Gabon

c) John Kufuor of Ghana

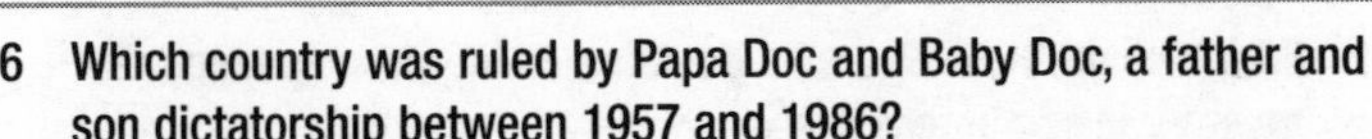

6 Which country was ruled by Papa Doc and Baby Doc, a father and son dictatorship between 1957 and 1986?

a) Dominican Republic

b) El Salvador

c) Haiti

7 Which member of the Kennedy family was killed by Palestinian gunman Sirhan Sirhan?

a) John F. Kennedy

b) Robert F. Kennedy

c) Edward Kennedy

8 Graca Machel, is the only woman to have married serving presidents of two different countries. The late Mozambican president Samora Machel was her first husband, but who was her second?

a) Nelson Mandela

b) Thabo Mbeki

c) Robert Mugabe

9 In which country did the president appoint her mother as prime minister in 1994?

a) India

b) Sri Lanka

c) Bangladesh

10 Harriet Harman is related to which former UK prime minister?

a) Clement Attlee

b) Edward Heath

c) Neville Chamberlain

A

1 b
2 b
3 c
4 a
5 b
6 c
7 b
8 a
9 b
10 c

Q POLITICAL QUOTATIONS

1 Which country did Churchill describe as 'a riddle wrapped in a mystery inside an enigma'?

a) Russia

b) Germany

c) France

2 Which prime minister said that the nation had 'never had it so good'?

a) Margaret Thatcher

b) Harold Wilson

c) Harold Macmillan

3 Which neo-con underestimated al-Qaida in April 2001 by asking 'Who cares about a little terrorist in Afghanistan'?

a) Donald Rumsfeld

b) Paul Wolfowitz

c) Dick Cheney

4 Who said: 'We will reduce and probably eliminate the homeless by 2008'?

a) Charles Clarke

b) John Prescott

c) Jacqui Smith

5 Which political philosopher declared 'An ideal form of government is democracy tempered with assassination'?

a) Jean-Jacques Rousseau

b) Voltaire

c) Alexis de Tocqueville

6 What event caused the British Foreign Secretary, Sir Edward Grey, to remark that 'the lamps are going out all over Europe'?

a) The death of Gladstone

b) The death of Queen Victoria

c) The outbreak of the First World War

7 Which Labour politician, according to Simon Hoggart, 'can skulk in broad daylight'?

a) Robin Cook

b) Peter Mandelson

c) Gordon Brown

8 'I believe there is something out there watching over us – unfortunately it's the government.' Who's view on extra-terrestrial life is this?

a) Oliver Stone

b) Woody Allen

c) Billy Crystal

9 Who said that a politician 'is a person who approaches every subject with an open mouth'?

a) Adlai Stevenson

b) Gore Vidal

c) Peter Cook

10 Who wrote that 'the broad mass of a nation . . . will more easily fall victim to a big lie than to a small one'?

a) Josef Stalin

b) Vladimir Lenin

c) Adolf Hitler

A

1 a
2 c
3 b
4 b
5 a
6 c
7 b
8 b
9 a
10 c

Q SPIES AND INTELLIGENCE

1 What is the name of the Israeli secret intelligence service?

a) Mossad

b) Eilat

c) Knesset

2 Which of the following official positions did Sir Anthony Blunt hold at the time he was revealed as a Soviet spy in 1979?

a) Poet Laureate

b) Master of Trinity College, Cambridge

c) Keeper of the Queen's Pictures

3 Who was Queen Elizabeth I's 'spymaster' who unravelled the treachery of Mary, Queen of Scots?

a) Sir Philip Sidney

b) Sir Francis Walsingham

c) Robert Devereux

4 Whose espionage efforts during the American War of Independence were rewarded with a statue outside the CIA headquarters at Langley, Virginia?

a) Nathan Hale

b) James J. Andrews

c) Daniel Bissell

5 Of which television show did former MI5 chief Dame Eliza Manningham-Buller say, 'In it everything is solved by half a dozen people who break laws to achieve results. I think . . . it is potentially quite damaging for the suggestion to prevail that we are totally above the law'?

a) *The Professionals*

b) *Spooks*

c) *Tinker, Taylor, Soldier, Spy*

6 Which French novelist wrote a pamphlet defending Alfred Dreyfus, who had been falsely convicted of spying for the Germans?

a) Emile Zola

b) Marcel Proust

c) Gustave Flaubert

---

7 Which of the following Soviet leaders was also once head of the KGB?

a) Leonid Brezhnev

b) Nikita Krushchev

c) Yuri Andropov

---

8 Franklin D. Roosevelt was president of the USA when J Edgar Hoover was appointed director of the FBI. Who was in office when Hoover died in the job?

a) Gerald Ford

b) Richard Nixon

c) Jimmy Carter

---

9 From the author of which book did Ian Fleming take the name James Bond?

a) *Birds of the West Indies*

b) *Flowers of the Blue Mountains*

c) *Fish of the Greater Antilles*

---

10 Whose activities were described in an FBI report as 'possibly the worst intelligence disaster in US history' and inspired the 2007 film *Breach* in which he was played by Chris Cooper?

a) Alger Hiss

b) Robert Hanssen

c) Julius Rosenberg

A

1 a
2 c
3 b
4 a
5 b
6 a
7 c
8 b
9 a
10 b

Q US PRESIDENTS

1 Who has served the shortest term in office as president?

a) Martin van Buren

b) William Henry Harrison

c) Harry S. Truman

2 Abraham Lincoln was the first American president to be assassinated. Who was the second?

a) James Garfield

b) William McKinley

c) John F. Kennedy

3 What is the most common Christian name among US presidents?

a) George

b) William

c) James

4 Whose administration was tainted by this association with the 'Ohio Gang'?

a) Herbert Hoover

b) Warren Harding

c) Woodrow Wilson

5 Who was the first president whose son also became president?

a) John Adams

b) Andrew Johnson

c) Theodore Roosevelt

6 **Which president's desk featured a sign with his catchphrase 'The buck stops here'?**

a) Dwight Eisenhower

b) Harry Truman

c) Lyndon Johnson

7 **Which of the following statements about Charles Dawes, vice-president to Calvin Coolidge in the 1920s, is true?**

a) He was a member of a religious sect which believed that the world was due to end in 1936

b) He wrote the music for a song which was a hit for Cliff Richard

c) He invented an early form of breathalyser called the 'drunkometer'

8 **Which president said, 'Sometimes I feel like a fire hydrant looking at a pack of dogs'?**

a) George W Bush

b) Bill Clinton

c) Richard Nixon

9 **Which TV show featured a fictional US president called David Palmer?**

a) *Heroes*

b) *The West Wing*

c) *24*

10 **Which vice-president was awarded the Education Ig Nobel prize for 'demonstrating, better than anyone else, the need for science education'?**

a) Walter Mondale

b) Dan Quayle

c) Al Gore

A

1 b
2 a
3 c
4 b
5 a
6 b
7 b
8 b
9 c
10 b

Q THE SCIENCE OF POLITICS

1 Who, according to Friedrich Engels, said 'All I know is I am not a Marxist'?

a) Vladimir Lenin

b) Leon Trotsky

c) Karl Marx

2 Coined by Aristotle, what general term is used to describe a form of government in which political power rests with a small elite distinguished by some attribute such as military power or wealth?

a) Aristocracy

b) Plutocracy

c) Oligarchy

3 'From each according to his abilities, to each according to his needs.' Which political theory can this statement be applied to?

a) Communism

b) Federalism

c) Capitalism

4 Who coined this well-known definition: 'Politics is the art of the possible'?

a) Margaret Thatcher

b) Otto von Bismark

c) Plato

5 With which of the following concepts is Francis Fukuyama associated?

a) The invisible hand

b) The end of history

c) Invention of tradition

6 Which of the following political ideologies has never been employed as the official ideology by any modern state?

a) Anarchism

b) Liberalism

c) Fascism

7 Who is most correctly referred to as the father of utilitarianism?

a) Jeremy Bentham

b) Adam Smith

c) John Stuart Mill

8 Who wrote 'tis better to be feared than loved if you cannot be both' in his work *The Prince*?

a) Bertrand Russell

b) Thomas Hobbes

c) Niccolo Machiavelli

9 Which of the following is not a political philosophy?

a) Zikism

b) Zenarchy

c) Zoroastrianism

10 Which of the following countries adopted social democracy as its chief political ideology in the late 20th century?

a) Japan

b) Mexico

c) Sweden

1 c
2 c
3 a
4 b
5 b
6 a
7 a
8 c
9 c
10 c

Q WORLD LEADERS

1 Who became the first chancellor of a newly united Germany in 1991?

a) Helmut Kohl

b) Gerhard Schroder

c) Helmut Schmidt

2 Which country appointed the first female prime minister?

a) India

b) Sri Lanka

c) Pakistan

3 Who did Mao Zedong choose as his successor?

a) Chiang Kai-Chek

b) Deng Xiaoping

c) Hua Guofeng

4 Who is the 'eternal president' of North Korea?

a) Kim Il-sung

b) Kim Jong-il

c) Kim Yong-ju

5 Which country had a prime minister and president who were twin brothers?

a) Switzerland

b) Poland

c) Norway

6 **Which Israeli leader was assassinated in November 1995?**

a) Moshe Dayan

b) Golda Meir

c) Yitzhak Rabin

7 **Which former prime minister later became the owner of an English football club?**

a) Nawaz Sharif of Pakistan

b) Thaksin Shinawatra of Thailand

c) Shinzo Abe of Japan

8 **Which state leader led a coup d'etat against King Idris I?**

a) Omar al-Bashir

b) Muammar Gaddafi

c) François Bozizé

9 **Which former African politician declared himself a CBE – that is, 'conqueror of the British Empire'?**

a) Louis Botha

b) Jomo Kenyatta

c) Idi Amin

10 **Which former South African prime minister was known as the 'architect of apartheid'?**

a) H. F. Verwoerd

b) P. W. Botha

c) B. J. Vorster

1 a
2 b
3 c
4 a
5 b
6 c
7 b
8 b
9 c
10 a

Q INTERNATIONAL ORGANISATIONS

1 **On which continent is the MERCOSUR organisation active?**

a) South America

b) Africa

c) Asia

2 **Which of these countries is not a member of the G8?**

a) Japan

b) Russia

c) Australia

3 **Which country left the Commonwealth following a suspension in 2002?**

a) Fiji

b) Pakistan

c) Zimbabwe

4 **In which country is the headquarters of Interpol?**

a) Belgium

b) France

c) The Netherlands

5 **Who preceded Kofi Annan as UN secretary-general?**

a) Dag Hammarskjold

b) Boutros Boutros-Ghali

c) Kurt Waldheim

A

1 a

2 c

3 c

4 b

5 b

SCIENCE

ANATOMY

SPACE

BIOLOGY

CALENDARS

CHEMISTRY

COMPUTING

CONSTELLATIONS

FAMOUS SCIENTISTS

PSYCHOLOGY

OPERATING THEATRE

INVENTIONS AND INVENTORS

MATHEMATICS

MEDICINE

PHYSICS

WEATHER

QUACKS AND FALLACIES

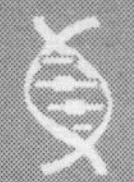

SCIENCE

ANATOMY

1 **How many bones are there in a fully developed human skeleton?**

a) 156

b) 176

c) 206

2 **Where in the body would you find the islands of Langerhans?**

a) Liver

b) Pancreas

c) Ear

3 **What is the correct scientific term for the nostrils?**

a) Philtrum

b) Nares

c) Cochlea

4 **Placed end-to-end, how far would all of the arteries, veins and capillaries from an average-sized man stretch for?**

a) 1,800 miles

b) 27,000 miles

c) 62,000 miles

5) Where in the body would you find metacarpals and metatarsals?

a) Hands and feet

b) Shins

c) Neck

6 **After the skin, what is the heaviest human organ?**

a) Liver

b) Brain

c) Lungs

---

7) **What takes blood away from the heart?**

a) Arteries

b) Veins

c) Capillaries

---

8 **The Edwin Smith Papyrus is thought to be the oldest medical text in existence, dating from 1600 BC – which ancient civilisation produced it?**

a) Greek

b) Chinese

c) Egyptian

---

9 **Apart from oxygen, what is the most abundant element in the human body, with about 16,000g in a 70kg person?**

a) Hydrogen

b) Carbon

c) Calcium

---

10 **Which of the following bones, found in the leg, is the longest in the human body?**

a) Femur

b) Tibia

c) Fibula

A

1 c
2 b
3 b
4 c
5 a
6 a
7 a
8 c
9 b
10 a

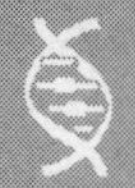

Q SPACE

1 Which was the first manned spacecraft to successfully orbit the moon?

a) Apollo 4

b) Apollo 8

c) Apollo 11

2 Which astronomical term derives its name from the Ancient Greek word for 'milk'?

a) Comet

b) Galaxy

c) Moon

3 Which planet orbits the sun once every 88 days?

a) Mars

b) Venus

c) Mercury

4 Which of the planets in the solar system was discovered in 1846 by the German astronomer Johann Galle?

a) Neptune

b) Pluto

c) Uranus

5 What is a parsec?

a) An incredibly bright object in space powered by the black hole at its centre

b) A large-distance unit equal to 3.26 light years

c) A gigantic cluster of more than 2,000 galaxies

6 Which make of watch was the first to have been worn on the moon, by Buzz Aldrin in 1969?

a) Rolex

b) Tag Heuer

c) Omega

7 What is unusual about the asteroid Vesta?

a) It's on a course to collide with the Earth in 12 million years time

b) It can occasionally be seen with the naked eye

c) It's the smallest asteroid so far discovered

8 Which planet contains the 'Great Dark Spot'?

a) Neptune

b) Jupiter

c) Uranus

9 If a person weighed 64kg on Earth, how much would they weigh on Mercury?

a) 8kg

b) 24kg

c) 98kg

10 Which planet's moons include Pan, Atlas and Prometheus?

a) Jupiter

b) Saturn

c) Neptune

A

1 b

2 b

3 c

4 a

5 b

6 c

7 b

8 a

9 b

10 b

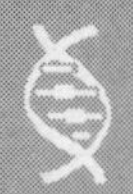

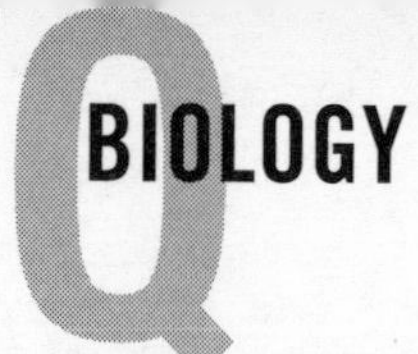

BIOLOGY

1 What does a herpetologist study?

a) Reptiles

b) Skin diseases

c) Bats

2 What is the scientific term for plants such as cacti, which live where it is difficult to obtain water?

a) Hydrophytes

b) Mesophytes

c) Xerophytes

3 Bile is secreted by which human organ?

a) Liver

b) Gall bladder

c) Pancreas

4 Of what are meiosis and mitosis both processes?

a) Cell division

b) Liquid absorption

c) Human digestion

5 What is the correct title of Charles Darwin's seminal work?

a) *The Origin of the Species*

b) *On the Origin of Species*

c) *The Origins of Species*

6 Which animal's brain weighs the least?

a) Dog

b) Cat

c) Pig

7 Straightened out, how long would a strand of DNA from a single cell be?

a) 20cm

b) 90cm

c) 200cm

8 Which biological process was first discovered by Jan Ingenhousz in the 18th century?

a) Asexual reproduction

b) Photosynthesis

c) Cell replication

9 How many chromosomes does a human being possess?

a) 46

b) 32

c) 23

10 Which of the following is not a genuine subcellular component of a eukaryotic cell?

a) Nucleus

b) Mitochondria

c) Tesicle

A

1 a

2 c

3 a

4 a

5 b

6 b

7 c

8 b

9 a

10 c

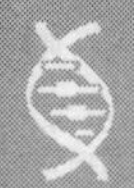

CALENDARS

1 Which day of the week was named for the Scandinavian goddess of love?

a) Monday for Mona

b) Wednesday for Wotan

c) Friday for Frigga or Freya

2 In the year 46 BC who ordered a reform of the calendar?

a) Alexander the Great

b) Julius Caesar

c) Ptolemy VII, Pharoah of Egypt

3 Which month was named for the Latin word for 'to open'?

a) March

b) April

c) May

4 Which month was the seventh month of the Roman calendar?

a) July

b) August

c) September

5 In order to have a Friday-the-13th, a month must start on which day of the week?

a) Sunday

b) Monday

c) Tuesday

6 **How many months were in the Mayan civil calendar, known as the Haab?**

a) 9

b) 13

c) 18

---

7 **Which of the following is a genuine zodiac animal, as featured in the Chinese calendar?**

a) Elephant

b) Duck

c) Sheep

---

8 **The Islamic year is roughly how many days shorter than a year in the Gregorian calendar?**

a) 11

b) 14

c) 17

---

9 **The earliest-known 'date' is thought to be 4236 BC, when the calendar of which ancient civilisation was founded?**

a) Chinese

b) Greek

c) Egyptian

---

10 **When did Britain abandon the Julian calendar in favour of the Gregorian calendar, resulting in 3 September instantly becoming 14 September?**

a) 1652

b) 1752

c) 1852

A

1 c
2 b
3 b
4 c
5 a
6 c
7 c
8 a
9 c
10 b

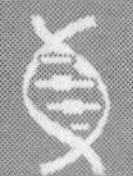

Q CHEMISTRY

1 **Which chemical element has the atomic number 78 and the chemical symbol Pt?**

a) Potassium

b) Platinum

c) Lead

2 **How was phosphorus first discovered in 1674?**

a) By subtracting salt from ocean water

b) By distilling human urine

c) By drying fish

3 **What, with only 25g occurring naturally, is the rarest element on Earth?**

a) Astatine

b) Polonium

c) Francium

4 **Which of the following elements is one of the so-called 'noble gases'?**

a) Chlorine

b) Fluorine

c) Argon

5 **Which of the following liquids has the highest pH, of around 4.3?**

a) Lime juice

b) Tomato juice

c) Orange juice

6 A cubic metre (m^3) of which material is the heaviest, weighing 1,030kg?

a) Milk

b) Grain

c) Apples

7 What metal is extracted from hematite ore?

a) Iron

b) Lead

c) Tin

8 From what or whom does the element Strontium derive its name?

a) A Norwegian chemist

b) The German word for 'heavy'

c) A village in Argyllshire

9 Which is the lightest of the chemical elements?

a) Helium

b) Oxygen

c) Hydrogen

10 Which acid is also known as oil of vitriol?

a) Sulphuric

b) Hydrochloric

c) Nitric

A

1 b

2 b

3 a

4 c

5 b

6 a

7 a

8 c

9 c

10 a

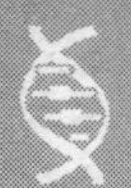

Q COMPUTING

1 **In November 2007 IBM's BlueGene/L System, then the world's fastest computer, achieved how many teraflops, or trillions of calculations, per second?**

a) 99.8

b) 280.6

c) 478.2

2 **When did Charles Babbage, who was credited with originating the idea for a programmable computer, devise his 'difference engine'?**

a) 1822

b) 1846

c) 1885

3 **Which of the following is not a genuine storage term?**

a) Zettabyte

b) Xittabyte

c) Yottabyte

4 **The first home video game system, the Magnavox Odyssey, was released in which year?**

a) 1972

b) 1976

c) 1979

5 **The programming language COBOL's name is derived from what?**

a) Computer Basic Object Language

b) Common Business Oriented Language

c) Coordinated Binary Original Language

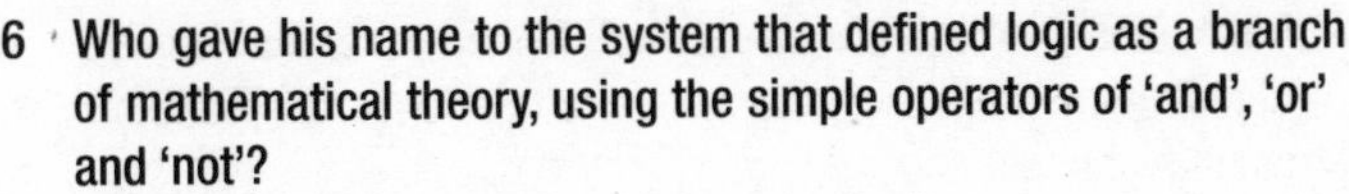

6 Who gave his name to the system that defined logic as a branch of mathematical theory, using the simple operators of 'and', 'or' and 'not'?

a) Blaise Pascal

b) Gottfried Leibniz

c) George Boole

7 The concept that microprocessors double in complexity and power every two years is known as what?

a) Craig's Law

b) Moore's Law

c) Connery's Law

8 Which of the following is not a genuine file format abbreviation?

a) JPEG

b) MPEG

c) HPEG

9 How much did the Pacific nation of Tuvalu receive for the ten-year lease of its .tv internet suffix in 1998?

a) $1m

b) $50m

c) $100m

10 The Apple iMac G3 came in 13 different 'flavours' – which of the following was a genuine option?

a) Blue Dalmatian

b) Red Labrador

c) Purple Alsatian

A

1 c

2 a

3 b

4 a

5 b

6 c

7 b

8 c

9 b

10 a

Q CONSTELLATIONS

1 Which cluster of stars is also called 'The Seven Sisters'?

a) Lyra

b) Orion's Belt

c) The Pleiades

2 How many constellations can be seen from the Earth?

a) 32

b) 88

c) 154

3 What does the constellation Cetus represent?

a) A serpent

b) A maiden

c) A whale

4 As seen from Earth, what is the brightest star in the night sky?

a) Sirius

b) Rigel

c) Canopus

5 Which constellation is also known as 'The Plough' and 'The Big Dipper'?

a) Leo Minor

b) Ursa Major

c) Bootes

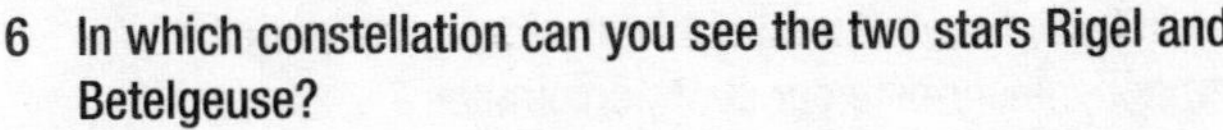

6 **In which constellation can you see the two stars Rigel and Betelgeuse?**

a) Gemini

b) Leo

c) Orion

7 **Which of the following is not a genuine constellation?**

a) Sculptor

b) Valaar

c) Fornax

8 **Which astronomer created the orders of magnitude by which the brightness of a star is measured?**

a) Johannes Kepler

b) Galileo

c) Hipparchus

9 **Which constellation is named after the woman whom Perseus, in Greek mythology, rescued from a sea monster?**

a) Andromeda

b) Cassiopeia

c) Virgo

10 **In which constellation is the Horsehead Nebula?**

a) Taurus

b) Orion

c) Pegasus

1 c
2 b
3 c
4 a
5 b
6 c
7 b
8 c
9 a
10 b

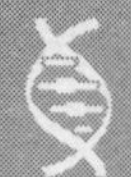

Q FAMOUS SCIENTISTS

1 Which scientist coined the phrase 'genius is one per cent inspiration, ninety-nine per cent perspiration'?

a) Benjamin Franklin

b) Thomas Edison

c) Robert Fulton

2 What is the name of Nicolaus Copernicus' most influential work?

a) *On the Revolutions of the Heavenly Spheres*

b) *Astronomia Nova*

c) *The Cosmos and its Origins*

3 How many laws of motion did Isaac Newton describe in his *Principia Mathematica*?

a) One

b) Two

c) Three

4 Where did Murray Gell-Mann find the word 'quark' which he used as a name for a type of sub-atomic particle?

a) In James Joyce's novel *Finnegans Wake*

b) In a medieval cookbook

c) In a German dictionary

5 In which element did the French scientist Henri Becquerel first discover naturally occurring radioactivity?

a) Radium

b) Plutonium

c) Uranium

6 **Which discovery in medicine was made by the 17th-century English physician William Harvey?**

a) The existence of bacteria

b) The circulation of the blood

c) The anaesthetic properties of ether

7 **What was the occupation of Gregor Mendel, whose scientific work became the basis for modern genetics?**

a) A monk

b) A doctor

c) A lawyer

8 **Which chemist first devised the periodic table, supposedly after seeing its basic structure in a dream?**

a) Sir Humphrey Davy

b) Dmitri Mendeleyev

c) Antoine Lavoisier

9 **How did the 18th-century French chemist Antoine Lavoisier die?**

a) He was killed in a duel

b) He inhaled poisonous gases during an experiment

c) He was guillotined during the French Revolution

10 **Who was the first person to be awarded two Nobel prizes?**

a) Louis Pasteur

b) Albert Einstein

c) Marie Curie

1 b
2 a
3 c
4 a
5 c
6 b
7 a
8 b
9 c
10 c

Q PSYCHOLOGY

1 **In an experiment by Stanley Milgram, what percentage of participants gave someone a 450-volt electric shock when told to by an authority figure?**

a) 5

b) 34

c) 65

2 **What did Ivan Pavlov condition dogs to do when he rang a bell?**

a) Bite

b) Salivate

c) Mate

3 **Which of these is not a theory of dreams proposed by Sigmund Freud or Carl Jung?**

a) We enter a collective unconscious of shared human experiences

b) Dreams act as wish-fulfilment

c) Dreams are a view of a parallel universe

4 **What is the female version of the Oedipus complex known as?**

a) Lolita complex

b) Electra complex

c) Helen complex

5 **What is the term coined by Roger Brown and James Kulick for a vivid memory of an emotional event?**

a) Flashbulb memory

b) Technicolor memory

c) Photographic memory

6 Who argued that behaviour is determined by reinforcement?

a) Ulric Neisser

b) Wilhelm Wundt

c) B. F. Skinner

7 What does the concept of 'chunking' refer to in a theory proposed by George A. Miller?

a) Memory

b) Relationships

c) Infant behaviour

8 Whose Stanford prison experiment on obedience was recreated in a programme on the BBC?

a) Philip Zimbardo

b) Abraham H. Maslow

c) Jean Piaget

9 Who spoke of introverted and extroverted psychological types?

a) Jacques Lacan

b) Carl Jung

c) Sigmund Freud

10 Which psychological theory features the law of closure, the law of proximity and the law of symmetry?

a) Social

b) Comparative

c) Gestalt

A

1 c
2 b
3 c
4 b
5 a
6 c
7 a
8 a
9 b
10 c

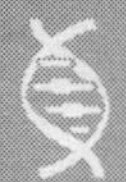

Q OPERATING THEATRE

1 **Which term refers to an operation to reduce the prominence of large ears?**

a) Blepharoplasty

b) Otoplasty

c) Rhinoplasty

2 **What was the connection between Burke and Hare, the notorious 19th-century murderers who supplied their victims to anatomists?**

a) Lodger and landlord

b) Publican and brewer

c) Librarian and publisher

3 **What is the oldest surgical procedure we have discovered evidence of?**

a) Trepanning (drilling a hole in the skull)

b) Lithotomy (removal of kidney stones)

c) Tooth extraction

4 **In which church can London's Old Operating Theatre be found?**

a) St Thomas', Southwark

b) Chelsea Old Church

c) St Paul's, Deptford

5 **What term was coined in 1798 by Pierre-Joseph Desault?**

a) Transplant

b) Plastic surgery

c) Pacemaker

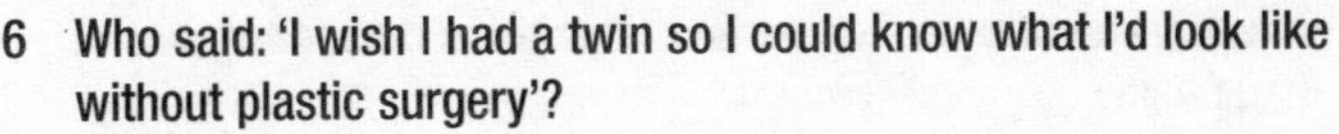

6 **Who said: 'I wish I had a twin so I could know what I'd look like without plastic surgery'?**

a) Dolly Parton

b) Joan Rivers

c) Cher

7 **What was the most common plastic surgery procedure in the UK in 2006?**

a) Liposuction

b) Breast enlargement

c) Eyebrow lift

8 **Which of these human organs was the first to be successfully transplanted?**

a) Kidney

b) Liver

c) Lung

9 **According to the WHO, what percentage of men worldwide have been circumcised?**

a) 15

b) 30

c) 45

10 **What is the Krukenberg procedure?**

a) The conversion of a forearm stump into a pincer

b) The attachment of a prosthesis to an amputated leg

c) The removal of surplus fingers and/or toes

1 b
2 a
3 a
4 a
5 b
6 b
7 b
8 a
9 b
10 a

Q INVENTIONS AND INVENTORS

1 In which country was paper first invented and used?

a) Egypt

b) India

c) China

2 What was invented by Jacques Cousteau and Emile Gagnan during the Second World War?

a) The drysuit

b) The aqualung

c) The BCD (buoyancy control device)

3 Which of these inventions was named after its inventor?

a) Lego

b) Stetson hat

c) Velcro

4 When was the earliest-known English patent granted, to the stained-glass maker John of Utynam?

a) 1449

b) 1625

c) 1801

5 How old was Louis Braille when he invented the raised-dot reading system that bears his name?

a) 15

b) 45

c) 75

6 **What did Friedrich Mohs invent a measurement system for?**

a) Electrical current

b) Mineral hardness

c) Radiation

7 **Which invention did the Yorkshireman Percy Shaw patent in 1934?**

a) Windscreen wipers

b) Parking meter

c) Cat's eyes

8 **When William Semple patented chewing gum in 1869, for what did he intend it to be used?**

a) As a means of exercising the jaw

b) As a glue for household use

c) As bait to catch birds

9 **Who is credited with the invention of the phonograph and the electric typewriter?**

a) Alexander Graham Bell

b) Thomas Edison

c) Michael Faraday

10 **Which of the following is also a creation of Trevor Baylis, the inventor of the wind-up radio?**

a) Wind-up media player

b) Wind-up laptop

c) Wind-up office lamp

A

1	c
2	b
3	b
4	a
5	a
6	b
7	c
8	a
9	b
10	a

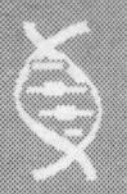

Q MATHEMATICS

1 What is a triangle with three sides of different lengths called?

a) An isosceles triangle

b) A scalene triangle

c) A congruent triangle

2 What were Napier's Bones?

a) An early form of calculating machine

b) Drawing tools for use in geometry

c) A binary system

3 Using a supercomputer, how many decimal places has Professor Yasumasa Kanada calculated π (pi) to?

a) 16 billion

b) 506 billion

c) 1.24 trillion

4 In measurements, if mega- is the prefix used for a million, giga- for a billion and tera- for a trillion, what is the prefix used for a quadrillion?

a) femto-

b) peta-

c) exa-

5 How would you calculate the volume of a cylinder?

a) $\pi \times \text{radius}^2 \times \text{height}$

b) $2 \times \pi \times \text{radius} \times \text{height}$

c) $\pi \times \text{radius} \times \text{length}$

6 Which of the following Greek scientists was renowned primarily as a mathematician and is known as the 'father of geometry'?

a) Apollonius

b) Hipparchus

c) Euclid

7 If two angles are complementary, what do they add up?

a) 90 degrees

b) 180 degrees

c) 360 degrees

8 In which branch of maths would you find a phenomenon known as the Witch of Agnesi?

a) Topology

b) Algebra

c) Geometry

9 Which of the following is a prime number?

a) 53

b) 63

c) 93

10 What is the name given to a number sequence where each new addition is the sum of the previous two numbers – 1, 1, 2, 3, 5, 8, 13, 21, etc?

a) Fibonacci series

b) Boolean series

c) Gauss series

A

1 b

2 a

3 c

4 b

5 a

6 c

7 a

8 c

9 a

10 a

MEDICINE

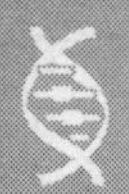

SCIENCE

1 **What is the chief symptom of the visual disorder known as diplopia?**

a) Seeing spots before the eyes

b) Blindness

c) Double vision

2 **Which of the following medical milestones was reached in 1967?**

a) The first human heart transplant

b) The first test-tube baby was born

c) The CAT scanner was invented

3 **What did 'doctor' originally mean in Latin?**

a) Priest

b) Teacher

c) Scientist

4 **Which painkiller was first patented in 1899?**

a) Paracetamol

b) Codeine

c) Aspirin

5 **Who discovered penicillin?**

a) Edward Jenner

b) Louis Pasteur

c) Alexander Fleming

6 The World Health Assembly confirmed the successful worldwide eradication of which disease in 1980?

a) Cholera

b) Smallpox

c) Plague

7 The disease scurvy is caused by a deficiency of which vitamin?

a) D

b) C

c) E

8 From which plant is the drug Digitalis obtained?

a) Deadly nightshade

b) Poppy

c) Foxglove

9 What is the more common name for the disease 'varicella'?

a) German measles

b) Mumps

c) Chicken-pox

10 Which Greek physician is known as the 'father of medicine'?

a) Hippocrates

b) Galen

c) Aristotle

A

1 c

2 a

3 b

4 c

5 c

6 b

7 b

8 c

9 c

10 a

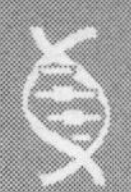

PHYSICS

1 What was the first man-made object to break the sound barrier?

a) An aeroplane

b) A bullet

c) A whip

2 What is the SI unit of resistance?

a) Ohm

b) Volt

c) Ampere

3 What does a pyrometer measure?

a) High temperatures

b) Low temperatures

c) Light intensity

4 Invented in 2004 with a thickness of one atom, what is the thinnest man-made material known as?

a) Nanocrya

b) Graphene

c) Miniester

5 Which of the following is the loudest sound, at a level of 188 decibels?

a) A jumbo jet taking off

b) A chainsaw

c) A blue whale's call

6 Which of the following do not travel through a vacuum?

a) Radio waves

b) Electromagnetic waves

c) Sound waves

7 At what temperature are the Celsius and Fahrenheit scales the same?

a) +40

b) –32

c) Zero

8 What colour light has the highest frequency?

a) Violet

b) Red

c) Indigo

9 Who said that 'to every action there is an equal and opposite reaction'?

a) Albert Einstein

b) Sir Isaac Newton

c) Stephen Hawking

10 What does the 'c' stand for in $E=mc^2$?

a) Coulomb

b) Candela

c) The speed of light

A

1 c

2 a

3 a

4 b

5 c

6 c

7 a

8 a

9 b

10 c

SCIENCE

WEATHER

1 **What is measured by an anemometer?**

a) Rainfall

b) Atmospheric pressure

c) Wind speed

2 **Where was the 20th century's highest temperature of 136°F (58°C) recorded in 1922?**

a) Pad Idan, Pakistan

b) Death Valley, California

c) Al Aziziyah, Libya

3 **From which language does the word 'monsoon', meaning a season of rain, originate?**

a) Arabic

b) Cantonese

c) Hindi

4 **What is the name of the area of low atmospheric pressure along the equator where calm winds can suddenly become storms?**

a) The Tropic of Cancer

b) The Doldrums

c) The Sargasso Sea

5 **Which of the following is a rain cloud?**

a) Stratus

b) Nimbus

c) Cumulus

6 Most snowflakes form regular patterns of how many sides?

a) Six

b) Eight

c) Twelve

7 Why do the Northern Lights usually only occur at the North and South Poles?

a) There is too much light pollution for us to see them elsewhere

b) The poles are not protected by the Earth's magnetic field

c) The rest of the world is not cold enough

8 What does SAD stand for?

a) Seasonal Affective Disorder

b) Sunshine-Affected Depression

c) Solar Adjusted Distress

9 What name refers to the cooling of the central and Eastern Pacific?

a) El Niña

b) La Niña

c) Los Niños

10 A drought in the UK used to be defined as how many days without rain?

a) 15

b) 30

c) 40

A

1 c

2 c

3 a

4 b

5 b

6 a

7 b

8 a

9 b

10 a

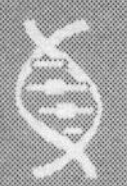

Q QUACKS AND FALLACIES

1 The name of which traditional Chinese medicine has become a synonym for fake, fraudulent or ineffective medicines?

a) Velvet antler

b) Pearl powder

c) Snake oil

2 What did American peddler John R. Brinkley propose as a cure for male impotence?

a) Exposure to the sea air on the coast of Brinkley's native North Carolina

b) Implanting goat glands into the testicles

c) Rubbing stem ginger on the rectum

3 What ailment was the soft drink 7 Up originally supposed to cure?

a) A hangover

b) Dyspepsia

c) A migraine

4 Which of the following statements about TV health specialist Gillian McKeith is not true?

a) She dropped the prefix Dr after complaints about her academic credentials

b) She was censored for selling unproven herbal sex aids

c) She used to weigh 22 stone

5 Which cereal magnate ran a sanatorium in the 19th century with an emphasis on holistic medicine?

a) John Harvey Kellogg

b) William Jordan

c) Robert Quaker

A

1 c

2 b

3 a

4 c

5 a

SPORT

BOXING

CRICKET

HORSE RACING

FOOTBALL

SPORTING INJURIES

SPORTING NICKNAMES

RIVALRIES

GOLF

OLYMPICS

GREAT COMEBACKS

RUGBY

YOUNG PRETENDERS AND GOLDEN OLDIES

MOTOR SPORTS

BIZARRE SPORTS

SNOW AND ICE

TENNIS

SPORTING TROPHIES

BOXING

1 Who did Muhammad Ali (then Cassius Clay) defeat to win his first world heavyweight title in 1965?

a) Bob Fitzsimmons

b) Sonny Liston

c) Joe Frazier

---

2 Who was the only undefeated world heavyweight champion of the last hundred years, winning all 49 of the professional bouts he fought?

a) Floyd Patterson

b) Jack Dempsey

c) Rocky Marciano

---

3 What is the lightest class in boxing, with a maximum weight of 48kg?

a) Flyweight

b) Strawweight

c) Featherweight

---

4 Which country was Lennox Lewis representing when he won his Olympic gold medal for boxing in 1988?

a) Canada

b) Great Britain

c) USA

---

5 Mike Tyson became the youngest heavyweight champion ever when he beat Trevor Berbick in 1986 – how old was he?

a) 17 years 11 months

b) 19 years 2 months

c) 20 years 4 months

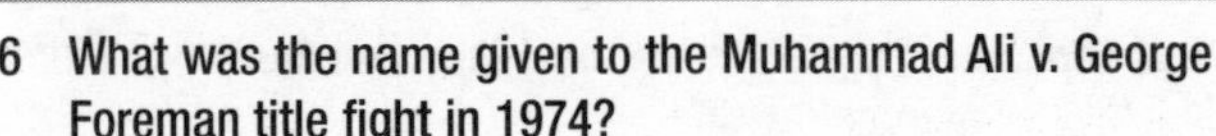

6 What was the name given to the Muhammad Ali v. George Foreman title fight in 1974?

a) The Fight of the Century

b) The Rumble in the Jungle

c) The Thriller in Manila

7 Which 21st-century singer-songwriter shares his name with an American boxing champion of the early 1900s?

a) Jack Johnson

b) Newton Faulkner

c) Ben Harper

8 At how many different weight divisions did 'Sugar' Ray Leonard win world titles?

a) 5

b) 4

c) 3

9 How did the pre-1914 British heavyweight champion Bombardier Billy Wells reach an even bigger audience after his boxing career ended?

a) He played the character of Tarzan in two silent movies

b) He was the BBC's boxing commentator for over 30 years

c) He was the man who banged the gong at the beginning of Rank films

10 Which boxer coined the phrase 'He can run, but he can't hide'?

a) Henry Cooper

b) Joe Louis

c) Sam Langford

A

1 b

2 c

3 b

4 a

5 c

6 b

7 a

8 a

9 c

10 b

CRICKET

1 Who has captained England in the most test matches?

a) Peter May

b) Mike Brearley

c) Mike Atherton

2 Who won the inaugural Cricket World Cup in 1975?

a) Australia

b) West Indies

c) England

3 Which English bowler was at the centre of the 'bodyline' controversy in the 1930s?

a) Freddie Trueman

b) Harold Larwood

c) Wilfred Rhodes

4 'The bowler's Holding, the batsman's Willey', but who was the commentator?

a) Jonathan Agnew

b) Brian Johnston

c) Henry Blofeld

5 The legendary Victorian cricketer W. G. Grace captained England at cricket and what other sport?

a) Bowls

b) Real Tennis

c) Billiards

SPORT

6 Which player scored a 57-ball century against England in December 2006?

a) Ricky Ponting

b) Matthew Hayden

c) Adam Gilchrist

7 In which city is cricket played at the Wankhede stadium?

a) Mumbai

b) Galle

c) Port Elizabeth

8 Which West Indian fast bowler was nicknamed 'Whispering Death'?

a) Joel Garner

b) Michael Holding

c) Malcolm Marshall

9 Which batsman was the victim of Shane Warne's 'ball of the century' at Old Trafford in 1993?

a) Alec Stewart

b) Graham Gooch

c) Mike Gatting

10 Who is the only player to score a double century and a century on his Test match debut?

a) Don Bradman (Australia)

b) Lawrence Rowe (West Indies)

c) Zaheer Abbas (Pakistan)

A

1 c

2 b

3 b

4 b

5 a

6 c

7 a

8 b

9 c

10 b

Q HORSE RACING

1 Which of the following races is not one of the five 'Classics' of English racing?

a) The Grand National

b) The Cheltenham Gold Cup

c) The Derby

2 Which race is renowned in its home country as being 'the most exciting two minutes in sports'?

a) The USA's Kentucky Derby

b) Australia's Melbourne Cup

c) France's Prix de l'Arc de Triomphe

3 The oldest of the five 'Classics', in which year was the first St Leger Stakes run?

a) 1749

b) 1776

c) 1791

4 What is the official name for jump racing?

a) Steeplechasing

b) Hurdle Races

c) National Hunt

5 Which of these races is for fillies only?

a) The Derby

b) The 2,000 Guineas

c) The Oaks

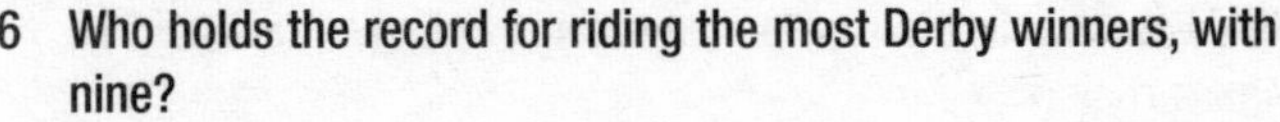

6 **Who holds the record for riding the most Derby winners, with nine?**

a) Willie Carson

b) Lester Piggott

c) Pat Eddery

7 **Coming home first in 1919 at 11/4, what was the shortest-priced winner of the Grand National?**

a) Poethlyn

b) Bogskar

c) Old Joe

8 **Which famous racehorse won the Cheltenham Gold Cup three years in succession in the 1960s?**

a) Red Rum

b) Desert Orchid

c) Arkle

9 **Which racecourse is said to be the oldest in England, with horse racing going back to 1539?**

a) Uttoxeter

b) Chester

c) Chepstow

10 **In which month of the year is Royal Ascot held?**

a) April

b) June

c) August

A

1 b
2 a
3 b
4 c
5 c
6 b
7 a
8 c
9 c
10 b

Q FOOTBALL

1 Who was the first million-pound signing in English football?

a) Trevor Francis

b) Kevin Keegan

c) Denis Law

2 For which team did David Beckham make his Football League debut, while on loan from Manchester United?

a) Preston North End

b) Blackburn Rovers

c) Bolton Wanderers

3 Which country won the first ever World Cup in 1930?

a) Italy

b) Brazil

c) Uruguay

4 In 1970 which African nation was the first ever to qualify for the World Cup finals?

a) Morocco

b) Cameroon

c) Tunisia

5 Who is the only player ever to have scored a hat-trick in a Wembley FA Cup final?

a) Stan Mortensen

b) Geoff Hurst

c) Jimmy Greaves

6 **Which manager was conned into signing Ali Dia, a part-time player, because he had been told Dia was the cousin of AC Milan legend George Weah?**

a) Kenny Dalglish

b) Graham Souness

c) Walter Smith

7 **Which goalkeeper was the first to save a penalty in an FA Cup Final?**

a) Pat Jennings

b) Dave Beasant

c) David Seaman

8 **What was the first club managed by Sir Alex Ferguson?**

a) East Stirling

b) St Mirren

c) Aberdeen

9 **In 2005, which club became the only European Cup winners to fall into its country's third tier?**

a) Nottingham Forest

b) Leeds United

c) Southampton

10 **Which Scottish team twice reached the English FA Cup Final in the 1880s and were twice beaten by Blackburn Rovers?**

a) Queen's Park

b) Dundee United

c) Rangers

A

1	a
2	a
3	c
4	a
5	a
6	b
7	b
8	a
9	a
10	a

SPORT

Q SPORTING INJURIES

1 **Which England cricketer broke an ankle trying to climb a drainpipe to get into his house after snapping a key in the lock of the front door?**

a) Ian Greig

b) Jonathan Agnew

c) Phil Tufnell

2 **Which Arsenal midfielder broke his arm whilst celebrating a goal with Tony Adams (and subsequently missed the FA Cup Final)?**

a) Paul Merson

b) Perry Groves

c) Steve Morrow

3 **Which goalkeeper played the last 15 minutes of the 1956 FA Cup Final with a broken neck?**

a) Bert Trautmann

b) William Foulke

c) Harald Schumacher

4 **What happened to long jumper Salim Sdiri as he waited to compete at a Golden League meeting in 2007?**

a) He was struck in the side by a javelin

b) A shot put landed on his foot

c) A discuss knocked him unconscious

5 **Whose ear did Mike Tyson take a liking to during a 1997 fight?**

a) Nigel Benn

b) Wladimir Klitschko

c) Evander Holyfield

6 After striking him in the face with a short-pitched delivery, whose nose cartilage did West Indian Malcolm Marshall pull out of the ball in a Test match against England in 1986?

a) Mike Atherton

b) Mike Gatting

c) Mike Smith

---

7 Which tennis player was stabbed in the back by Gunter Parche, a fan of her opponent, Steffi Graf, in 1993?

a) Jennifer Capriati

b) Monica Seles

c) Conchita Martinez

---

8 Which unfortunate AC Milan player was both hit by a flare thrown by a member of the crowd in 2005 and punched by a fan during a pitch invasion in 2007?

a) Dida

b) Serginho

c) Ronaldo

---

9 How did Swiss footballer Paulo Diogo injure himself while celebrating an assist in 2004?

a) He ripped a finger off when hurdling the fence separating the pitch from the supporters

b) He broke a leg after an incorrect landing from a backflip

c) He caught his foot on the advertising boards and fell, breaking his nose

---

10 Which Formula One circuit saw the death of Ayrton Senna in 1994?

a) Monaco

b) Hockenheim

c) Imola

A

1 a
2 c
3 a
4 a
5 c
6 b
7 b
8 a
9 a
10 c

Q SPORTING NICKNAMES

1 Why are Dundee United FC nicknamed the Arabs?

a) They used to play on a very sandy pitch

b) They used to be owned by an Arab oil sheikh

c) Their ground is on Arabian Road

2 In American football, what are the San Diego Chargers also known as?

a) The Bolts

b) The Nuts

c) The Screws

3 What is former cricket umpire 'Dickie' Bird's first name?

a) William

b) Richard

c) Harold

4 The Barbarians, an invitational rugby union team, is also known by which nickname?

a) The Barbies

b) The Baa-Baas

c) The Baboons

5 What is the official name of West Ham United FC's ground, commonly called by its nickname of Upton Park?

a) Boleyn Ground

b) Seymour Park

c) Aragon Lane

6 Which former England football captain was known as Captain Marvel?

a) Bobby Moore

b) Bryan Robson

c) Billy Wright

7 Phil 'The Power' Taylor, Jelle 'The Love Machine' Klaasen and Andy 'The Viking' Fordham are associated with which sport?

a) Bowls

b) Snooker

c) Darts

8 Panamanian boxer Roberto Durán earned which nickname?

a) Hands of Stone

b) Bonecrusher

c) The Real Deal

9 Which American football team did William 'The Fridge' Perry play, and win a Super Bowl in 1986, with?

a) Chicago Bears

b) Washington Redskins

c) San Francisco 49ers

10 El Niño is the nickname of which golfer?

a) Seve Ballesteros

b) José Maria Olazábal

c) Sergio Garcia

A

1 a
2 a
3 c
4 b
5 a
6 b
7 c
8 a
9 a
10 c

SPORT

Q RIVALRIES

1 Who won more Grand Slam singles tennis titles – Bjorn Borg or John McEnroe?

a) Borg

b) McEnroe

c) They won the same number

2 Where did Bobby Fischer and Boris Spassky contest the World Chess Championship?

a) St Petersburg

b) Las Vegas

c) Reykjavik

3 Which member of the *Blackadder* cast rowed for Cambridge in the University Boat Race?

a) Stephen Fry

b) Hugh Laurie

c) Rowan Atkinson

4 Phil Chisnall in 1964 was the last player to transfer between which two rival football clubs?

a) Liverpool and Manchester United

b) Arsenal and Tottenham Hotspur

c) Celtic and Rangers

5 Which two teams contest Rugby Union's Calcutta Cup?

a) England and Scotland

b) Australia and New Zealand

c) Wales and Ireland

SPORT

6 **Which English striker has scored a hat-trick in the Barcelona v Real Madrid derby?**

a) Mark Hughes

b) Michael Owen

c) Gary Lineker

7 **Which golfer has won the most points in Ryder Cup history?**

a) Nick Faldo

b) Seve Ballesteros

c) Sam Torrence

8 **Martina Navratilova and Chris Evert won 18 of the 19 tennis grand slams between 1982 and 1986. Who won the other?**

a) Tracy Austin

b) Hana Mandlikova

c) Mima Jausovec

9 **How many times has Stephen Hendry beaten Jimmy White in the final of snooker's World Championship?**

a) 2

b) 3

c) 4

10 **Who has taken the most wickets in the history of the Ashes?**

a) Glenn McGrath

b) Shane Warne

c) Ian Botham

A

1 a
2 c
3 b
4 a
5 a
6 c
7 a
8 b
9 c
10 b

GOLF

1 Three players have won back-to-back Masters titles. Jack Nicklaus and Tiger Woods are two, who is the other?

a) Nick Faldo

b) Seve Ballesteros

c) Bernhard Langer

2 Which US Open winner was killed in a plane crash in 1999?

a) Curtis Strange

b) Payne Stewart

c) Fuzzy Zoeller

3 When was the British Open first held?

a) 1860

b) 1875

c) 1890

4 Which British golfer was quoted as saying that once he reaches his potential, 'it will just be me and Tiger'?

a) Ian Poulter

b) Lee Westwood

c) Justin Rose

5 Who captained the European team that won the Ryder Cup in 2006?

a) Bernhard Langer

b) Colin Montgomerie

c) Ian Woosnam

6 **Which Scottish golf course has a hole nicknamed 'the Postage Stamp'?**

a) Muirfield

b) Troon

c) St Andrews

7 **What is the name of the women's equivalent of the Ryder Cup?**

a) Littlejohn Vase

b) Segrave Trophy

c) Solheim Cup

8 **Which of the following is a genuine name of a wooden-shafted pre-1900 golf club?**

a) Mashie

b) Bashie

c) Crashie

9 **If one under par is a birdie and two under par is an eagle, what is three under?**

a) Emu

b) Turkey

c) Albatross

10 **What are the yips?**

a) A slang term for the crowd who follow a particular player obsessively

b) An involuntary muscle movement often blamed for missed putts

c) Divots left in a fairway from a previous player's driver

A

1 a
2 b
3 a
4 a
5 c
6 b
7 c
8 a
9 c
10 b

Q OLYMPICS

1 What was the name of the French nobleman who initiated the revival of the Olympic Games in the 1890s?

a) De Richelieu

b) De Lesseps

c) De Coubertin

2 Which US swimmer won a record seven gold medals in the 1972 Munich Olympics?

a) Mark Spitz

b) John Naber

c) Don Schollander

3 In which year did women first compete in the Olympic Games?

a) 1900

b) 1908

c) 1920

4 What is the Latin motto of the Olympic movement?

a) Per Ardua ad Astra

b) Ad Valorem

c) Citius, Altius, Fortius

5 Who won gold in the men's 200m freestyle at the Athens Olympics in 2004, dubbed the 'Race of the Century' because it contained the four fastest swimmers in history?

a) Ian Thorpe

b) Grant Hackett

c) Michael Phelps

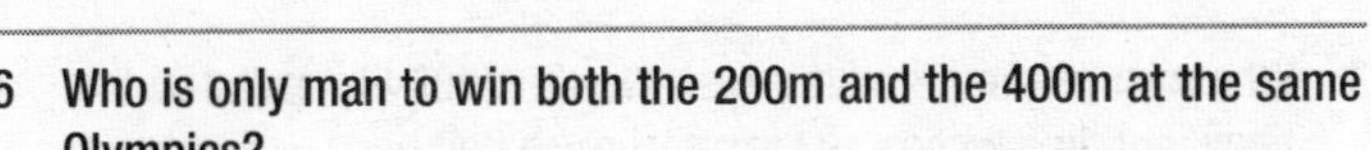

6 **Who is only man to win both the 200m and the 400m at the same Olympics?**

a) Carl Lewis

b) Jesse Owens

c) Michael Johnson

7 **How old was Merlene Ottey when she won bronze in the women's 100m at the Sydney Olympics in 2000?**

a) 36

b) 38

c) 40

8 **Which of the following sports was an Olympic sport from 1900 to 1920?**

a) Croquet

b) Tug of War

c) Lacrosse

9 **Who was the first female gymnast to gain a perfect score of 10.00 in an Olympic competition?**

a) Olga Korbut

b) Nadia Comaneci

c) Ludmilla Tourischeva

10 **At which Olympics was Ben Johnson disqualified from the men's 100m after setting a new world record?**

a) 1984

b) 1988

c) 1992

A

1 c
2 a
3 a
4 c
5 a
6 c
7 c
8 b
9 b
10 b

GREAT COMEBACKS

1 Who missed the decisive penalty in the 2005 European Cup Final, handing victory to Liverpool, who had been 3–0 down at half-time?

a) Kaka

b) Clarence Seedorf

c) Andriy Shevchenko

2 Which Indian batsman scored 281 against Australia in 2001 to win a test match after being forced to follow on?

a) Rahul Dravid

b) Sachin Tendulkar

c) V. V. S. Laxman

3 Which tennis player recovered from breaking his neck in a collision with the net post in 2004 to reach the top ten in the world rankings?

a) Mardy Fish

b) James Blake

c) Andy Roddick

4 Who took 8–43 in the 1981 Ashes Test at Headingley to bowl out Australia for 111 and win the match for England?

a) Bob Willis

b) Phil Edmonds

c) Chris Old

5 Who recovered from 8–0 down to beat Steve Davis 18–17 at the 1985 World Snooker Championship?

a) Cliff Thorburn

b) Joe Johnson

c) Dennis Taylor

6 **Who scored 28 points for France as they came back from 24–10 down to beat New Zealand 43–31 in their 1999 Rugby World Cup semi-final?**

a) Christophe Dominici

b) Raphael Ibanez

c) Christophe Lamaison

7 **Who scored the winning goal in Manchester United's European Cup Final win over Bayern Munich in 1999?**

a) Andy Cole

b) Teddy Sheringham

c) Ole Gunnar Solskjaer

8 **What was Goran Ivanisevic's world ranking when he won Wimbledon in 2001?**

a) 12

b) 125

c) 1,250

9 **Which F1 driver returned to the track just six weeks after a crash so severe that a priest performed his last rites?**

a) Alain Prost

b) Niki Lauda

c) Jean Alesi

10 **How many consecutive Tour de France wins did Lance Armstrong achieve after recovering from testicular cancer?**

a) 3

b) 5

c) 7

A

1 c
2 c
3 b
4 a
5 c
6 c
7 c
8 b
9 b
10 c

RUGBY

1 **Which All Black player scored four tries against England in the semi-final of the 1995 Rugby Union World Cup?**

a) Andrew Mehrtens

b) Jonah Lomu

c) Sean Fitzpatrick

2 **Who won the rugby gold medal in 1924, the last time the sport was played at the Olympics?**

a) Australia

b) France

c) USA

3 **In which year did a number of clubs in northern England break away from Rugby Union, leading to the founding of Rugby League as a separate sport?**

a) 1895

b) 1909

c) 1926

4 **Which Rugby League club play at The Jungle?**

a) Wakefield Trinity Wildcats

b) Castleford Tigers

c) Hull Kingston Rovers

5 **Who scored England's try in the Rugby Union 2003 World Cup Final?**

a) Will Greenwood

b) Josh Lewsey

c) Jason Robinson

6 Which English Rugby Union player is known as 'the fun bus'?

a) Jason Leonard

b) Andrew Sheridan

c) Martin Johnson

7 In 1972, Salford's David Watkins embarked on the longest scoring run in Rugby League history – how many consecutive matches did he score in?

a) 48

b) 92

c) 134

8 Who was the first English player to win 50 Rugby Union international caps?

a) Jonny Wilkinson

b) Rob Andrew

c) Rory Underwood

9 Which Rugby League player has won the Challenge Cup a record nine times?

a) Shaun Edwards

b) Iestyn Harris

c) Frano Botica

10 What is the country of birth of England Rugby Union players Matt Stevens and Mike Catt?

a) New Zealand

b) Australia

c) South Africa

A

1 b

2 c

3 a

4 b

5 c

6 a

7 b

8 c

9 a

10 c

YOUNG PRETENDERS AND GOLDEN OLDIES

1 Who was the 20th century's youngest tennis grand slam singles champion, at the age of 16 years and 3 months?

a) Martina Hingis

b) Maria Sharapova

c) Steffi Graf

2 Who scored his first Premier League goal against Arsenal in 2002 at the age of 16?

a) Michael Owen

b) Theo Walcott

c) Wayne Rooney

3 Who competed in his last Test match aged 50?

a) Donald Bradman

b) Richie Benaud

c) W. G. Grace

4 How old was Steve Redgrave when he won his fifth and final Olympic gold in 2000?

a) 36

b) 38

c) 40

5 Who is the youngest person to win a Formula One grand prix?

a) Lewis Hamilton

b) Kimi Raikkonen

c) Fernando Alonso

6 **How many years separated Martina Navaratilova's first and last grand slam wins?**

a) 26

b) 29

c) 32

7 **Who is the oldest goal scorer at the World Cup finals?**

a) Romario

b) Roger Milla

c) Gabriel Batistuta

8 **How old was British golfer Justin Rose when he finished fourth at The Open in 1998?**

a) 17

b) 19

c) 21

9 **Who was the youngest member of England's victorious 1966 World Cup squad?**

a) Alan Ball

b) Geoff Hurst

c) Martin Peters

10 **What age was the oldest Olympic champion Oscar Swahn, who won gold in a team event in 1920?**

a) 52

b) 62

c) 72

A

1 a

2 c

3 c

4 b

5 c

6 c

7 b

8 a

9 a

10 c

MOTOR SPORTS

1 Which Formula One driver was the youngest to become world champion, at the age of 24?

a) Emerson Fittipaldi

b) Michael Schumacher

c) Fernando Alonso

2 Which manufacturer is by far the most successful in the history of the Superbike World Championship?

a) Ducati

b) Honda

c) Suzuki

3 Which driver became the first Briton to win the World Rally Championship?

a) Richard Burns

b) Colin McRae

c) Roger Clark

4 What instrument does motorcyclist James Toseland play?

a) Bass guitar

b) Piano

c) Drums

5 With 31 race victories, who is Britain's most successful Formula One driver?

a) Jim Clark

b) Jackie Stewart

c) Nigel Mansell

6 **Andy Priaulx won three consecutive world championships between 2005–2007 in which category of motor sport?**

a) Touring car racing

b) Powerboat racing

c) Speedway

7 **How was Formula One driver Lewis Hamilton honoured in his home town of Stevenage?**

a) The council granted him use of all bus lanes

b) A supermarket kept a reserved space for him at all times

c) His portrait was painted on to all mini-roundabouts

8 **What speeds can drag racers reach in competition?**

a) 260mph

b) 295mph

c) 330mph

9 **Which of the following is the only driver to win the Formula One world championship, the Indianapolis 500 and Le Mans in his career?**

a) Mario Andretti

b) Graham Hill

c) Jochen Rindt

10 **Who was the last British motorcyclist to win any category (MotoGP, 250cc or 125cc) of FIM Grand Prix World Championship?**

a) Barry Sheene

b) John Surtees

c) Phil Read

A

1 c
2 a
3 b
4 b
5 c
6 b
7 b
8 c
9 b
10 a

Q BIZARRE SPORTS

1 Which of the following is a genuine sport, founded in 2003, with its own governing body and world championships?

a) Sand hockey

b) Rugby golf

c) Chess boxing

2 When was the Mobile Phone Throwing World Championships, an annual event in Finland, first held?

a) 1994

b) 2000

c) 2006

3 Sepak takraw, originating in South-East Asia, is best described as containing elements of which two sports?

a) Squash and handball

b) Football and volleyball

c) Darts and bowls

4 The World Bog Snorkelling Championships are contested in Wales over two 60m peat bog trenches – what is the world record time for completing the course?

a) 1min 35sec

b) 4min 05sec

c) 9min 15sec

5 The Cooper's Hill cheese rolling festival in Gloucestershire involves running and tumbling down a very steep hill after a cheese travelling at up to what speed?

a) 35mph

b) 50mph

c) 70mph

6 What is the main prize awarded for the winners of the Wife Carrying World Championships?

a) The wife's weight in beer

b) The wife's weight in potatoes

c) The wife's weight in live poultry

7 What must an attacking team member do at all times during the Bangladeshi game of kabbadi?

a) Hop on one leg

b) Hold their breath

c) Run backwards

8 Tejo, played by throwing a metallic plate at a gunpowder-filled target, is a traditional game from which country?

a) Colombia

b) Guatemala

c) Mexico

9 In the Central Asian sport of buzkashi, what must be cleared over the opponents' goal line to score a point?

a) A 20kg stone column

b) An eagle egg

c) A headless calf or goat

10 Which English county is home to the obscure game of dwile flonking?

a) Suffolk

b) Dorset

c) Staffordshire

A

1 c
2 b
3 b
4 a
5 c
6 a
7 b
8 a
9 c
10 a

Q SNOW AND ICE

1 Where does the 1,150 mile Iditarod, an annual dog sled race, take place?

a) Iceland

b) Russia

c) Alaska

2 Bjorn Einar Romoren was airborne for over eight seconds and travelled how far while setting the ski-jumping world record?

a) 192m

b) 239m

c) 278m

3 What is unusual about the Stanley Cup, ice hockey's most famous trophy?

a) It is only 8cm tall, making it one of the smallest trophies in world sport

b) Each player on the winning team takes possession of it for 24 hours

c) It is the fifth incarnation of the trophy, the others having been lost or stolen

4 Bjorn Daehlie of Norway is the most successful Winter Olympian of all time, with eight golds and four silvers – in what discipline?

a) Cross-country skiing

b) Luge

c) Figure skating

5 Which of the following is not true of Steven Bradbury, an Australian skater who won gold at the 1,000m short track event at the 2002 Winter Olympics?

a) He won following crashes of opponents in the semi-final and final

b) He was mistaken for an Austrian and the wrong national anthem was played

c) His was the first gold medal won by a southern hemisphere country

6 Other than skiing, what is the other pursuit of the biathlon cross-country event?

a) Rifle shooting

b) Archery

c) Crossbow shooting

7 Which city has been chosen to host the 2014 Winter Olympics?

a) Salzburg, Austria

b) Sochi, Russia

c) Pyeongchang, South Korea

8 What was the name of the book written by Eddie 'The Eagle' Edwards, Britain's one-time ski-jumping record holder?

a) *Where Eagle's Dared*

b) *Snow Joke*

c) *On the Piste*

9 Which of the following was not an event included at the first Winter Olympics in 1924?

a) Ice hockey

b) Figure skating

c) Luge

10 Shaun White from the USA is a renowned competitor in which winter sport?

a) Snowboarding

b) Freestyle skiing

c) Bob skeleton

A

1 c
2 b
3 b
4 a
5 b
6 a
7 b
8 c
9 c
10 a

SPORT

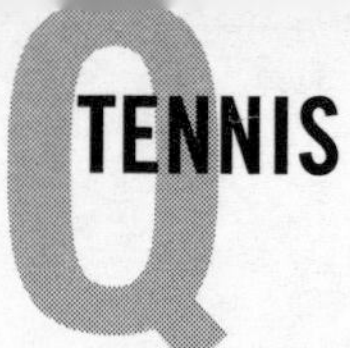

TENNIS

1 Who did Roger Federer beat at Wimbledon in 2003 to win his first grand slam title?

a) Goran Ivanisevic

b) Andre Agassi

c) Mark Philippoussis

2 Which female tennis player cried on the shoulder of the Duchess of Kent after losing a Wimbledon final to Steffi Graf?

a) Jana Novotna

b) Arantxia Sanchez Vicario

c) Monica Seles

3 Who defeated Greg Rusedski at the US Open in 1997?

a) Todd Martin

b) Pat Rafter

c) Marat Safin

4 Who was the only player to beat Pete Sampras at Wimbledon between 1993 and 2000?

a) Richard Krajicek

b) Tim Henman

c) Carlos Moya

5 Which female player holds the record for the most grand slam singles titles?

a) Margaret (Smith) Court

b) Martina Navratilova

c) Chris Evert

6 Who was the last British male player to win a grand slam singles title?

a) Tim Henman

b) Roger Taylor

c) Fred Perry

7 On what surface are the French Open championships played?

a) Grass

b) Clay

c) Hard Court

8 Who played fictional champion Peter Colt in the 2004 film *Wimbledon*?

a) Christian Bale

b) Paul Bettany

c) Jonathan Rhys Meyers

9 Who did Virginia Wade beat in the final to win her 1977 Wimbledon women's singles title?

a) Billie Jean King

b) Betty Stove

c) Martina Navratilova

10 What unenviable feat was set by Lleyton Hewitt in 2004?

a) He recorded the longest losing run on the ATP tour

b) He became the first man to be defeated by the eventual winner in each of the four grand slams

c) He made the most unforced errors recorded in a match

A

1 c

2 a

3 b

4 a

5 a

6 c

7 b

8 b

9 b

10 b

Q SPORTING TROPHIES

In which sports can individuals or teams win the following trophies or awards?

1 Doggett's Coat and Badge

a) Croquet

b) Rowing

c) Shooting

2 Cartier Award

a) Real Tennis

b) Polo

c) Horse racing

3 Curtis Cup

a) Hockey

b) Tennis

c) Golf

4 Man of Steel Award

a) Rugby League

b) Boxing

c) Triathlon

5 Lorenzo Bandini Trophy

a) Formula One

b) Cycling

c) Baseball

6 Ballon d'Or

a) Boules

b) Football

c) Snooker

7 Webb Ellis Cup

a) Darts

b) Rugby Union

c) Cricket

8 Louis Vuitton Cup

a) Ice Skating

b) Skiing

c) Yachting

9 Golden Bagel Award

a) Basketball

b) Tennis

c) Weightlifting

10 Lugano Cup

a) Race walking

b) Cycling

c) Skiing

A

1 b
2 c
3 c
4 a
5 a
6 b
7 b
8 c
9 b
10 a

GENERAL KNOWLEDGE

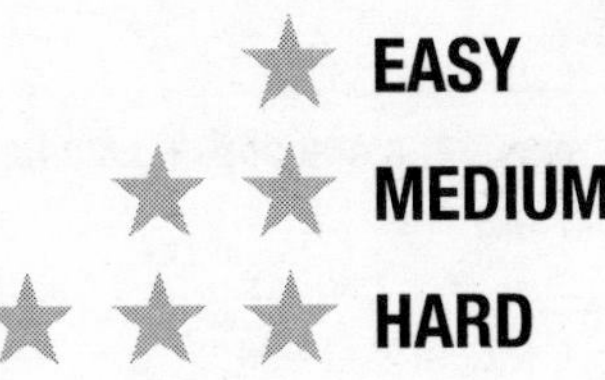

EASY – PART 1

1 What was the name of the Lone Ranger's horse?

a) Trigger

b) Champion

c) Silver

2 Who played the Sheriff of Nottingham to Kevin Costner's Robin Hood in *Robin Hood, Prince of Thieves*?

a) Alan Rickman

b) Steven Berkoff

c) Anthony Hopkins

3 What type of animal is a taipan?

a) Rodent

b) Snake

c) Tortoise

4 What do the French call custard?

a) Crème anglais

b) Crème brulée

c) Coutarde

5 Who wrote Sinead O'Connor's 1989 hit single 'Nothing Compares 2 U'?

a) Madonna

b) Prince

c) Phil Collins

GENERAL KNOWLEDGE ★

6 **What did Sid James and Tommy Cooper have in common?**

a) They both died on stage

b) They both fathered nine children

c) They were both nominated for, but failed to win, BAFTAs

7 **How did Mary Queen of Scots meet her death in 1587?**

a) She was beheaded

b) She was poisoned

c) She was hung, drawn and quartered

8 **If David Bowie is the Thin White Duke and Elvis is the King, what is Jim Morrison?**

a) The Reptile King

b) The Crocodile King

c) The Lizard King

9 **When was George Lucas' *Star Wars* released?**

a) 1971

b) 1977

c) 1983

10 **The highest temperature recorded in Britain occurred in Gravesend, Kent, in 2003 – how hot was it?**

a) 36.3°C

b) 38.1°C

c) 41.8°C

A

1 c

2 a

3 b

4 a

5 b

6 a

7 a

8 c

9 b

10 b

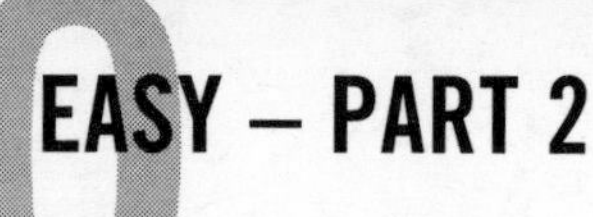

EASY – PART 2

1 What was the name of Steven Spielberg's first full-length feature film?

a) *Jaws*

b) *The Sugarland Express*

c) *Duel*

2 Who succeeded Magnus Magnusson as the quizmaster on *Mastermind*?

a) Jeremy Paxman

b) John Humphrys

c) Michael Aspel

3 In which decade was Parliament first televised?

a) 1970s

b) 1980s

c) 1990s

4 What is the name of Edina's daughter in *Absolutely Fabulous*?

a) Posy

b) Saffron

c) Bluebell

5 What colour is a giraffe's tongue?

a) Blue

b) Yellow

c) Red

GENERAL KNOWLEDGE ★

6 **Which salad vegetable is the main ingredient in the Greek dish tzatziki?**

a) Tomato

b) Cucumber

c) Lettuce

7 **How many upper-case typewritten letters in the English alphabet would be identical to their mirror image?**

a) 10

b) 11

c) 12

8 **What colour does a Chinese bride traditionally wear?**

a) Red

b) White

c) Purple

9 **What is the highest valued poker hand?**

a) Full house

b) Four-of-a-kind

c) Royal flush

10 **Which of the following is not one of the 'three cardinal virtues'?**

a) Hope

b) Temperance

c) Charity

1 c
2 b
3 b
4 b
5 a
6 b
7 b
8 a
9 c
10 b

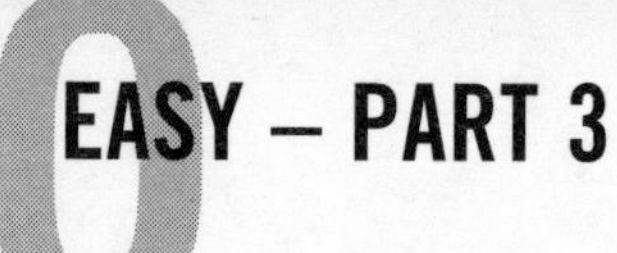

EASY – PART 3

1 What was the name of the TV and film production company founded by Prince Edward?

a) Ardent

b) Argent

c) Urgent

2 In which English county is Tewkesbury?

a) Shropshire

b) Gloucestershire

c) Herefordshire

3 How many names were there in the first British telephone directory, issued in 1880?

a) 55

b) 255

c) 1,555

4 In which body of water is Iceland?

a) Arctic Ocean

b) Atlantic Ocean

c) Baltic Sea

5 How many toes do camels have on each foot?

a) 2

b) 3

c) 4

6 What is the code name of Coca Cola's secret ingredient?

a) 7X

b) 10CC

c) 007K

7 How many sheets of paper are there in a ream?

a) 192

b) 500

c) 770

8 Which art gallery was founded by a 19th-century sugar magnate?

a) The Wallace Collection

b) The Guggenheim Museum of Modern Art

c) The Tate Gallery

9 Which of these pioneer women aviators disappeared while trying to fly around the world?

a) Amy Johnson

b) Amelia Earhart

c) Beryl Markham

10 Which of the following is not a rule of Shrovetide Football, a sporting event dating from the 12th century, played annually in Ashbourne, Derbyshire?

a) Do not murder or intentionally harm other players

b) Do not trespass on private property

c) Do not continue to play after 7pm

1 a

2 b

3 b

4 b

5 a

6 a

7 b

8 c

9 b

10 c

Q EASY – PART 4

1 Which Suffolk town is home to an annual music festival?

a) Southwold

b) Felixstowe

c) Aldeburgh

2 Who was the youngest of the Bronte sisters?

a) Emily

b) Charlotte

c) Anne

3 In which county is the botanical site known as the Eden Project?

a) Cornwall

b) Devon

c) Somerset

4 The grave of which legendary Briton supposedly lies under a platform at King's Cross station?

a) Robin Hood

b) King Arthur

c) Boudicca

5 Which poet of the First World War wrote *Anthem for Doomed Youth*?

a) Siegfried Sassoon

b) Wilfred Owen

c) Laurence Binyon

6 What was the name of Shakespeare's only son?

a) Hamlet

b) William

c) Hamnet

7 What is a natterjack?

a) Toad

b) Frog

c) Lizard

8 What are the principal ingredients of a Waldorf salad?

a) Apples, carrots and mayonnaise

b) Apples, celery and walnuts

c) Apples, cheese and grapes

9 Which of the following is a member of MENSA, the high intelligence society?

a) Geena Davis

b) Sandra Bullock

c) Charlize Theron

10 Which of the following ranks of the Order of the British Empire is the highest?

a) CBE

b) MBE

c) OBE

1 c
2 c
3 a
4 c
5 b
6 c
7 a
8 b
9 a
10 a

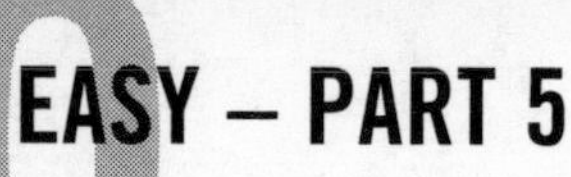

EASY – PART 5

1 In which British city is there a statue of the cartoon character Desperate Dan?

a) Cardiff

b) Birmingham

c) Dundee

2 To which institution are the royalties of J. M. Barrie's play Peter Pan paid?

a) The Red Cross

b) Great Ormond Street Hospital

c) The Natural History Museum

3 Henri Cartier-Bresson is best remembered for his work in which art form?

a) Dance

b) Architecture

c) Photography

4 How many pairs of legs does a house centipede have?

a) 5

b) 15

c) 100

5 Where was Worcestershire sauce invented?

a) England

b) Australia

c) India

6 Which is the highest mountain in the UK?

a) Ben Nevis

b) Scafell Pike

c) Snowdon

7 Which of the following languages has the most native speakers?

a) Russian

b) Arabic

c) Spanish

8 In the song, 'The Twelve Days of Christmas', how many ladies dancing were there?

a) Eight

b) Nine

c) Ten

9 What star-sign would you be if you were born on the 1 July?

a) Gemini

b) Cancer

c) Leo

10 In Cluedo, what was the name of the murder victim?

a) Dr Black

b) Lady Grey

c) Mr Pink

A

1 c

2 b

3 c

4 b

5 c

6 a

7 c

8 b

9 b

10 a

Q EASY – PART 6

1 What is another name for the snow leopard?

a) Ocelot

b) Ounce

c) Okapi

2 What were the names of the two ethnic groups involved in the Rwandan genocide of 1994?

a) Hutu and Tutsi

b) Masai and Kikuyu

c) Ibo and Yoruba

3 In which country did Aung San Suu Kyi lead a party that won national elections while she was under house arrest?

a) Burma

b) South Korea

c) Cambodia

4 What does an ichthyologist study?

a) Reptiles

b) Beetles

c) Fish

5 What does a sphygmomanometer measure?

a) Brain activity

b) Hearing

c) Blood pressure

6 Which famous sports team was established by former members of The Savoy Big Five?

a) The New York Yankees

b) The Harlem Globetrotters

c) The New York Knickerbockers

7 What is the first name of the Saatchi brother married to celebrity chef Nigella Lawson?

a) Charles

b) Maurice

c) Kevin

8 In what town do the Flintstones live?

a) Boulderville

b) Bedrock

c) Great Rock

9 What does the following description refer to: a quadrilateral whose opposite sides are parallel and equal in length?

a) Kite

b) Trapezium

c) Parallelogram

10 Where in London is Speakers' Corner?

a) Hyde Park

b) Piccadilly Circus

c) Trafalgar Square

1	b
2	a
3	a
4	c
5	c
6	b
7	a
8	b
9	c
10	a

Q EASY – PART 7

1 Which domestic dog breed is the heaviest?

a) Saint Bernard

b) Irish Wolfhound

c) English Setter

2 Which game is thought to have been invented in 1875 by a British army officer stationed in India?

a) Snooker

b) Table Tennis

c) Polo

3 Which car manufacturer's slogan is 'Vorsprung Durch Technik'?

a) Mercedes

b) Audi

c) Volkswagen

4 Which golfer was nicknamed 'The Golden Bear'?

a) Arnold Palmer

b) Jack Nicklaus

c) Lee Trevino

5 Which is the world's smallest independent state?

a) Liechtenstein

b) San Marino

c) Vatican City

6 **After how many years of marriage do you celebrate your tin wedding anniversary?**

a) 5

b) 10

c) 15

7 **In which British city can Haymarket and Waverley railway stations be found?**

a) Leeds

b) Manchester

c) Edinburgh

8 **What was the name of the police officer in the cartoon series *Top Cat*?**

a) Officer Drabble

b) Officer Dibble

c) Officer Dumble

9 **How many sides does a 50p coin have?**

a) 6

b) 7

c) 8

10 **Which of these characteristics is typical of a Siamese cat?**

a) Long hair

b) Loud meow

c) Striped coat

1 a
2 a
3 b
4 b
5 c
6 b
7 c
8 b
9 b
10 b

Q EASY – PART 8

1 In Monopoly which street joins Bow Street and Marlborough Street to complete a set?

a) Bond Street

b) Coventry Street

c) Vine Street

2 In a hockey game how many players in one team are allowed on the field at any one time?

a) 22

b) 16

c) 11

3 Who was the first member of the royal family to be interviewed on TV?

a) George VI

b) The Queen

c) Prince Philip

4 What breed of dog is Snoopy in the strip cartoon 'Peanuts'?

a) Beagle

b) Basset hound

c) Dachshund

5 In which year did *EastEnders* first appear on our TV screens?

a) 1982

b) 1985

c) 1988

6 What is the flavouring in ouzo?

a) Bergamot

b) Aniseed

c) Peppermint

7 What is a fox's den called?

a) Earth

b) Holt

c) Lair

8 In which gangster film did Al Pacino star as Tony Montana?

a) *Scarface*

b) *The Godfather*

c) *Donnie Brasco*

9 In which year did the £1 note cease to be legal tender in Britain?

a) 1986

b) 1988

c) 1990

10 What kind of creature is a pipistrelle?

a) Bird

b) Bat

c) Beetle

1 c

2 c

3 c

4 a

5 b

6 b

7 a

8 a

9 b

10 b

EASY – PART 9

1 Who was Dan Dare's evil enemy?

a) Lex Luthor

b) Emperor Ming the Merciless

c) The Mekon

2 In which country is there a leading football club called Boca Juniors?

a) Brazil

b) Argentina

c) Spain

3 Which James Bond film's theme song was written by Paul McCartney?

a) *Live and Let Die*

b) *The Living Daylights*

c) *You Only Live Twice*

4 Which famous annual sporting event did Miguel Indurain win every year from 1991 to 1995?

a) The Indianopolis 500

b) The Tour de France

c) The US Golf Masters

5 Who was the author of the books about Thomas the Tank Engine?

a) Reverend W. Awdry

b) Enid Blyton

c) Roger Dean

6 Which vegetable has varieties called 'globe' and 'Jerusalem'?

a) Artichoke

b) Cabbage

c) Broad bean

7 Which Roman goddess was the equivalent of Artemis, the Greek goddess of hunting?

a) Ceres

b) Diana

c) Venus

8 Which US president authorised the dropping of the atomic bombs on Hiroshima and Nagasaki?

a) Dwight Eisenhower

b) Franklin D. Roosevelt

c) Harry S. Truman

9 Which parts of the rhubarb are poisonous?

a) The stems

b) The leaves

c) The flowers

10 Of which legendary rock band was Syd Barrett once a member?

a) Deep Purple

b) Black Sabbath

c) Pink Floyd

A

1	c
2	b
3	a
4	b
5	a
6	a
7	b
8	c
9	b
10	c

GENERAL KNOWLEDGE

Q EASY – PART 10

1 In Ancient Rome, what colour was considered the symbol of imperial power?

a) Red

b) Purple

c) Yellow

2 On a dartboard which number is directly opposite 20?

a) 3

b) 2

c) 1

3 What do the initials V.S.O.P. stand for on a bottle of brandy?

a) Very Special Old Pale

b) Very Special Over Proof

c) Veritas Semper Omnia Plaudit

4 Which Shakespearean heroine spoke of her 'salad days when I was green in judgement'?

a) Lady Macbeth

b) Cleopatra

c) Juliet

5 Which comedian once said, 'I don't care to belong to any club that will have me as a member'?

a) Woody Allen

b) Charlie Chaplin

c) Groucho Marx

6 **Which classic English novel begins with the line, 'It is a truth universally acknowledged, that a single man in possession of a good fortune, must be in want of a wife'?**

a) Persuasion

b) Sense and Sensibility

c) Pride and Prejudice

7 **In which branch of science did Edwin Hubble achieve success?**

a) Physics

b) Biology

c) Astronomy

8 **What was lost and regained by John Milton?**

a) Reason

b) Paradise

c) Love

9 **What is the symbol for a mini roundabout on British roads?**

a) A red circle with a white background

b) A blue circle with white arrows

c) A white circle with black arrows

10 **Which road crossings are designed for both pedestrians and cyclists?**

a) Toucan

b) Pelican

c) Pegasus

A

1 b

2 a

3 a

4 b

5 c

6 c

7 c

8 b

9 b

10 a

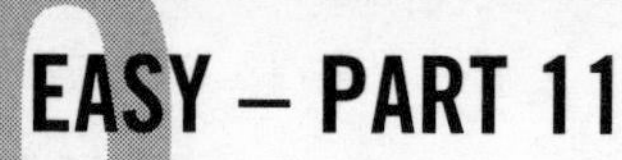

EASY – PART 11

1 Which vegetable did Mark Twain describe as 'nothing but a cabbage with a college education'?

a) Broccoli

b) Lettuce

c) Cauliflower

2 Who was the presenter of the first *Top of the Pops* programme?

a) Jimmy Savile

b) Tony Blackburn

c) Kenny Everett

3 Which American dramatist was once the husband of Marilyn Monroe?

a) Tennessee Williams

b) Arthur Miller

c) Eugene O'Neill

4 If you suffer from kleptophobia what do you fear?

a) Walking

b) Sleeping

c) Stealing

5 Which Hollywood actor was originally named Thomas Mapother IV?

a) Tom Hanks

b) Tom Waits

c) Tom Cruise

6 Which Charles Dickens novel features the character Uriah Heep?

a) *Dombey and Son*

b) *A Tale of Two Cities*

c) *David Copperfield*

7 How many hairs are on the average head?

a) 1,000

b) 100,000

c) 1,000,000

8 What ailment was Thalidomide first prescribed to treat?

a) Morning sickness

b) Bad breath

c) Headaches

9 What was the name of the voice who offered contestants 'a quick recap' on *Blind Date*?

a) George

b) Graham

c) Geoff

10 Which has the greatest area – North or South America?

a) North

b) South

c) They are both equal

1	c
2	a
3	b
4	c
5	c
6	c
7	b
8	a
9	b
10	a

EASY – PART 12

1 What gas mark is equivalent to 200°C?

a) 5

b) 6

c) 7

2 If 'Monday's child is fair of face, Tuesday's child is full of grace', what is Wednesday's child?

a) Has far to go

b) Loving and giving

c) Full of woe

3 Which of the following can fly backwards?

a) Woodpecker

b) Hummingbird

c) Kingfisher

4 What was the name of The Beatles' debut album?

a) *With the Beatles*

b) *Please Please Me*

c) *Help!*

5 According to the legend, in which street did Sweeney Todd keep his barbershop?

a) Oxford Street

b) Regent Street

c) Fleet Street

6 Who wrote *A Journey to the Centre of the Earth*?

a) Jules Verne

b) H. G. Wells

c) Robert Louis Stevenson

7 Which film features Roger Moore, Christopher Lee and Britt Ekland?

a) *Goldeneye*

b) *The Man with the Golden Gun*

c) *Goldfinger*

8 Who was the first winner of the UK *Big Brother*?

a) Brian Dowling

b) Kate Lawler

c) Craig Phillips

9 What is the capital of Turkey?

a) Ankara

b) Istanbul

c) Konya

10 Shylock is the central character in which Shakespeare play?

a) *As You Like It*

b) *The Winter's Tale*

c) *The Merchant of Venice*

1	b
2	c
3	b
4	b
5	c
6	a
7	b
8	c
9	a
10	c

Q EASY – PART 13

1 Where is Reykjavik?

a) Iceland

b) Sweden

c) Norway

2 Laurence Olivier is famous for acting in which type of film?

a) Silent

b) Comedy

c) Shakespearean adaptation

3 Which sea borders Romania?

a) Mediterranean

b) Black

c) North

4 How many people usually make up a jury for a criminal trial in England and Wales?

a) 8

b) 10

c) 12

5 In computing, what does RAM stand for?

a) Ready-altered Modem

b) Read All Messages

c) Random Access Memory

6 Which blood type can be given to anyone in a blood transfusion?

a) O negative

b) AB positive

c) A positive

7 St Mary's, Trevelyan and Hatfield are all colleges in which university?

a) Oxford

b) Cambridge

c) Durham

8 What rank in the Royal Navy is equivalent to General in the Army or Air Chief Marshal in the Royal Air Force?

a) Commodore

b) Admiral

c) Captain

9 Which is the correct spelling?

a) Allege

b) Alledge

c) Aledge

10 What was the first name of the Norwegian playwright Ibsen?

a) Henry

b) Henri

c) Henrik

1 a

2 c

3 b

4 c

5 c

6 a

7 c

8 b

9 a

10 c

Q EASY – PART 14

1 What is the name of the portable tent used by nomads in the Gobi Desert?

a) Tepee

b) Yurt

c) Trullo

2 What is the etymology of the word 'dodo'?

a) It is Portuguese for 'stupid'

b) It is Mauritian for 'large beak'

c) It is Tamil for 'dead'

3 In chemistry, what is the process of changing from a solid to a gas state?

a) Evaporation

b) Sublimation

c) Deposition

4 Which of the following is not a type of nuclear radiation?

a) Alpha

b) Beta

c) Theta

5 Which film's tagline is, 'A motion picture destined to offend nearly two thirds of the civilised world. And severely annoy the other third'?

a) *Borat: Cultural Learnings of America for Make Benefit Glorious Nation of Kazakhstan*

b) *The Life of Brian*

c) *Fahrenheit 9/11*

GENERAL KNOWLEDGE ★

6 **Which of the following do astronauts not have in space?**

a) Weight

b) Mass

c) Volume

7 **In computing, what does PDF stand for?**

a) Portable document format

b) Postscript document file

c) Printable document font

8 **What is one of the main ingredients of the breakfast dish kedgeree?**

a) Smoked eel

b) Smoked haddock

c) Smoked salmon

9 **Which London railway station serves the East Midlands cities of Leicester, Nottingham and Derby?**

a) St Pancras

b) Euston

c) King's Cross

10 **Which common ancestor is shared by Queen Elizabeth II and her husband Prince Philip, the Duke of Edinburgh?**

a) Queen Victoria

b) William IV

c) George VI

A

1 b

2 a

3 b

4 c

5 b

6 a

7 a

8 b

9 a

10 a

Q EASY – PART 15

1 **What is the name for a musical note that is played for half the duration of a semibreve?**

a) Crotchet

b) Quaver

c) Minim

2 **Which of these coniferous trees is not evergreen?**

a) Pine

b) Spruce

c) Larch

3 **What was the most common type of car in the socialist state of East Germany?**

a) VW Beetle

b) Trabant

c) Fiat 500

4 **Which household item did supermarkets in the UK agree to stop selling by 2012, to help reduce carbon emissions?**

a) Triple-ply toilet tissue

b) Traditional light bulbs

c) Non-recyclable kitchen foil

5 **What is the symbol for a lamp in a circuit diagram?**

a) A circle with a rectangle inside it

b) A rectangle with an arrow through it

c) A circle with a cross inside it

6 What is Britain's second largest city?

a) Manchester

b) Birmingham

c) Liverpool

7 Which is the correct spelling?

a) Accomodate

b) Accommodate

c) Acommodate

8 Lincoln is the capital of which US state?

a) Alabama

b) Nevada

c) Nebraska

9 Which chef opened a restaurant in the UK called Fifteen?

a) Jamie Oliver

b) Gordon Ramsay

c) Nigella Lawson

10 How many lines are there on a musical stave?

a) 4

b) 5

c) 6

A

1 c

2 c

3 b

4 b

5 c

6 b

7 b

8 c

9 a

10 b

Q EASY – PART 16

1 The Agatha Christie play *The Mousetrap* has been running continuously in the West End of London since when?

a) 1952

b) 1972

c) 1992

2 Which desert can be found in Mongolia?

a) Kalahari

b) Eastern

c) Gobi

3 Frittata means omelette in what language?

a) Spanish

b) Italian

c) Portuguese

4 What is actor Ben Kingsley's real name?

a) Krishna Bhanji

b) Cyril Bouganvillea

c) Marcellus Singh

5 Which number comes next in the series 3, 5, 8, 13 . . .?

a) 15

b) 21

c) 25

6 Which of the following is Latin for 'I roll'?

a) Audi

b) Volvo

c) Nissan

7 Which animal represents the star sign Taurus?

a) Crab

b) Sheep

c) Bull

8 Which of the following video games was the first to be released?

a) Pong

b) Tetris

c) Space invaders

9 In the international radio alphabet, what word represents the letter T?

a) Tango

b) Thomas

c) Tokyo

10 The last British king to be killed in battle, when did Richard III die?

a) 1066

b) 1485

c) 1789

1 a
2 c
3 b
4 a
5 b
6 b
7 c
8 a
9 a
10 b

Q EASY – PART 17

1 Which is not a character that traditionally appears in Punch and Judy puppet shows?

a) A baby

b) A crocodile

c) A badger

2 How often does Halley's comet orbit Earth?

a) Every 12 years

b) Every 76 years

c) Every 114 years

3 Which of these is a genuine style of dance, which evolved in New York in the 1920s?

a) Bindy Bop

b) Lindy Hop

c) Windy Pop

4 What instrument plays the lowest notes in the woodwind family?

a) Bassoon

b) Clarinet

c) Piccolo

5 What was the nationality of Dame Nellie Melba, the opera singer after whom melba toast and peach melba were named?

a) Canadian

b) New Zealander

c) Australian

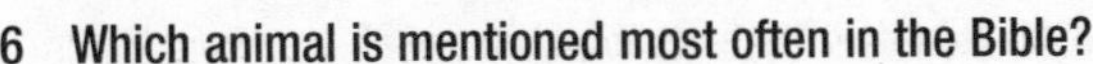

6 **Which animal is mentioned most often in the Bible?**

a) Lion

b) Sheep

c) Ox

7 **Which year saw the deaths of Princess Diana, Deng Xiaoping and the Notorious B.I.G.?**

a) 1997

b) 1999

c) 2001

8 **Who wrote the play *The History Boys*?**

a) David Hare

b) Alan Bennett

c) Willy Russell

9 **Portsmouth, Southampton and Winchester are found in which English county?**

a) Sussex

b) Hampshire

c) Berkshire

10 **Who played Barbarella in the film of the same name?**

a) Jane Fonda

b) Carrie Fisher

c) Mia Farrow

A

1 c
2 b
3 b
4 a
5 c
6 b
7 a
8 b
9 b
10 a

Q EASY – PART 18

1 The disease myxomatosis affects which animal?

a) Cows

b) Chickens

c) Rabbits

2 Who was the first host of University Challenge?

a) Bamber Gascoigne

b) Magnus Magnusson

c) Henry Kelly

3 Which cheese is traditionally made from buffalo milk?

a) Parmesan

b) Mozzarella

c) Gorgonzola

4 Which anniversary did the modern bikini celebrate in 2006?

a) 25th

b) 60th

c) 100th

5 How many seconds are there in a day?

a) 36,000

b) 69,000

c) 86,400

6 In which year was the first Red Nose Day?

a) 1992

b) 1980

c) 1988

7 In which English county are Grantham, Scunthorpe and Grimsby?

a) Lincolnshire

b) Cambridgeshire

c) Northumberland

8 Who wrote *The Turn of the Screw*?

a) Henry James

b) Bram Stoker

c) Robert Louis Stevenson

9 In which city is the Millennium Stadium?

a) London

b) Cardiff

c) Edinburgh

10 How old was Tiger Woods when he won his first Masters title in 1997?

a) 17

b) 21

c) 25

1 c
2 a
3 b
4 b
5 c
6 c
7 a
8 a
9 b
10 b

Q EASY – PART 19

1 Which team won the inaugural football World Cup held in 1930?

a) Brazil

b) Argentina

c) Uruguay

2 If it is noon in London, what time is it in New York?

a) 5am

b) 7am

c) 9am

3 What is Uluru (Ayers Rock) in Australia made of?

a) Sandstone

b) Limestone

c) Mudstone

4 What is the total number of sides of a hexagon, decagon and octagon?

a) 20

b) 22

c) 24

5 Which year saw the launch of BBC Two, the release of the Rolling Stones' debut album and the opening of the first Habitat store?

a) 1957

b) 1964

c) 1971

GENERAL KNOWLEDGE ★

6 **In which sport are stones aimed at a button inside a house?**

a) Shinty

b) Curling

c) Hailes

7 **Who became prime minister of Australia in 2008?**

a) Kevin Rudd

c) Zola Budd

c) Elmer Fudd

8 **What is UK prime minister Gordon Brown's real first name?**

a) Fred

b) Angus

c) James

9 **Which of the following countries is in the same time zone as the UK?**

a) Spain

b) Portugal

c) France

10 **What type of fish is used for kippers?**

a) Herring

b) Mackerel

c) Trout

A

1	c
2	b
3	a
4	c
5	b
6	b
7	a
8	c
9	b
10	a

Q EASY – PART 20

1 In cricket, which legendary player finished his career with a Test average of 99.94?

a) W. G. Grace

b) Len Hutton

c) Donald Bradman

2 How old was James Dean when he died?

a) 19

b) 24

c) 29

3 Which year saw the first call by mobile phone in Britain, *Amadeus* win Best Picture at the Oscars and the Heysel Stadium disaster?

a) 1979

b) 1985

c) 1991

4 In US currency, how many cents are there in a nickel?

a) Five

b) Ten

c) Twenty-five

5 Which of the following is a unit of force?

a) Newton

b) Ohm

c) Joule

6 **What does the chemical symbol 'Au' represent in the periodic table?**

a) Iron

b) Gold

c) Lead

7 **Where is New South Wales?**

a) Australia

b) Africa

c) America

8 **From which country has Angelina Jolie not adopted a child?**

a) Cambodia

b) China

c) Ethiopia

9 **Which is the fastest sprinter of the big cats?**

a) Cheetah

b) Leopard

c) Panther

10 **In which European country is the region of Transylvania?**

a) Slovakia

b) Hungary

c) Romania

A

1 c

2 b

3 b

4 a

5 a

6 b

7 a

8 b

9 a

10 c

MEDIUM – PART 1

1 Which world-renowned sculpture was created by Frederic-Auguste Bartholdi?

a) The Statue of Liberty

b) The Burghers of Calais

c) The Thinker

2 Which illustrator created the girls' school St Trinian's?

a) Ronald Searle

b) Gerald Scarfe

c) Ralph Steadman

3 Who directed the 1980 film *The Elephant Man*?

a) Mel Brooks

b) David Lynch

c) Tim Burton

4 On a horse where would you find the 'frog'?

a) On its leg

b) On its head

c) On its hoof

5 Of what is oology the study?

a) Grasses

b) Birds' eggs

c) Moths

6 If you suffer from suriphobia what do you fear?

a) Mice

b) Rats

c) Voles

7 Which Hollywood star was originally named Caryn Johnson?

a) Whoopi Goldberg

b) Demi Moore

c) Halle Berry

8 Which of the following witticisms is not attributed to the writer Dorothy Parker?

a) 'Brevity is the soul of lingerie'

b) 'You can lead a horticulture, but you can't make her think'

c) 'One morning I shot an elephant in my pyjamas. How he got into my pyjamas I'll never know'

9 In what year was Nelson Mandela released from jail after 27 years?

a) 1987

b) 1990

c) 1993

10 In the RAF version of the phonetic alphabet (*c.*1930), 'a' was 'ace', 'b' was 'beer' and so on – what word represented the letter 'm'?

a) Mike

b) Monkey

c) Marble

A

1	a
2	a
3	b
4	c
5	b
6	a
7	a
8	c
9	b
10	b

MEDIUM – PART 2

1 **Which band's *Liege & Lief* album was voted the best folk album ever in a BBC poll?**

a) Fairport Convention

b) The Chieftains

c) Pentangle

2 **How many times was the US rapper 50 Cent shot in an attack in 2000?**

a) 2

b) 5

c) 9

3 **How is the letter A expressed in Morse code?**

a) dah-di-dit

b) di-dit

c) di-dah

4 **Which of the following film studios used to claim that they had 'more stars than there are in heaven'?**

a) Warner Brothers

b) MGM

c) Paramount

5 **What type of alcohol is used to make a Daiquiri?**

a) Vodka

b) Gin

c) Rum

6 Which of these drinks contains the most calories?

a) A single measure of tequila

b) A small glass of white wine

c) Half a pint of lager

7 Who was the first Prime Minister to occupy Chequers?

a) David Lloyd George

b) Winston Churchill

c) William Pitt the Younger

8 What was the name of Saddam Hussein's oldest son?

a) Ali

b) Qusay

c) Uday

9 Which comedian once said that all he needed to make a film was 'a park, a policeman and a pretty girl'?

a) Charlie Chaplin

b) Buster Keaton

c) Woody Allen

10 From which 1960s film did the band Duran Duran take their name?

a) Yellow Submarine

b) Barbarella

c) One Million Years BC

1 a
2 c
3 c
4 b
5 c
6 a
7 a
8 c
9 a
10 b

MEDIUM – PART 3

1 In which American state is the Coen Brothers' film *Fargo* set?

a) Wisconsin

b) Kansas

c) Minnesota

2 How many sides does a dodecagon have?

a) 10

b) 12

c) 20

3 In Roman numerals, how is 500 represented?

a) C

b) D

c) L

4 What is the correct orientation of the Union Flag when flying?

a) With the broader diagonal band of white uppermost in the hoist and the narrower band of white uppermost in the fly

b) With the narrower diagonal band of white uppermost in the hoist and the broader band of white uppermost in the fly

c) With the broader diagonal band of white uppermost in the hoist and the fly

5 Which actor made his debut as a director with the 2002 film *Confessions of a Dangerous Mind*?

a) Gary Oldman

b) George Clooney

c) Nicolas Cage

6 **From which series was *Knots Landing* a spin-off?**

a) Dynasty

b) Hawaii Five-0

c) Dallas

7 **Which long-running British TV series was first shown on the day after the assassination of John F. Kennedy?**

a) Panorama

b) Doctor Who

c) Blue Peter

8 **On which long-running series is Carenza Lewis a resident expert?**

a) Antiques Roadshow

b) Time Team

c) The Sky at Night

9 **Which film composer links *Gladiator*, *The Lion King* and *Hannibal*?**

a) Hans Zimmer

b) John Williams

c) James Horner

10 **Which novel by Khaled Hosseini was adapted into a film directed by Marc Forster?**

a) *The Poisonwood Bible*

b) *The Kite Runner*

c) *Half of a Yellow Sun*

1 c
2 b
3 b
4 a
5 b
6 c
7 b
8 b
9 a
10 b

Q MEDIUM – PART 4

1 Who conducted the first British TV interview with Nelson Mandela after his release from prison in 1990?

a) Jeremy Paxman

b) Trevor McDonald

c) Robin Day

2 For what are the outlaws searching in Sergio Leone's 1966 film *The Good, the Bad and the Ugly*?

a) Buried cash

b) The man who killed their partner

c) A goldmine

3 Which town on the south coast of England became a city as part of the Millennium celebrations?

a) Plymouth

b) Bournemouth

c) Brighton

4 Which ocean contains the deepest trench in the world?

a) Atlantic

b) Arctic

c) Pacific

5 In which capital city was Osama bin Laden born?

a) Riyadh, Saudi Arabia

b) Sana'a, Yemen

c) Kabul, Afghanistan

GENERAL KNOWLEDGE ★ ★

6 **How is Lesley Hornby better known?**

a) Twiggy

b) Cilla Black

c) Marianne Faithfull

7 **What was the name of Ross's pet primate in *Friends*?**

a) Jean-Claude

b) Marcel

c) Fifi

8 **Which Premier League football club were bought by US businessman Randy Lerner in 2006?**

a) Aston Villa

b) Portsmouth

c) Manchester City

9 **How is the most severe form of earthquake described on the Modified Mercalli scale?**

a) Cataclysmic

b) Catastrophic

c) Calamitous

10 ***Marion and Geoff* launched the career of which comedy actor?**

a) Steve Coogan

b) Rob Brydon

c) Peter Kay

1 b
2 a
3 c
4 c
5 a
6 a
7 b
8 c
9 b
10 b

Q MEDIUM – PART 5

1 What does Llan mean in Welsh place names like Llanberis, Llangollen and Llanelli?

a) An enclosed area where a church is often built

b) An area adjacent to a lake or river

c) A valley with a river or stream running through it

2 What name was given to the followers of John Wycliffe?

a) The Lollards

b) The Chartists

c) The Luddites

3 Who spoke the only line in Mel Brooks's 1976 film *Silent Movie*?

a) Marty Feldman

b) Mel Brooks

c) Marcel Marceau

4 Who wrote 'The Executioner's Song', a book about the life and death of the American murderer Gary Gilmore?

a) Truman Capote

b) Norman Mailer

c) George Plimpton

5 The actress Jane Asher had a relationship with which Beatle?

a) John

b) Paul

c) George

GENERAL KNOWLEDGE ★★

6 **Who was the presenter of the first series of *Robot Wars*?**

a) Philippa Forrester

b) Craig Charles

c) Jeremy Clarkson

7 **Becky Sharp was the protagonist of which Victorian novel?**

a) *Vanity Fair*

b) *Middlemarch*

c) *The Tenant of Wildfell Hall*

8 **Which footballer played for both Merseyside clubs, Newcastle United and the Vancouver Whitecaps?**

a) Paul Parker

b) Peter Beardsley

c) Paul Ince

9 **The Hanging Gardens of Babylon – one of the original seven wonders of the world – were located in which modern-day country?**

a) Syria

b) Iran

c) Iraq

10 **What is the name of Jack Bauer's ill-fated daughter in the TV show *24*?**

a) Kate

b) Kim

c) Kath

A

1 a
2 a
3 c
4 b
5 b
6 c
7 a
8 b
9 c
10 b

MEDIUM – PART 6

1 The mother of which famous politician was an American heiress called Jenny Jerome?

a) Stanley Baldwin

b) Clement Attlee

c) Winston Churchill

2 What is the name of Sherlock Holmes's elder brother?

a) Ashcroft

b) Mycroft

c) Sancroft

3 Which of the following women writers was born in Wellington, New Zealand?

a) Iris Murdoch

b) Katherine Mansfield

c) Muriel Spark

4 Which Shakespeare play features the line 'The course of true love never did run smooth'?

a) *Romeo and Juliet*

b) *Antony and Cleopatra*

c) *A Midsummer Night's Dream*

5 Which of the following TV shows was created by Simon Pegg and Jessica Stevenson?

a) *Big Train*

b) *The Royle Family*

c) *Spaced*

GENERAL KNOWLEDGE ★★

6 **In which decade did Jack Cohen open the first Tesco store?**

a) 1920s

b) 1930s

c) 1940s

7 **On which mountain range did Joe Simpson – author of *Touching the Void* – and Simon Yates come unstuck?**

a) Himalayas

b) Andes

c) Alps

8 **How long ago did the South American landmass break away from Africa?**

a) 105 million years

b) 65 million years

c) 25 million years

9 **Which of the following is the birthstone for April?**

a) Topaz

b) Emerald

c) Diamond

10 **Which member of The Rolling Stones married Mandy Smith, a woman he began dating when she was 13-years-old?**

a) Keith Richards

b) Brian Jones

c) Bill Wyman

A

1 c

2 b

3 b

4 c

5 c

6 a

7 b

8 a

9 c

10 c

MEDIUM – PART 7

1 Which television comedy follows the lives of flatmates Mark and Jeremy?

a) *Spaced*

b) *Peep Show*

c) *Flight of the Conchords*

2 In which year did Kate Bush's 'Wuthering Heights' reach number one?

a) 1968

b) 1978

c) 1988

3 Who played Yorick in the Kenneth Branagh film version of 'Hamlet'?

a) Tommy Cooper

b) Ken Dodd

c) Frankie Howerd

4 For what type of music is Ira D. Sankey best remembered?

a) Music hall songs

b) Hymns

c) Brass band music

5 In which of the performing arts did Merce Cunningham make his name?

a) Theatre

b) Music

c) Dance

6 Which Russian word meaning 'destruction' can be applied to any organised massacre?

a) Putsch

b) Pogrom

c) Ghetto

7 What is the capital of the Isle of Man?

a) St Helier

b) St Peter Port

c) Douglas

8 What do you do in bed if you suffer from bruxism?

a) Snore

b) Grind your teeth

c) Occasionally stop breathing

9 In *The Devil's Dictionary*, what did Ambrose Bierce define as 'a spiritual pickle preserving the body from decay'?

a) Learning

b) Life

c) Religion

10 In logic, what term is used to describe a proposition that is not proved or demonstrated but considered self-evident?

a) Theorem

b) Axiom

c) Hypothesis

A

1 b

2 b

3 b

4 b

5 c

6 b

7 c

8 b

9 b

10 b

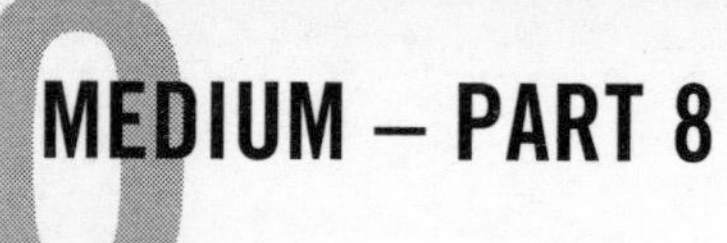

MEDIUM – PART 8

1 Which group had a picture of Jerry Hall as a mermaid on the cover of one of their albums?

a) Roxy Music

b) Rolling Stones

c) The Who

2 The last book Charles Darwin published was about which creature widely found in Britain?

a) Earthworm

b) Slug

c) Snail

3 Which of the following cheeses is made from sheep's milk?

a) Gorgonzola

b) Roquefort

c) Edam

4 Which Northern Irish band wrote the theme tune to *Father Ted*?

a) Ash

b) The Divine Comedy

c) The Undertones

5 Why was Judith Keppel newsworthy in November 2000?

a) She became the BNP's first member of parliament

b) She was the first £1m winner on *Who Wants to be a Millionaire?*

c) She received an MBE for creating the Teletubbies

GENERAL KNOWLEDGE ★★

6 Which film's tagline is 'The first casualty of war is innocence'?

a) *Platoon*

b) *The Deer Hunter*

c) *Apocalypse Now*

7 The phrase 'McJob' which caused McDonalds to campaign against its inclusion in the Oxford English Dictionary, was popularised by which author?

a) Douglas Coupland

b) Chuck Palahniuk

c) Kurt Vonnegut

8 Where is the only unclaimed piece of land on Earth?

a) In the Atlantic ocean

b) In the Antarctic

c) In the Arctic ocean

9 What is wrapped in bacon to make the dish Angels on Horseback?

a) Prunes

b) Oysters

c) Potatoes

10 How did the X in Xmas originate?

a) It represents the cross

b) It comes from the Greek letter *chi*, used as an abbreviation for Christ

c) It is a common abbreviation for the first name Chris

1 a

2 a

3 b

4 b

5 b

6 a

7 a

8 b

9 b

10 b

Q MEDIUM – PART 9

1 To what family of plants does garlic belong?

a) Rose

b) Magnolia

c) Lily

2 Which metal is extracted from bauxite?

a) Lead

b) Tin

c) Aluminium

3 What is measured by a hygrometer?

a) Pressure

b) Humidity

c) Force

4 Which viral disease takes its name from a river in the Republic of Congo?

a) Yellow fever

b) Ebola

c) Dengue fever

5 Who was the first England footballer to be sent off in an international match?

a) Alan Mullery

b) Ray Wilkins

c) Alan Ball

6 What is frankincense?

a) Perfumed oil

b) An aromatic resin obtained from trees

c) Smoke used in religious ceremonies

7 In economics what term represents a market with only one buyer?

a) Monopsony

b) Monopoly

c) Oligopoly

8 Where is the headquarters of the United Nations?

a) Brussels

b) New York

c) Geneva

9 What does the distress signal SOS stand for?

a) Nothing, it is an easy combination in Morse code

b) Save our souls

c) Survivors on shore

10 Chisinau is the capital of which European country?

a) Romania

b) Belarus

c) Moldova

A

1	c
2	c
3	b
4	b
5	a
6	b
7	a
8	b
9	a
10	c

Q MEDIUM – PART 10

1 Which English physician coined the word 'vaccination' to describe a method of inoculation he was using?

a) William Harvey

b) Edward Jenner

c) Lord Lister

2 Of which sports commentator did Clive James once remark, 'In his quieter moments, he sounds like his trousers are on fire'?

a) Murray Walker

b) Jonathan Pearce

c) David Coleman

3 What name was shared by the second and sixth US presidents?

a) Adams

b) Jackson

c) Jefferson

4 What is an appaloosa?

a) a striped wild cat

b) a spotted riding horse

c) a flying lizard

5 Which Victorian artist painted *The Light of the World*?

a) John Everett Millais

b) Edwin Landseer

c) William Holman Hunt

6 Which English city was called Eboracum by the Romans?

a) Chester

b) St Albans

c) York

7 Who wrote the Mary Poppins stories?

a) Dodie Smith

b) Joyce Lankester Brisley

c) P. L. Travers

8 The Atacama Desert is found in which South American country?

a) Peru

b) Chile

c) Argentina

9 Which planet do the Daleks in *Doctor Who* call home?

a) Durko

b) Pharos

c) Skaro

10 Which ship did Captain Scott sail on his last expedition to the Antarctic?

a) The Terra Nova

b) The Discovery

c) The Endurance

1	b
2	a
3	a
4	b
5	c
6	c
7	c
8	b
9	c
10	a

MEDIUM – PART 11

1 Which fictional character lived in the village of Puddleby-on-the-Marsh?

a) Dr Dolittle

b) Willy Wonka

c) Miss Marple

2 Which of the following is not a true nut?

a) Peanut

b) Chestnut

c) Hazelnut

3 What is the name of the island in New York harbour on which the Statue of Liberty stands?

a) Ellis Island

b) Harbour Island

c) Liberty Island

4 From what plant is saffron obtained?

a) Poppy

b) Crocus

c) Aconite

5 Who was the king of England at the time of the Great Fire of London?

a) Charles I

b) Charles II

c) James II

6 **What was the name of Desmond Dekker's backing group on the 1960s hit 'The Israelites'?**

a) The Aces

b) The Deuces

c) The Jokers

7 **In which city is Fenner's cricket ground?**

a) Cambridge

b) Canterbury

c) Oxford

8 **Who played Sebastian Flyte in the TV series *Brideshead Revisited*?**

a) Jeremy Irons

b) Anthony Andrews

c) Lawrence Olivier

9 **In the animal world, what is a monotreme?**

a) A mammal that rears its young in a pouch

b) A mammal that lays eggs

c) A mammal with webbed feet

10 **What does the word Zorro mean in Spanish?**

a) Fox

b) Sword

c) Avenger

1 a
2 a
3 c
4 b
5 b
6 a
7 a
8 b
9 b
10 a

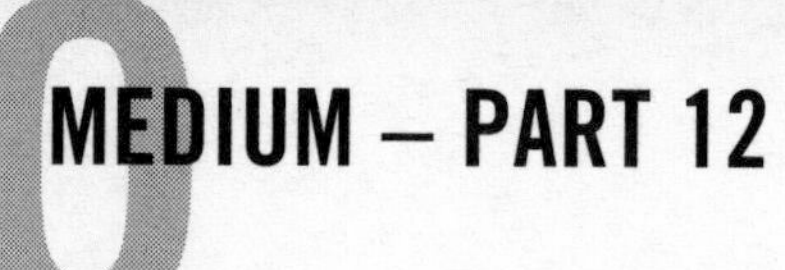

MEDIUM – PART 12

1 Who was British Prime Minister when Edward VIII abdicated in 1936?

a) Winston Churchill

b) Neville Chamberlain

c) Stanley Baldwin

2 In Stanley Kubrick's film *2001: A Space Odyssey*, what song does the computer HAL sing?

a) 'Hey Jude'

b) 'Home, Sweet Home'

c) 'Daisy Bell (A Bicycle Built for Two)'

3 Which empire dominated Central America in the 15th century?

a) The Mayan

b) The Inca

c) The Aztec

4 What was The Clash's only No. 1 single?

a) 'Rock the Casbah'

b) 'Should I Stay Or Should I Go'?

c) 'London Calling'

5 What is the inscription on the Victoria Cross?

a) For valour

b) For courage

c) For gallantry

6 **What 1760s invention by John Spilsbury became a popular pastime?**

a) The jigsaw puzzle

b) The spinning top

c) The yo-yo

7 **For which area of the British Isles did Alfred Wainwright write a series of famous guidebooks?**

a) The Lake District

b) The Pennines

c) The Scottish Highlands

8 **Of which Native American tribe was Geronimo a leader?**

a) Sioux

b) Navajo

c) Apache

9 **What was the route of the original Orient Express in the 1920s?**

a) Paris to Venice

b) Paris to Istanbul

c) Paris to Shanghai

10 **What was Disney's second animated feature film?**

a) *Dumbo*

b) *Pinocchio*

c) *Fantasia*

1	c
2	c
3	c
4	b
5	a
6	a
7	a
8	c
9	b
10	b

MEDIUM – PART 13

1 Which famous horse race was won in three successive years in the 1960s by Arkle?

a) The Cheltenham Gold Cup

b) The Derby

c) The St Leger

2 Mitch Buchannon was one of the central characters in which American TV series?

a) *Saved by the Bell*

b) *Hawaii 5–0*

c) *Baywatch*

3 What did Elisha Otis invent in 1853?

a) The lift

b) The moving staircase

c) The dumb waiter

4 Who designed the giant flying boat that was nicknamed the Spruce Goose?

a) Charles Lindbergh

b) Barnes Wallis

c) Howard Hughes

5 Under which London bridge was the Italian banker Roberto Calvi found hanging in 1982?

a) London Bridge

b) Blackfriars Bridge

c) Tower Bridge

GENERAL KNOWLEDGE ★★

6 Which of the following singers was a gravedigger before he hit the big time?

a) Julio Iglesias

b) Barry Manilow

c) Rod Stewart

7 Which of the following has the most sheep per person?

a) New Zealand

b) Falkland Islands

c) Wales

8 In which novel does the character Major Major Major Major appear?

a) *Catch 22*

b) *Gravity's Rainbow*

c) *Empire of the Sun*

9 Which author created the character of the Scarlet Pimpernel?

a) Arthur Conan Doyle

b) Baroness Orczy

c) Nathaniel Hawthorne

10 Apart from potato, what is the principal vegetable in vichyssoise soup?

a) Leek

b) Onion

c) Asparagus

A

1 a
2 c
3 a
4 c
5 b
6 c
7 b
8 a
9 b
10 a

MEDIUM – PART 14

1 What is the literal meaning of 'vermicelli'?

a) Little hairs

b) Little worms

c) Little snakes

2 What is the principal ingredient of couscous?

a) Wheat

b) Beans

c) Rice

3 Of what did Dr Johnson say, 'There is nothing which has yet been contrived by man, by which so much happiness is produced'?

a) A good book

b) A good meal

c) A good tavern

4 Who said, 'The only difference between me and a madman is that I'm not mad'?

a) Salvador Dali

b) Spike Milligan

c) George III

5 What was the Christian name of Mrs Beeton, author of *Mrs Beeton's Book of Household Management*?

a) Jane

b) Elizabeth

c) Isabella

6 Who was the first black tennis player to win a Wimbledon title?

a) Arthur Ashe

b) Althea Gibson

c) Venus Williams

7 What was the name of the aeroplane in which Charles Lindbergh made the first solo flight across the Atlantic?

a) Columbia

b) Spirit of St Louis

c) Belle of New York

8 Which two of Henry VIII's six wives survived him?

a) Catherine Howard and Catherine Parr

b) Catherine Parr and Anne of Cleves

c) Catherine of Aragon and Anne of Cleves

9 Which famous couple, then husband and wife, starred in the 1966 film version of Edward Albee's play *Who's Afraid of Virginia Woolf*?

a) Richard Burton and Elizabeth Taylor

b) Laurence Olivier and Vivien Leigh

c) Paul Newman and Joanne Woodward

10 Which movie star named their son Satchel?

a) Tom Hanks

b) Woody Allen

c) Robert Downey Jr

1 b
2 a
3 c
4 a
5 c
6 b
7 b
8 b
9 a
10 b

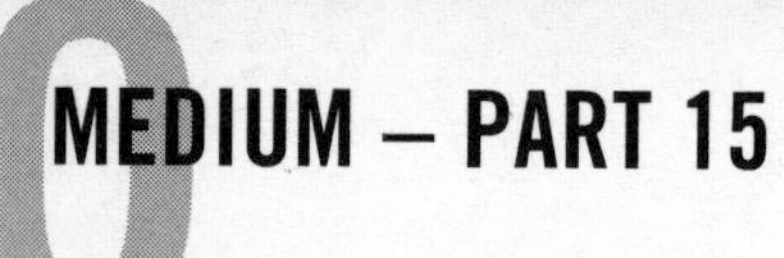

MEDIUM – PART 15

1 In whose memory did Don McLean write the song 'American Pie'?

a) Elvis Presley

b) Eddie Cochrane

c) Buddy Holly

2 What nationality is the former Secretary General of the UN Boutros Boutros-Ghali?

a) Egyptian

b) Greek

c) Algerian

3 What was the name of the South African surgeon who performed the world's first open heart transplant in 1967?

a) Dr Christiaan Barnard

b) Dr Ali Bacher

c) Dr Richard Vorster

4 What useful household object was first invented and patented by William Lyman in 1870?

a) The sewing machine

b) The can opener

c) The screw-top lid

5 Which actress was described by Clive James as 'good at playing abstract confusion in the same way a midget is good at being short'?

a) Marilyn Monroe

b) Doris Day

c) Judy Garland

6 **If you suffer from gynophobia what do you fear?**

a) Pregnancy

b) Women

c) Sex

7 **Which Hollywood star was originally named Issur Danielovitch?**

a) Kirk Douglas

b) Tony Curtis

c) Burt Lancaster

8 **Which of the following was not a genuine episode of the popular sitcom *Fawlty Towers*?**

a) 'The Germans'

b) 'Waldorf Salad'

c) 'The Birthday'

9 **Who designed the iconic London Underground map, first issued in 1933?**

a) George Dow

b) Ralph Gray

c) Harry Beck

10 **Chortle, napalm, galumphing and Oxbridge are all examples of what?**

a) Portmanteau words

b) Spoonerisms

c) Palindromes

1 c
2 a
3 a
4 b
5 a
6 b
7 a
8 c
9 c
10 a

MEDIUM – PART 16

1 Who succeeded Herbert Asquith as British prime minister in 1916?

a) Stanley Baldwin

b) David Lloyd George

c) Henry Campbell-Bannerman

2 The US dollar bill features the Latin saying 'E pluribus unum' – what does it mean?

a) Prosperity, together

b) United we stand

c) Out of many, one

3 Which of the following was not designed by Christopher Wren?

a) Somerset House

b) The Royal Observatory

c) St Paul's Cathedral

4 What is a titmouse?

a) A rodent

b) A marsupial

c) A bird

5 What was the largest ever lottery jackpot, split by two winners in the USA in 2007?

a) $160m

b) $390m

c) $510m

6 What is the famous last line of Karl Marx and Friedrich Engels' *Communist Manifesto*?

a) 'Workers of the world unite'

b) 'From each according to his abilities, to each according to his needs'

c) 'Political power grows out of the barrel of a gun'

7 What work of art was sold at auction for a record $140m in 2006?

a) *Boy with a Pipe (The Young Apprentice)* by Pablo Picasso

b) *No 5, 1948* by Jackson Pollock

c) *For the Love of God* by Damien Hirst

8 Which of the following celebrities has not been declared bankrupt at some point in their lives?

a) Kim Basinger

b) Francis Ford Coppola

c) Sharon Stone

9 Whose face graces the most recent version of the £20 note, introduced in 2007?

a) Sir Edward Elgar

b) Adam Smith

c) Charles Darwin

10 In what year was 'Decimal Day', when the old monetary system of ha'pennies, sixpence and bob was replaced?

a) 1967

b) 1971

c) 1975

A

1 b
2 c
3 a
4 c
5 b
6 a
7 b
8 c
9 b
10 b

MEDIUM – PART 17

1 What is the hardest substance in the human body?

a) Bone

b) Tooth enamel

c) Nail

2 From which type of flower are vanilla pods obtained?

a) Lilies

b) Orchids

c) Carnations

3 Which part of the body is affected by otitis?

a) Liver

b) Ear

c) Pancreas

4 What did the American businessman Joseph Gayetty invent in 1857?

a) Toilet paper

b) Scissors

c) Vacuum cleaner

5 Aside from Russia/USSR, which nation has won the most medals at the Winter Olympics?

a) USA

b) Austria

c) Norway

6 Which US city was the first to have a subway, in 1897?

a) Boston

b) Chicago

c) New York

7 In which county is the source of the River Thames?

a) Oxfordshire

b) Berkshire

c) Gloucestershire

8 Which of the following English words is not of Hindi origin?

a) Sofa

b) Cummerbund

c) Shampoo

9 When were the first Wimbledon tennis championships held?

a) 1851

b) 1877

c) 1902

10 What do Tony Blair, Delia Smith and Evelyn Waugh have in common?

a) Support Norwich City Football Club

b) Educated at Oxford University

c) Converted to Roman Catholicism as adults

1 b
2 b
3 b
4 a
5 c
6 a
7 c
8 a
9 b
10 c

Q MEDIUM – PART 18

1 What is 'Hispaniola'?

a) The name of the island shared by Haiti and the Dominican Republic

b) A blood disease to which Latin Americans are particularly susceptible

c) The debut album by Buena Vista Social Club

2 Which chef owns the restaurants Maze, Petrus and the Boxwood Cafe?

a) Marco Pierre White

b) Gordon Ramsay

c) Raymond Blanc

3 Which of the following is synaesthesia?

a) A type of anaesthetic

b) A painful inherited nerve disorder

c) The involuntarily association of numbers, letters or words with particular colours

4 How long was the Eiffel Tower originally intended to stand for?

a) 5 years

b) 20 years

c) Indefinitely

5 What is the longest underground railway in the world by total length of track?

a) The Paris Metro

b) The London Underground

c) The New York Subway

6 **What do the initials 'P. G.' of P. G. Wodehouse stand for?**

a) Paul Galahad

b) Peregrine Green

c) Pelham Grenville

7 **Which of the following is not an official team suffix used by a Rugby Super League team?**

a) Warriors

b) Wolves

c) Wizards

8 **What is the symbol for a nature reserve on an Ordnance Survey map?**

a) Tree

b) Flower

c) Bird

9 **What colour is the neutral wire in a plug?**

a) Brown

b) Blue

c) Green and yellow

10 **What are freemen and liverymen members of?**

a) Freemasons

b) The Royal household

c) City guilds

1	a
2	b
3	c
4	b
5	b
6	c
7	c
8	c
9	b
10	c

MEDIUM – PART 19

1 What is the ballet term used for the rapid crossing and uncrossing of the feet during a jump?

a) Pas de deux

b) Entrechat

c) Glissade

2 What was unusual about Neil Oram's play *The Warp*, first performed in 1979?

a) Its actors were all under nine years old

b) It was performed entirely in the dark

c) It ran for over 18 hours

3 Which of the following is a type of novel that follows the development of a central character?

a) Epistolary

b) Hagiography

c) Bildungsroman

4 On sheet music, which of the following indicates that a piece should be played quietly?

a) *f*

b) *p*

c) rit.

5 What is the meaning of 'bellwether'?

a) A male sheep that leads the herd

b) An experiment used to predict future trends

c) A navigational buoy fitted with a bell

6 **Which of the following was one of the original six 'redbrick' universities?**

a) Reading

b) Leicester

c) Sheffield

7 **Which royal house in Britain had the most ruling monarchs?**

a) Plantagenet

b) Tudor

c) Lancaster

8 **Which unit of measurement is used in relation to astronomical temperatures?**

a) Celsius

b) Fahrenheit

c) Kelvin

9 **Which of the following sports has been contested at every Olympic Games since the modern era began in 1896?**

a) Judo

b) Weightlifting

c) Cycling

10 **What does the W stand for in the name George W. Bush?**

a) Walter

b) Walker

c) Winston

1	b
2	c
3	c
4	b
5	a
6	c
7	a
8	c
9	c
10	b

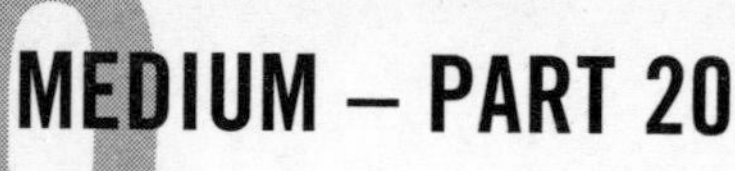

MEDIUM – PART 20

1 What does the Dewey decimal system classify?

a) Books

b) Coins

c) Stamps

2 When was Amnesty International founded?

a) 1941

b) 1961

c) 1981

3 Dactylology is the study of what?

a) Skulls

b) Prehistoric flying animals

c) Sign language communication

4 If something is said to be circadian, how long does it last?

a) An hour

b) A day

c) A year

5 Which of the following is the shortest distance from the United Kingdom?

a) Havana

b) Hong Kong

c) Honolulu

6 **Who had a UK number one hit with 'Magic Moments' in 1958?**

a) Lonnie Donegan

b) Perry Como

c) Bing Crosby

7 **Which country hosted the first Commonwealth Games in 1978?**

a) Canada

b) Australia

c) Great Britain

8 **Which of the following cites has an area called the Jordaan?**

a) Amsterdam

b) New York City

c) Brussels

9 **A game in which sport is divided into six chukkas?**

a) Polo

b) Squash

c) Lacrosse

10 **What would you do with a kohlrabi?**

a) Eat it

b) Drink it

c) Wear it

A

1 a

2 b

3 c

4 b

5 a

6 b

7 a

8 a

9 a

10 a

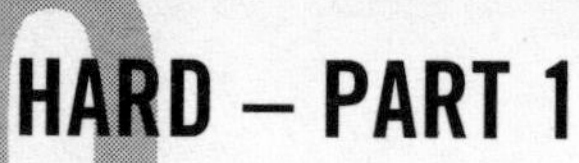

HARD – PART 1

1 Which of the following French artists worked for most of his life as a customs inspector?

a) Paul Gauguin

b) Henri Rousseau

c) Claude Monet

2 Which veteran film-maker directed *A Fish Called Wanda*, starring John Cleese and Jamie Lee Curtis?

a) Jack Clayton

b) Charles Crichton

c) Michael Powell

3 How many grandchildren did Queen Victoria have?

a) 40

b) 60

c) 80

4 Which Los Angeles neighbourhood has been home to many famous residents, including: 'Mama' Cass Elliot, Frank Zappa and the Red Hot Chili Peppers?

a) Topanga Canyon

b) Feeny Canyon

c) Laurel Canyon

5 Which of these bands was the first on stage at the Live Aid concert in 1985 at Wembley Stadium?

a) Status Quo

b) Spandau Ballet

c) Queen

GENERAL KNOWLEDGE ★★★

6 The furthest distance from Earth that an astronaut has travelled was during the Apollo 13 mission. How far was it?

a) 220,000km

b) 310,000km

c) 400,000km

7 Orson Welles' character of Citizen Kane was loosely based on which person?

a) William Randolph Hearst

b) Howard Hughes

c) John D. Rockefeller

8 Britain joined the European Economic Community, Pablo Picasso died and US forces withdrew from South Vietnam – in which year did these events occur?

a) 1971

b) 1973

c) 1975

9 Which London prison has been home to Titus Oates, Daniel Defoe and Ben Jonson?

a) Wormwood Scrubs

b) Pentonville

c) Newgate

10 What connects the bands Moloko and Heaven 17?

a) Each has recorded with David Bowie

b) Both featured on a Band Aid single

c) Both band names were taken from the film *A Clockwork Orange*

A

1 b

2 b

3 a

4 c

5 a

6 c

7 a

8 b

9 c

10 c

Q HARD – PART 2

1 Which work by which philosopher advocates an ideal state based on rational order, ruled by philosopher kings?

a) Nietzsche's *Thus Spake Zarathustra*

b) Plato's *Republic*

c) Machiavelli's *The Prince*

2 Of what is epistemology the study?

a) Logic

b) The theory of knowledge

c) Ethics

3 Which Italian film-maker directed the movies *8½* and *Juliet of the Spirits*?

a) Federico Fellini

b) Sergio Leone

c) Michelangelo Antonioni

4 Which of the following was a name originally intended to be given to *Coronation Street*?

a) Northern Echoes

b) Victoria Road

c) Florizel Street

5 Which Native American tribe featured in the 1990 Kevin Costner western *Dances with Wolves*?

a) Sioux

b) Apache

c) Cheyenne

6 **On which island can you find Fingal's Cave?**

a) Mull

b) Staffa

c) Skye

7 **What did George Shillibeer introduce to London in 1829?**

a) Street lights

b) Horse-drawn bus service

c) Newspaper kiosks

8 **Which woman mathematician, astronomer and Platonic philosopher was murdered in Alexandria in 415 AD?**

a) Thais

b) Heloise

c) Hypatia

9 **Which American crime writer worked as a detective for Pinkerton's Agency before ill-health forced him to retire and take up writing?**

a) Raymond Chandler

b) Dashiell Hammett

c) James Ellroy

10 **Which American crime writer published an autobiography called *My Dark Places* in which he wrote about his own investigations into the murder of his mother?**

a) James Lee Burke

b) Elmore Leonard

c) James Ellroy

A

1 b

2 b

3 a

4 c

5 a

6 b

7 b

8 c

9 b

10 c

HARD – PART 3

1 For which work is the medieval writer William Langland best known?

a) *Piers Plowman*

b) *Ancrene Wisse*

c) *The Owl and the Nightingale*

2 What do Malory's *Morte d'Arthur*, Bunyan's *The Pilgrim's Progress* and Adolf Hitler's *Mein Kampf* have in common?

a) Each was the author's only book

b) They were all written in prison

c) They were all published without the author's knowledge

3 Which well-known British novelist once played Ken Barlow's girlfriend in an episode of *Coronation Street*?

a) Beryl Bainbridge

b) Margaret Drabble

c) Margaret Forster

4 Which was the relationship between Christina and Dante Gabriel Rossetti?

a) Husband and wife

b) Brother and sister

c) Mother and son

5 In what year was the First Folio of Shakespeare's plays published?

a) 1613

b) 1623

c) 1633

6 In which city was Antonio Vivaldi born?

a) Venice

b) Naples

c) Rome

7 Ford's Model T was the world's first mass-produced car – approximately how many were manufactured?

a) 16 million

b) 26 million

c) 48 million

8 What is the name of the national weapon of Nepal (also the traditional weapon of the Gurkhas)?

a) Lajinaa

b) Khukuri

c) Sgian dubh

9 Set in 1971, what is the record for the greatest distance covered during the Le Mans 24-hour race?

a) 3,890km

b) 4,530km

c) 5,335km

10 In Prokofiev's *Peter and the Wolf*, what instrument is the wolf represented by?

a) Flute

b) French horn

c) Clarinet

A

1	a
2	b
3	a
4	b
5	b
6	a
7	a
8	b
9	c
10	b

HARD – PART 4

1 Which Russian composer wrote the score for Sergei Eisenstein's film *Alexander Nevsky*?

a) Stravinsky

b) Shostakovich

c) Prokofiev

2 Which of the following is an alternative name for the scaly anteater?

a) Armadillo

b) Wapiti

c) Pangolin

3 Where was Mother Teresa born?

a) Bucharest, Romania

b) Skopje, Macedonia

c) Tirana, Albania

4 What is 'nutation'?

a) A method of measuring the speed at which stars are travelling away from us

b) A small variation in the spinning of the Earth on its axis

c) A type of mammalian hibernation

5 What kind of plant is an epiphyte?

a) One with exceptionally speedy growth

b) A non-parasitic growth on another plant

c) One which grows towards a light source

GENERAL KNOWLEDGE ★★★

6 **To which of the following do Messier numbers refer?**

a) Elements in the Periodic Table

b) Sub-atomic particles

c) Star clusters

7 **In which sport do toxophilists compete?**

a) Archery

b) Clay pigeon shooting

c) Water Polo

8 **Whose reliability did David Niven describe thus: 'You always knew where you stood with him because he always let you down'?**

a) John Barrymore's

b) Dylan Thomas'

c) Errol Flynn's

9 **What are Mildred and Patty Hill remembered for?**

a) Composing the tune now known as 'Happy Birthday to You'

b) Writing the words to the carol 'Away in a Manger'

c) Writing the poem which became the hymn 'Morning Has Broken'

10 **If you suffer from pogonophobia what do you fear?**

a) Beards

b) Thunder

c) Cats

1 c
2 c
3 b
4 b
5 b
6 c
7 a
8 c
9 a
10 a

HARD – PART 5

1 The music of which composer, according to Mark Twain, was 'better than it sounds'?

a) Richard Wagner

b) Richard Strauss

c) Ludwig van Beethoven

2 Which musician and singer appeared as a boy in a West End production of *Oliver!* playing the Artful Dodger?

a) David Bowie

b) Sting

c) Phil Collins

3 To which of the following animals is the rock hyrax or rock rabbit most closely related?

a) Tiger

b) Kangaroo

c) Elephant

4 What sport do the New Jersey Devils and the San Jose Sharks play?

a) Baseball

b) Basketball

c) Ice Hockey

5 Which is the first bridge under which the crews pass in the University Boat Race?

a) Hammersmith Bridge

b) Barnes Bridge

c) Chiswick Bridge

6 In which year was Joseph Stalin named *Time* magazine's Person of the Year?

a) 1929

b) 1934

c) 1939

7 When was the board game Monopoly patented?

a) 1915

b) 1925

c) 1935

8 Snail-mail, birth-mother and church wedding are all examples of what?

a) Eponyms

b) Retronyms

c) Antonyms

9 Approximately, how many days did the siege of Leningrad last for?

a) 450

b) 900

c) 1,350

10 Which of the following actors has not played the role of God in a film?

a) John Candy

b) Morgan Freeman

c) Val Kilmer

1 a
2 c
3 c
4 c
5 a
6 c
7 c
8 b
9 b
10 a

Q HARD – PART 6

1 Which sport, other than tennis, originally had its UK headquarters at Wimbledon?

a) Badminton

b) Crown bowls

c) Croquet

2 Who assisted Gertrude Jekyll in the design and planting of many of her famous gardens?

a) Sir Edward Lutyens

b) Vita Sackville-West

c) Charles Rennie Mackintosh

3 How many standard bottles of champagne make up a balthazar?

a) 12

b) 16

c) 24

4 Which German composer wrote the opera *Hansel and Gretel*, first performed in 1893?

a) Richard Strauss

b) Engelbert Humperdinck

c) Richard Wagner

5 What common word is officially defined as 1/100th of a second?

a) a tick

b) a trice

c) a jiffy

6 **Which fictional character was imprisoned in the Chateau D'If?**

a) The Scarlet Pimpernel

b) The Count of Monte Cristo

c) The Barber of Seville

7 **In the New Testament who was chosen as an apostle to take the place of Judas Iscariot?**

a) Matthias

b) Thomas

c) Zacharias

8 **Who said that 'nothing is really work unless you would rather be doing something else'?**

a) J. M. Barrie

b) Rudyard Kipling

c) Katherine Mansfield

9 **Which of the following countries is a permanent member of the Security Council of the United Nations?**

a) Germany

b) China

c) Australia

10 **Where was the world's first automatic telephone exchange, linking ten phones, installed in 1886?**

a) The Vatican

b) The House of Commons

c) The White House

A

1	c
2	a
3	b
4	b
5	c
6	b
7	a
8	a
9	b
10	a

HARD – PART 7

1 Who was the president of the Confederate States of America at the time of the American Civil War?

a) Robert E. Lee

b) Jefferson Davis

c) Ulysses S. Grant

2 Which London monument now stands on the original site of the gallows at Tyburn?

a) Admiralty Arch

b) Marble Arch

c) Nelson's Column

3 What is a wampee?

a) A root vegetable

b) A flowering shrub

c) A fruit

4 Of which famous ship was Benjamin Briggs the captain?

a) Titanic

b) Mary Celeste

c) Exxon Valdez

5 Which country is the Przewalski horse native to?

a) Poland

b) Mongolia

c) Kyrgyzstan

6 In which sport would you perform a 'randolph'?

a) Figure skating

b) Trampolining

c) Diving

7 Launched in 1977, *Voyager 1* is the most distant man-made object from Earth – how far away is it?

a) 130 million km

b) 1.3 billion km

c) 13 billion km

8 There is enough carbon in the average human body to fill roughly how many pencils?

a) 60

b) 900

c) 1,400

9 Which pop musician used to be a professional upholsterer?

a) Morrissey

b) Jack White

c) Elvis Costello

10 Which ancient Egyptian coined the phrase 'Eat, drink and be merry, for tomorrow we shall die'?

a) Cleopatra

b) Imhotep

c) Nefertiti

1 b
2 b
3 c
4 b
5 b
6 b
7 c
8 b
9 b
10 b

HARD – PART 8

1 Which European people speak Euskara?

a) The Basques

b) The Catalans

c) The Galicians

2 In which Shakespearean play do two characters called Gobbo appear?

a) *Measure for Measure*

b) *The Merchant of Venice*

c) *All's Well That Ends Well*

3 Which section of line was the first to be opened on the London Underground in 1863?

a) Between Paddington and Kensington

b) Between Farringdon and Moorgate

c) Between Paddington and Farringdon

4 Which of the following, at 4352km, is the longest stretch of straight railroad track in the world?

a) The Trans-Siberian Railway, on the route from Moscow to Irkutsk

b) The Indian Pacific rail service from Sydney to Perth, Australia

c) The Alamosa-Salida section in Colorado, USA

5 Which bridge over the Seine in Paris is a footbridge only?

a) Pont Neuf

b) Pont des Arts

c) Pont Henri IV

GENERAL KNOWLEDGE ★ ★ ★

6 In which city was Malcolm X assassinated at a rally in 1965?

a) Los Angeles

b) Chicago

c) New York

7 If feline is cat-like and equine is horse-like, what is ranine?

a) Frog-like

b) Wolf-like

c) Hare-like

8 What can be referred to as pseudocyesis?

a) A compulsion to lie

b) A phantom pregnancy

c) A sensory illusion

9 The band Boo Radleys were named after a character in which classic novel?

a) *Breakfast at Tiffany's*

b) *To Kill a Mockingbird*

c) *The Catcher in the Rye*

10 In which African country was author Alexander McCall Smith born?

a) Ghana

b) Zimbabwe

c) Botswana

1 a

2 b

3 c

4 b

5 b

6 c

7 a

8 b

9 b

10 b

HARD – PART 9

1 Which actor was Al Gore's room-mate at Harvard?

a) Richard Dreyfuss

b) Dustin Hoffman

c) Tommy Lee Jones

2 What is Orange Pekoe?

a) a tea

b) a variety of pineapple

c) a liqueur

3 Which bridge was captured by British Commandos on the 5th June 1944?

a) Arnhem

b) Pegasus

c) The bridge on the River Kwai

4 If food is described as 'impanato', what does this mean?

a) Breaded

b) Boiled

c) Baked

5 Which sauce takes its name from a 17th-century French financier at the court of Louis XIV?

a) Béarnaise

b) Mornay

c) Béchamel

6 **Ada, Countess of Lovelace, an early pioneer of computing, was the daughter of which English Romantic poet?**

a) Byron

b) Shelley

c) Keats

7 **Of which famous English actress did Dorothy Parker cruelly remark, 'She looks like something that would eat its young'?**

a) Peggy Ashcroft

b) Edith Evans

c) Margaret Rutherford

8 **How did Charlotte Brew achieve a sporting first in 1977?**

a) First woman to swim the English Channel

b) First woman to ride in the Grand National

c) First woman to compete in the University Boat Race

9 **Who wrote the Restoration drama *The Country Wife*?**

a) William Congreve

b) William Wycherley

c) Oliver Goldsmith

10 **Which US president was nicknamed 'the Illinois Baboon'?**

a) Abraham Lincoln

b) George Washington

c) Ulysses S. Grant

1 c
2 a
3 b
4 a
5 c
6 a
7 c
8 b
9 b
10 a

HARD – PART 10

1 Which star of the silent movies was the original 'it' girl?

a) Gloria Swanson

b) Clara Bow

c) Mary Pickford

2 Which Russian author wrote the novel *Fathers and Sons*?

a) Dostoevsky

b) Turgenev

c) Tolstoy

3 Which French novel begins, 'Mother died today. Or, maybe, yesterday; I can't be sure'?

a) Michel Houellebecq's *Atomised*

b) Jean-Paul Sartre's *Nausea*

c) Albert Camus's *The Outsider*

4 Which poet kept a pet bear when he was at Cambridge University?

a) Byron

b) Tennyson

c) Wordsworth

5 Which of the following statements is true of the nineteenth century politician William Huskisson?

a) He was the illegitimate son of George IV

b) He was the first person killed in a railway accident

c) He was blinded in a childhood accident

6 What did Colonel Thomas Blood attempt to steal in 1671?

a) The skull of Oliver Cromwell

b) The Mona Lisa

c) The Crown Jewels

7 Who died in 1798, at a castle in Bavaria where he was working as a librarian?

a) Rousseau

b) Casanova

c) Voltaire

8 How was Jean-Baptiste Poquelin better known?

a) Nostradamus

b) Molière

c) Voltaire

9 Which former British prime minister was described as 'a modest little man with much to be modest about'?

a) Clement Attlee

b) David Lloyd George

c) Stanley Baldwin

10 Norwegian inventor Johan Vaaler became the first person to patent the design for which commonly used office object?

a) The stapler

b) The paper clip

c) The hole punch

A

1 b

2 b

3 c

4 a

5 b

6 c

7 b

8 b

9 a

10 b

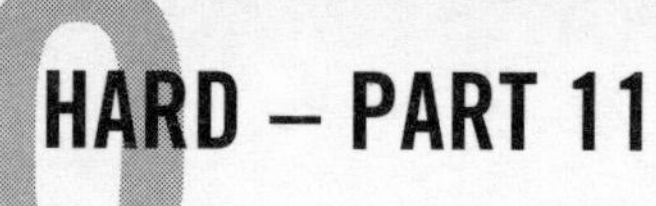

HARD – PART 11

1 Many 19th-century British denture-wearers took pride in knowing that their teeth came from the dead at what great battle?

a) Waterloo

b) Rorke's Drift

c) Khartoum

2 How does the Duke meet his death in the *Revenger's Tragedy*?

a) He is slain by his son and fed to wild pigs

b) He is duped into kissing the poisoned skull of his enemy's betrothed

c) He is eaten alive by rats whilst watching his wife's infidelity

3 What are the names of the leaders of *West Side Story*'s rival gangs, the Jets and the Sharks?

a) Biff and Reynaldo

b) Riff and Bernardo

c) Rolf and Benito

4 Which of these US states does not have an active volcano?

a) Texas

b) Washington

c) California

5 At birth, a baby has about 305, while an adult has roughly 206 – of what?

a) Nerve endings in the scalp

b) Bones

c) Muscles

GENERAL KNOWLEDGE ★★★

6 What is the hardest of all metallic elements?

a) Caesium

b) Cadmium

c) Chromium

7 How old was the youngest person to be awarded a Nobel prize?

a) 18

b) 25

c) 35

8 Most toilets flush in which key?

a) C major

b) E flat

c) F sharp

9 The horse decapitated in *The Godfather* and left in the bed of studio executive Jack Woltz was named after which African capital?

a) Khartoum

b) Cairo

c) Kinshasa

10 Which cricket umpire is also known as 'Slow Death'?

a) Billy Bowden

b) Steve Bucknor

c) David Shepherd

A

1	a
2	b
3	b
4	a
5	b
6	c
7	b
8	b
9	a
10	b

HARD – PART 12

1 Which of the following makes up the highest percentage of the Earth's atmosphere?

a) Carbon dioxide

b) Argon

c) Methane

2 What is the capital city of Burkina Faso?

a) Murwillumbah

b) Yarramalong

c) Ouagadougou

3 Which animal has the fastest ground speed?

a) Roe deer

b) Lion

c) Greyhound

4 In which of the following countries would you drive on the left?

a) Malta

b) Canada

c) Nigeria

5 What was recited in the first sound recording of a human voice?

a) The first chapter of the Bible

b) Keats' poetry

c) 'Au Clair de la Lune'

6 Which future political leader once worked as a vegetable cook at the Carlton Hotel in London?

a) Fidel Castro

b) Ho Chi Minh

c) Mao Zedong

7 Which composer was also a trained football referee?

a) Bela Bartok

b) Dmitri Shostakovich

c) Igor Stravinsky

8 The peyote cactus contains which hallucinatory drug?

a) LSD

b) Phencyclidine

c) Mescaline

9 In the cartoon series *South Park*, the character of Saddam Hussein was often romantically involved with whom?

a) Satan

b) Adolf Hitler

c) Charles Manson

10 In mixed martial arts, who were the inaugural inductees into the Ultimate Fighting Championship Hall of Fame in 2003?

a) Randy Couture and Mark Coleman

b) Royce Gracie and Ken Shamrock

c) Tito Ortiz and Matt Serra

1	b
2	c
3	a
4	a
5	c
6	b
7	b
8	c
9	a
10	b

HARD – PART 13

1 In which year was the Booker prize for fiction first awarded?

a) 1959

b) 1969

c) 1979

2 The Bronx, Brooklyn, Manhattan and Queens are four of the five boroughs of New York. What is the other?

a) Long Island

b) Ellis Island

c) Staten Island

3 Which country abolished its monarchy in 2007?

a) Thailand

b) Nepal

c) Malaysia

4 In the 'death pack' of playing cards issued to US soldiers in Iraq, who was the king of spades?

a) 'Chemical' Ali Hassan Al-Majid

b) Tariq Aziz

c) Uday Hussein

5 What was Sharron Davies' *Gladiator* name in the UK TV series?

a) Jet

b) Lightning

c) Amazon

6 From which newspaper was Boris Johnson sacked for falsifying a quotation?

a) *The Times*

b) *The Daily Mail*

c) *The Daily Telegraph*

---

7 Which football club's Latin motto means 'To dare is to do'?

a) Arsenal

b) Chelsea

c) Tottenham Hotspur

---

8 In *Sex and the City*, what is Mr Big's real name?

a) John

b) Michael

c) Thomas

---

9 *ER* was created by which bestselling author based on his own experiences as a medical student?

a) James Patterson

b) Stephen King

c) Michael Crichton

---

10 Which city is served by the Metrolink tram service?

a) Brighton

b) Manchester

c) Croydon

1 b
2 c
3 b
4 a
5 c
6 a
7 c
8 a
9 c
10 b

Q HARD – PART 14

1 In 2007 how many hotdogs did International Federation of Competitive Eating champion Joey Chestnut eat in 12 minutes?

a) 22

b) 44

c) 66

2 The first known usage of the phrase 'in a pickle' appears in which Shakespeare play?

a) *A Comedy of Errors*

b) *Richard III*

c) *The Tempest*

3 Where was North America's first commercial oil well drilled in 1858?

a) Ontario

b) Texas

c) California

4 What is the only country in the world not to have a flag in the shape of a quadrilateral?

a) Bhutan

b) Nepal

c) Cambodia

5 C. P. Scott edited which British newspaper for 57 years from 1872?

a) *The Guardian*

b) *The Daily Telegraph*

c) *The Times*

6 In which century did Dante Alighieri write his *Divine Comedy*?

a) 12th

b) 13th

c) 14th

7 Who is the only female vocalist to have appeared on a Led Zeppelin song?

a) Joni Mitchell

b) Sandy Denny

c) Carole King

8 To the nearest whole number, how many revolutions does the Moon make around the Earth in a calendar year?

a) 11

b) 12

c) 13

9 In which sport did the Whitaker family achieved a 1-2-3 finish in an international event in 2008?

a) Indoor bowls

b) Show jumping

c) Rifle shooting

10 Which country has the world's largest Muslim population?

a) Indonesia

b) Pakistan

c) Bangladesh

1 c

2 c

3 a

4 b

5 a

6 c

7 b

8 c

9 b

10 a

HARD – PART 15

1 How many novels were written by the Bronte sisters?

a) 7

b) 9

c) 11

2 Whose debut album was *My Aim Is True*?

a) Mariah Carey

b) George Michael

c) Elvis Costello

3 Which river burst its banks in 1931 and killed up to 3.7 million people?

a) Yellow

b) Yangtze

c) Mekong

4 Who said: 'There is no sincerer love than the love of food'?

a) George Bernard Shaw

b) Friedrich Nietzsche

c) Ralph Waldo Emerson

5 Which of the following was not an alumnus of Trinity College Dublin?

a) Oscar Wilde

b) Samuel Beckett

c) James Joyce

GENERAL KNOWLEDGE ★★★

6 How many British prime ministers has the Oxford University college of Christ Church produced?

a) 0

b) 6

c) 13

7 Which saint is Salisbury Cathedral dedicated to?

a) St Peter

b) St Mary

c) St Paul

8 Which of the following fruits grows on a herb?

a) Banana

b) Kiwi

c) Strawberry

9 Which Scottish singer provided vocals for the Prince song 'You've Got the Look'?

a) Lulu

b) Sheena Easton

c) Annie Lennox

10 In which country did the sport of jai-alai originate?

a) Spain

b) Japan

c) Korea

1 a
2 c
3 a
4 a
5 c
6 c
7 b
8 a
9 b
10 a

HARD – PART 16

1 What was the name of the house that lent its name to The Band's debut album in 1968?

a) Big Pink

b) Old Yellow

c) Little Green

2 In the British parliament who is the 'father of the house'?

a) The MP whose service in parliament is the longest

b) The oldest MP

c) The MP with the highest majority

3 Which 16th-century church stands in the Red Square in Moscow?

a) The Kremlin

b) St Basil's Cathedral

c) Cathedral of Christ the Saviour

4 Apart from Ireland, St Patrick is the patron saint of which other country?

a) Canada

b) Spain

c) Nigeria

5 What does the Latin phrase *per se* literally mean?

a) Through itself

b) By reason of which

c) For the time

6 In which European city are the poets Shelley and Keats buried?

a) Paris

b) London

c) Rome

7 In January of which year did the first annual letter appear on British number plates?

a) 1948

b) 1955

c) 1963

8 What was enshrined in the Bern Convention, signed in 1886?

a) The international agreement on the treatment of prisoners of war

b) The establishment of the International Federation of the Red Cross

c) The protection of literary and artistic copyright

9 *Ivanov*, premiered in 1887, was the first full-length play by which Russian dramatist?

a) Alexander Pushkin

b) Anton Chekhov

c) Leo Tolstoy

10 What is the largest satellite of Uranus?

a) Titan

b) Titania

c) Triton

1 a
2 a
3 b
4 c
5 a
6 c
7 c
8 c
9 b
10 b

HARD – PART 17

GENERAL KNOWLEDGE ★★★

1 Which of the following statements is Boyle's Law?

a) The volume of a mass of gas changes in relation to its pressure

b) The volume of a mass of gas that is at a fixed pressure is determined by its temperature

c) The pressure exerted by a gas at constant volume increases as the temperature of the gas rises

2 In mathematics, what name is given to a hypothetical point where two parallel lines join at infinity?

a) Asymptote

b) Ideal point

c) Antipodal point

3 Which of the following titles is not given to diplomatic representatives of the Pope?

a) Nuncio

b) Legate

c) Cardinal

4 Which Mozart opera features 'The Bird Catcher's Aria'?

a) *The Magic Flute*

b) *The Marriage of Figaro*

c) *Don Giovanni*

5 Which of the following does not quote the 17th-century Baroque work 'Pachelbel's Canon'?

a) Kylie Minogue, I Should Be So Lucky'

b) Britney Spears, 'Toxic'

c) Coolio, 'C U When U Get There'

6 **In all of Shakespeare's plays, only one reference to America can be found – where?**

a) *The Tempest*

b) *King Lear*

c) *The Comedy of Errors*

7 **Which of the following was the first feature-length film to be released on DVD?**

a) *The Godfather*

b) *Titanic*

c) *Twister*

8 **Who was the first official poet laureate?**

a) John Dryden

b) William Wordsworth

c) Alfred Tennyson

9 **Carl Fogarty holds the record for most Superbike World Championships – how many?**

a) 3

b) 4

c) 5

10 **Which literary figure co-founded the Hogarth Press?**

a) Virginia Woolf

b) George Bernard Shaw

c) E. M. Forster

1 a
2 b
3 c
4 a
5 b
6 c
7 c
8 a
9 b
10 a

Q HARD – PART 18

1 **How many books are there in the Bible?**

a) 55

b) 66

c) 77

2 **How many countries share a border with Poland?**

a) 5

b) 6

c) 7

3 **Which of the following cities has only hosted the Winter Olympics once?**

a) Innsbruck, Austria

b) St Moritz, Switzerland

c) Calgary, Canada

4 **Which of the following is not an expression invented by Shakespeare?**

a) 'Without rhyme or reason'

b) 'Don't put all your eggs in one basket'

c) 'Pushing up the daisies'

5 **Which of the following Italian footballers has won the FIFA World Player of the Year award?**

a) Gianluca Vialli

b) Fabio Cannavaro

c) Paolo Maldini

6 What are Qin, Tang and Song?

a) Musical instruments

b) Dishes in Taiwanese cuisine

c) Chinese dynasties

7 Which of the following indicates the highest quality of Italian wine?

a) IGT

b) DOCG

c) DOC

8 Which is the first animal in the Chinese calendar cycle?

a) Rat

b) Pig

c) Rooster

9 Which of the following countries are tulips native to?

a) The Netherlands

b) Turkey

c) Switzerland

10 What is the company Yahoo! named after?

a) A race of creatures in *Gulliver's Travels*

b) An Austrian communication system

c) A desert rodent known for its ability to search for food

1	b
2	c
3	c
4	b
5	b
6	c
7	b
8	a
9	b
10	a

HARD – PART 19

1 Which city is home to the arch known as the Gateway of India?

a) Mumbai

b) Kolkata

c) Delhi

2 Who wrote the short stories 'The Legend of Sleepy Hollow' and 'Rip Van Winkle'?

a) Edgar Allan Poe

b) Washington Irving

c) Nathaniel Hawthorne

3 What is Dr Jekyll's first name?

a) Harold

b) Henry

c) Horace

4 In which year was the first Superbowl held?

a) 1927

b) 1947

c) 1967

5 Which country has the world's longest coastline?

a) Russia

b) USA

c) Canada

GENERAL KNOWLEDGE ★★★

6 **Which of the following was invented the earliest?**

a) Ice cream cone

b) Crossword

c) Sellotape

7 **In cricket, against which team did Graham Gooch score 333 in 1990?**

a) India

b) Australia

c) West Indies

8 **In the 'cosmic calendar', if 1 January was the Big Bang and midnight on 31 December is now, on what day did the earliest known life forms appear?**

a) 22 July

b) 27 August

c) 1 October

9 **In snooker, how many points are awarded for a break of red-black-red?**

a) 9

b) 11

c) 13

10 **In radio which self-styled antidote to panel games was first broadcast in 1972?**

a) Desert Island Discs

b) Mornington Crescent

c) I Am Sorry I Haven't a Clue

1 a
2 b
3 b
4 c
5 c
6 a
7 a
8 c
9 a
10 c

HARD – PART 20

1 Tegucigalpa is the capital of which country?

a) Mexico

b) Venezuela

c) Honduras

2 In what year did The Beatles officially split up?

a) 1967

b) 1970

c) 1973

3 Which is the only country to have a flag that is just one colour?

a) Libya

b) Liberia

c) Lesotho

4 What type of insect does an apiarist keep?

a) Ants

b) Bees

c) Butterflies

5 What is the official language of Guinea-Bissau?

a) English

b) Portuguese

c) French

GENERAL KNOWLEDGE ★★★

6 If MSP means Member of the Scottish Parliament, what is the abbreviation used for members of the Welsh Assembly?

a) MWA

b) AM

c) WAM

7 Which of the following rappers was born Dylan Mills?

a) Dizzee Rascal

b) Shaggy

c) 50 Cent

8 In which city is the DAX stock exchange based?

a) Tokyo

b) Paris

c) Frankfurt

9 In which ocean would you find the Barents Sea?

a) Arctic

b) North Atlantic

c) Pacific

10 What is the collective noun for a group of starlings?

a) Chattering

b) Scattering

c) Puddling

A

1 c

2 b

3 a

4 b

5 b

6 a

7 a

8 c

9 a

10 a